Reforming Reading, Writing, and Mathematics

Teachers' Responses and the Prospects for Systemic Reform

Reforming Reading, Writing, and Mathematics

Teachers' Responses and the Prospects for Systemic Reform

S. G. Grant
State University of New York at Buffalo

LEA LAWRENCE ERLBAUM ASSOCIATES, PUBLISHERS
1998   Mahwah, New Jersey   London

Lawrence Erlbaum Associates, Inc., Publishers
10 Industrial Avenue
Mahwah, NJ 07430

Cover design by Kathryn Houghtaling Lacey

Library of Congress Cataloging-in-Publication Data
Grant, S. G.
Reforming reading, writing, and mathematics: teachers' responses and the prospects for systemic reform / S. G. Grant
  p. cm.
Includes bibliographical references (p.) and index.
ISBN 0–8058–2840–0 (cloth). — ISBN 0–8058–3279–1 (pbk. : alk. paper)
1. Language arts (Elementary)—Michigan—Case studies. 2. Mathematics—Study and teaching (Elementary)—Michigan—Case studies. 3. Educational change—Michigan—Case studies. I. Title.
LB1576.G7263   1998
372.19—dc21   98–20837
                                                    CIP

Books published by Lawrence Erlbaum Associates are printed on acid-free paper, and their bindings are chosen for strength and durability.

Printed in the United States of America
10 9 8 7 6 5 4 3 2 1

To
Anne, Alexander, and Claire
ಏ✧ಚ

Contents

Preface

This book represents a study within a study. The core study examines how teachers make sense of multiple subject matter reforms. More specifically, I examine the responses of four Michigan elementary school teachers to recent reforms in reading, writing, and mathematics and why their responses vary across both teachers and reforms. The outer study explores the prospects for the current movement known as *systemic reform*, which promotes coherence through the alignment of educational policies. Although conceptually separate, the two studies necessarily interact. The study of teachers' responses to multiple reforms helps us to understand some of the problems and possibilities the systemic agenda holds, and the systemic reform study provides a context for the study of teachers' reform responses.

Although it is becoming more common, the notion of talking to teachers as a means of understanding the importance of educational policy is relatively new. This approach challenges traditional conceptions of policy analysis in two ways: by elevating the perspective of teachers in relation to the policy process, and by promoting an alternative conception of that process that interprets policy as an instance of teaching and learning rather than one strictly of implementation. Considering these challenges, I argue that teachers play a different, but no less important, role than policymakers when policies are constructed (and reconstructed).

Chapter 1 provides the groundwork for both studies by sketching some of the ways that recent reform efforts differ from those in the past, and by introducing the four teachers and the cross-teacher and cross-reform variations in their reform responses. The chapter concludes with an overview of the many reasons advanced for those varied responses.

Chapters 3 through 6 are individual case studies where I describe and compare how teachers made sense of, and responded to, new and challenging subject matter reforms. I examine those responses along three dimensions: (a) the reforms encountered and each teacher's reaction to them; (b) the evidence of reform-minded ideas in each teacher's current instruction; and (c) the changes in each teacher's assumptions about teaching and learning reading, writing, and mathematics.

I present the teacher case studies in two sets. The first two cases feature Bonnie Jones and Frank Jensen. Both teach at Donnelly-King Elementary in Derry, a rural, White, working-class district. Jones teaches grade 5; Jensen teaches a split class of third and fourth graders. The second set of cases pairs two teachers in Hamilton, a mid-sized metropolitan area. Marie Irwin teaches grade 6 at Sanford Heights Elementary, a predominately White, middle- to upper-middle class suburban school. Paula Goddard, a second-grade teacher, teaches in the same school district, but in a very different school context. Sheldon Court Academic Center is an alternative, inner-city school whose students are African American and poor. A prologue describes each set of schools and communities and establishes the local context of reform. An epilogue describes the cross-teacher and cross-reform variation in the teachers' responses.

Chapter 7 wraps up the study of teachers and reforms by explaining the teachers' responses and the variation among them. I first discuss the specific influences of personal, organizational, and policy factors, and then explore these factors in interaction. I conclude that explaining teachers' behavior is much more complex than suggested by traditional discrete explanations.

Two chapters devoted to systemic reform frame the study of teachers and reforms. Chapter 2 outlines the systemic change argument. I describe the problems systemic reformers identify with U.S. education, the solutions they offer, and the assumptions that guide their agenda. I present Michigan as a case of systemic change by describing the state and local reform contexts. Those contexts, viewed in light of the systemic agenda, foreshadow several tensions which relate directly to the prospects for systemic reform. I analyze those prospects in chapter 8, using the teacher cases to explore a series of slippages between the rhetoric of systemic reform and the reality of life in classrooms, schools, districts, and a state department of education.

Finally, chapter 9 looks ahead by sketching two alternatives to the systemic argument. These are the bottom-up and middle-ground approaches. I propose focusing on ideas as a lever of change and adopting the middle-ground strategy.

ACKNOWLEDGMENTS

Books are rarely the effort of one individual and this book is no exception. I owe enormous intellectual debts to a range of people who have guided my work (whether or not they know it). One group includes the many teachers, administrators, and policymakers who graciously and openly talked with me during this project. I would particularly like to thank the four teachers—Bonnie Jones, Frank Jensen, Marie Irwin, and Paula Goddard—who tirelessly endured my questions and visits, and whose stories became central to this book. The other group includes colleagues and mentors—David Cohen, Catherine Cornbleth, Helen Featherstone, Ruth Heaton, Nancy Jennings, Bill McDiarmid, Dennis Mike, Hugh Petrie, James Spillane, Gary Sykes, Sam Weintraub, and Suzanne Wilson. Busy people all, they kindly gave both me and my work much needed time, energy, and support.

I also owe a profound debt to my family for the emotional support that is so critical to writing. Thanks first to my two children, Alexander and Claire, who gave their dad enough time to write when he needed to, and enough diversion when he didn't. Thanks also to my wife and friend, Anne, whose confidence and faith were harder to shake than my own.

—*S. G. Grant*

TEACHERS, REFORMS, AND SYSTEMIC CHANGE

Teachers and Reforms

Educational reforms are "as American as apple pie" (Warren, 1989, p. 1). Reforming schools and classrooms has been "steady work" since World War II (Elmore & McLaughlin, 1988), but that activity increased dramatically beginning in the mid-1980s when reports like *A Nation at Risk* (National Commission on Excellence in Education, 1983) portrayed America's public schools in serious decline. The first wave of reforms tinkered with regulations such as student graduation credits and teacher certification standards. Such efforts altered some aspects of schooling, but they left important dimensions of teaching and learning largely untouched. As Kirp and Driver (1995) note, these policies led to "great bookkeeping," but made "little pedagogical sense" (p. 590).

This is changing. A second wave of reforms speaks more directly to these issues.[1] This new breed of educational policies—the California frameworks in mathematics and language arts, the National Council of Teachers of Mathematics (NCTM) curriculum and professional standards, and the National Center for History in the Schools content standards—promote ambitious intellectual and pedagogical goals.

These initiatives are notable in at least three ways. First, they promote new educational goals. Past efforts alternately aimed low or only at selected students.[2] Newer reforms express a promising, if problematic objective: high academic standards for all students. Second, current reforms challenge teachers' modal knowledge, practices, and assumptions about subject matter knowledge, teaching, and learning. Prevailing approaches reflect traditional views: Knowledge is viewed as discrete bits, which are sequential, hierarchical, and fixed. Teaching is didactic and emphasizes drill, practice, and evaluation. Learning is passive, a reflex of teaching. Reflecting constructivist thinking, recent reforms challenge these views by tendering new perspectives about knowledge, teaching, and learning. In this light, knowledge is neither fixed nor hierarchical, but instead is constructed as individuals interact with ideas and with one another. Teaching is no longer viewed as delivering material and supervising practice, but is viewed as guiding or facilitating learning. Learning is no longer viewed as passive, but as actively constructive with students developing understandings based on new information and the ideas, experiences, and theories they bring with them.

The third way new policies differ from those of the past is that they represent efforts at systemic reform. Advocates of systemic change argue that past reforms have resulted in an education system that is "uncoordinated, piecemeal, fragmented, project centered, and irrational" (Fuhrman, 1993a, p. 15). Moreover, previous reforms have failed to include the least advantaged students. The solution, as proposed by Smith and O'Day (O'Day & Smith, 1993; Smith & O'Day, 1991) and their followers, focuses on making the educational system itself more coherent. Three changes are highlighted: creating new and intellectually ambitious curriculum frameworks, aligning key state education policies, and restructuring school governance.

Consider Michigan as an example. In the mid-1980s, state-level policymakers began work on new curriculum policies in reading, writing, and mathematics. They revised the state assessment tests, the Michigan Educational Assessment Program (MEAP). They also encouraged local educators to pursue site-based decision-making strategies. These efforts came together in 1990 when a comprehensive state policy, Public Act 25 (PA 25), was signed into law. Subsequent legislation furthered the systemic reform agenda.

Systemic efforts are visible in numerous states with California, New York, Kentucky, and Vermont most frequently mentioned. Reformers believe that, if enacted, systemic reform will have a profound effect on schooling. But what does all this reform-minded activity mean? Some observers answer that question by looking at state department of education activity (Lusi, 1997). Others look at district responses (Brouillette, 1996; Spillane, 1996). I propose to answer the question by looking at those actors closest to the action—teachers. Advocates of systemic reform presume that teachers can and will embrace new policies and will effect fundamental changes in their classroom practices. But how do teachers interpret these efforts? What do their responses look like? What explains the variation in their responses? And what does the variation in teachers' responses imply about the prospects for systemic reform?

At its core, this book is a study of the responses of four Michigan elementary school teachers to new and challenging reforms in reading, writing, and mathematics. Using case studies, I describe and analyze each teacher's response along three dimensions:

1. how each teacher learns about and makes sense of the reforms in light of his or her past practice;
2. changes in each teacher's instructional practice; and
3. changes in each teacher's assumptions about teaching and learning.

Comparing responses across teachers and across reforms provides insight into the various ways teachers interpret and manage reforms in their classrooms. That analysis, in turn, provides the context for an examination of the prospects for systemic reform. Using Michigan as a case in point, I describe how the systemic agenda developed at the state, district, school, and classroom levels. Examination of the actions of actors at each level and comparison of them to the rhetoric of systemic reform suggests a series of tensions or slippages—instances where the reality of educational policy and practice rubs against the grain of educational change.

MAKING SENSE OF REFORMS: A PREVIEW

A blizzard of reform swirls around teachers, but if the systemic reformers are right, it should. They argue that only by reexamining all elements of the education system will real change occur. We begin with a glimpse at the ways in which four Michigan elementary school teachers respond to a subset of the reforms that blow around them, those in reading, writing, and mathematics:

Bonnie Jones[3] teaches grade 5 in a small, working-class school in the rural town of Derry. After several personal tragedies, Jones began an intense effort to transform her teaching. She eagerly embraces reading and mathematics reforms; until recently she ignored reforms in writing.

Jones interprets all reforms as challenges to her traditional skills-based instruction and she aggressively pursues opportunities to learn about new ideas and practices. She has made several changes in her reading and mathematics teaching. Some appear superficial and tacked-on, but others, such as using trade books[4] in reading, and taking a conceptual approach in mathematics, seem profound. In writing, however, Jones generally maintains her traditional grammar instruction. She occasionally adds a reform-minded activity, but the bulk of her practice is little changed.

Beyond her daily instruction, Jones is also questioning her basic assumptions about teaching and learning. Her questions run deepest in reading. There she is making wholesale changes in her view of reading, her role as teacher, and her expectations of students. The questions are less deep and the changes are less profound in mathematics, and they are virtually nonexistent in writing.

Frank Jensen teaches a combination third- and fourth-grade class in the same school. Jensen's reform responses are more modest. He uses the language of reforms, but his reading and mathematics instruction is quite conventional. In contrast, Jensen recently developed a writing project that reflects several reform-minded ideas.

Jensen sees no significant differences between his extant practice and reading and mathematics reforms. In fact, he believes these reforms "justify" his approaches and he seeks no new learning opportunities. Jensen has been more attentive to reading than to mathematics reforms. He uses an occasional trade book and reading strategy. These changes, however, are added to an instructional practice which is eclectic in the extreme. Beyond his talk, there is virtually no evidence of reform in his mathematics teaching. In neither case is Jensen questioning his underlying beliefs about teaching and learning.

Some of the same could be said about writing reforms, but here Jensen has moved more ambitiously. Some traditional elements persist. With assistance from his wife, the district reading coordinator, however, Jensen created an expansive writing project that integrated reading, social studies, and computer skills. Reform-minded elements such as having an authentic writing task and using the writing process are evident. Jensen reports being satisfied with this effort, and he has no plans to push the project or his practice any further.

Marie Irwin teaches grade 6 in a middle- to upper-middle-class school in the city of Hamilton. Irwin's responses are also relatively modest. Reforms are evident, but only as supplements to a largely conventional classroom practice.

Irwin's cautious response is not uniform, however. She claims that reading reforms hold no challenge for her and she has sought no particular opportunities to learn more about them. Nevertheless, Irwin has adopted a range of reform-minded practices such as using trade books and teaching skills in context. Reforms are also evident in Irwin's writing practice. Rather than integrate new approaches into her writing instruction as she does in reading, Irwin keeps them separate. Her writing instruction stresses mechanics; reform-minded practices like journal writing are done separately. Different again is Irwin's response to mathematics reforms. Until recently, she ignored them. She knew reforms presented a new approach to mathematics teaching, but her personal discomfort with mathematics, and the district's emphasis on basic facts and procedures supported her avoidance of new ideas and approaches. Last year, however, she began confronting her feelings and she is now considering a number of modest changes.

Irwin's responses vary at the level of daily practice, but no evidence indicates she is pushing beyond that level and exploring her basic assumptions about teaching and learning.

Paula Goddard teaches grade 2 in Hamilton, in an unusual school setting. Sheldon Court Academic Center is a public alternative school where students are largely poor and African American. Teachers, parents, and administrators are committed to the school's strong disciplinary code and basic skills curriculum. Until 3 years ago, Goddard taught traditional reading, writing, and mathematics skills in traditional ways. Then she began experimenting with new mathematics approaches. A year later, she returned to a more conventional approach. Her reading and writing instruction, however, continue to push toward reform-minded goals.

Initially, Goddard responded eagerly to mathematics reforms. She took a mathematics education course at a local university, adopted several reform-minded practices, and seemed poised to make fundamental changes. A combination of school and personal factors, however, urged her to reverse course. Her practice today stresses mathematical rules and procedures. Goddard is more attentive to reading and writing reforms. A new literature-based textbook, a university course, and her own children's positive experience in a whole language classroom increase her interest in reading. Numerous changes have resulted, and in her own way, Goddard is reconstructing her reading practice and rethinking her beliefs about teaching and learning. She avers similar goals in writing, but her interest there is brand new and her responses are just developing.

There is a lot going on here. These teachers face multiple reforms that, for some, challenge long-held views of teaching, learning, and knowledge. Some teachers take advantage of opportunities to learn about these ideas. Others do not. Some personal and organizational factors encourage change, but not all. These and other issues surface throughout these vignettes. Two issues in particular—the variation in teachers' responses and the influences on those responses—have important implications for the systemic agenda.

Variation in Teachers' Responses

Throughout the vignettes, similarities and differences surface in the ways teachers respond to reforms. This is complicated territory, in part because multiple comparisons are possible. One set of comparisons can be made across the four teachers' reactions (e.g., how each teacher interprets reading reforms). A second set of comparisons can be made across an individual teacher's responses to multiple reforms (e.g., how Bonnie Jones responds to reforms in reading, writing, and mathematics). An overview of the cross-teacher and cross-reform variation follows.

Some similarities emerge across the four teachers' reactions to each reform. First, these teachers respond most ambitiously to reading reforms. Each incorporated new texts and new instructional strategies, and though not mentioned previously, each also abandoned a mainstay of traditional reading instruction—ability-based reading groups. Second, while reform-minded changes are also evident in writing, they appear to be more superficial than those in reading. Frank Jensen aside, these teachers generally maintain their conventional writing instruction. Finally, with the exception of Bonnie Jones, the teachers' responses to mathematics reforms are relatively weak. Frank Jensen ignores them completely. Marie Irwin did so until just recently. And after a trial run, Paula Goddard settled back into a more conventional practice.

There are also conspicuous differences. First, these teachers interpret reforms and the relationship between reforms and their extant practices quite differently. For example, Jones views reforms as a promising challenge to her current approaches. Jensen, by contrast, generally views his extant practice as consistent with reforms. Second, teachers vary in what they believe they need to learn. For example, Goddard senses she has much to learn and she pursues a variety of opportunities to do so. Irwin is more sanguine. She seeks no learning opportunities in reading and writing, and it is not clear that she will do so in mathematics. Third, the instructional changes teachers make range broadly. Jones and Goddard are after big changes, especially in reading. Irwin and Jensen, although different in many ways, pursue more modest changes. Finally, while one could conclude that little change occurs beyond the level of daily practice, there are indications that reforms can provoke questions about traditional teaching and learning assumptions. But again this varies. Irwin and Jensen entertain no such questions; Jones and Goddard do.

Just as there are similarities and differences across teachers, so too are there similarities and differences in each individual teacher's responses across reforms. Some similarities emerge within each teacher's responses. For example, Bonnie Jones' ambitious responses to reading and mathematics reforms share several commonalties. In each area, Jones uses new curriculum materials, emphasizes strategic learning and real-world applications, and organizes students in a range of work settings. Moreover, she pursues opportunities to learn more in each subject.

These similarities notwithstanding, it is the differences that stand out. Consider the example of Marie Irwin. Reading and writing reforms inspire no particular challenge or concern. Irwin makes some instructional changes in both areas, but she senses no profound incompatibilities between her views and reformers'. The situation is quite different with mathematics. Irwin ignored mathematics reforms for years. She recently concluded, however, that reforms offer new and different approaches, and that her practice is not in "sync." Among other things, Irwin's personal discomfort with mathematics encouraged her to avoid reforms. Her professional discomfort in believing that her practice is out of "sync" encourages her to entertain thoughts of reform-minded change. What this will mean for Irwin's future mathematics practice is not clear, but Irwin's nascent interest in mathematics reforms illustrates both how her responses differ from other teachers' and from her attention to other reforms.

The variation across teachers is, in some sense, predictable. More surprising, however, is the variation across reforms. This is no small point.

Whereas many studies illustrate the first condition, virtually none recognize the second. Systemic reformers appear bent on bundling reforms together, yet the variation across teachers and across reforms has important implications for systemic assumptions about creating instructional coherence and consistency.

Factors in Explaining Teachers' Varied Responses

Recent reforms promote new views of knowledge as constructed and mutable rather than fixed, of teaching as guiding rather than telling, and of learning as active rather than passive. As the vignettes show, however, teachers' interpretations of, and classroom responses to, such challenges vary across teachers and across reforms. Explaining this variation poses a challenge because no one set of factors accounts for the range of responses that emerge. I take up this challenge more fully in chapter 7. Here, I sketch some prevailing explanations for teachers' reform responses.

The Nature of Policy. One category of explanations centers on the nature of policy. One relevant feature is the ambiguity of policy. By definition, policy sets directions, defines broad goals, and establishes parameters. Observers have long noted, however, that policy is not sufficiently clear, coherent, or authoritative to ensure consistent interpretations or responses (Cohen & Ball, 1990; Grant, 1997b; Jennings, 1996; Kirst & Walker, 1971; Lusi, 1997; Pressman & Wildavsky, 1974; Weatherly & Lipsky, 1977). Rather than communicating a single message, policy is more likely to provide fodder for multiple responses.[5]

A second feature is the competition among policies. That competition comes in two forms. One is the competition among policies related to the same subject matter. In reading, for example, each teacher in this study encountered state policies such as the *Essential Goals and Objectives for Reading Education* (Michigan State Board of Education, 1986) and the revised reading portion of the state test. But state policy holds no special privilege. Jones and Goddard also encountered national initiatives such as *Becoming a Nation of Readers* (Anderson, Hiebert, Scott, & Wilkenson, 1985). All four teachers encountered local reading policies through revised curriculum guides and new textbook adoptions.[6] Whereas these efforts may push a common constructivist view of reading, that result is not assured. Teachers who see only a new textbook or a new test may respond quite differently from colleagues engaged in more substantive representations.

The second form of competition is among policies related to different subject matters. It is not always the case, but teachers routinely face multiple reforms. Jones, for example, faces health, science, cooperative learning, and outcomes-based education initiatives in addition to reading, writing, and mathematics reforms. This seemingly endless swirl of reforms takes its toll on teachers' time, energy, and enthusiasm such that even the most conscientious teachers must continually decide what they will attend to and what they will let fall aside. Inevitably, those decisions will vary from teacher to teacher and from subject matter to subject matter.

Systemic reformers expect that their policy efforts will redirect teachers' practices and make them more coherent. Past experience, however, suggests just the reverse: Policy fosters greater variability rather than greater consistency (McLaughlin, 1990). Policy may stimulate and support powerful changes. The competition among policies for teachers' attention and the inherent ambiguity of policy, however, provides fertile ground for alternative responses.

Subject Matter Reforms. Nowhere is the complex nature of policy clearer than in the case of subject matter reforms. Policies dealing with regulatory matters (e.g., graduation and certification requirements) are relatively straightforward. Subject matter reforms are a different story. Recent initiatives are complicated and require deep and profound changes in the classroom lives of teachers and learners. As a special case of policy, then, the nature of subject matter reforms helps explain the variation in teachers' responses across teachers and across reforms.

Consider the scope of changes reformers ask teachers to make. The new Michigan reading policy discounts conventional views of reading as a series of sequential and hierarchical skills and promotes a view of reading as a constructive activity emphasizing understanding (Michigan State Board of Education, 1986). The Michigan mathematics policy strikes a similar tone: "Conceptualization of mathematics and understanding of problems should be valued more highly than just correct solutions to routine exercises" (Michigan State Board of Education, 1990, p. 3). This statement recalls the National Council of Teachers of Mathematics (1991) position that "learning occurs as students actively assimilate new information and experiences and construct their own meanings" (p. 2). The meanings students construct are also emphasized in the Michigan writing policy which advises, "Be primarily interested in the content, not the mechanics of expression. . . . Perfection in mechanics develops slowly. Be patient" (Michigan State Board of Education, 1985, p. 6).

Reforms also challenge conventional views of teaching as telling. The NCTM *Professional Standards* (National Council of Teachers of Mathematics, 1991), for example, suggest, "Instead of the teacher doing virtually all of the talking, modeling, and explaining themselves, teachers must encourage and expect students to do more" (p. 36). To do that, reformers expect teachers will know their subject matters deeply and will develop rich instructional repertoires. The NCTM *Curriculum and Evaluation Standards*

(National Council of Teachers of Mathematics, 1989), for example, caution against using only traditional abstract or symbolic representations. It urges teachers to use multiple representations (e.g., manipulatives, diagrams, journals) and to emphasize problem solving, estimation, and other mathematical strategies. Reading reforms advocate similarly rich instruction. Although basal reading series are not abandoned, reformers promote use of multiple text types (e.g., poetry, science fiction, biography, magazine articles, reference books) and instructional strategies (e.g., predicting, summarizing, and accessing the reader's prior knowledge) aimed at helping students to construct meaning.

New ideas about teaching are linked to new views of learning. Creating rich learning opportunities from which all students can draw on prior knowledge and experience is a common theme in reading reforms. Writing reforms advocate multiple and meaningful occasions for students to write—journals, stories, poetry, and reports. Mathematics reforms advocate "doing" mathematics wherein students have opportunities to "explore, develop, test, discuss, and apply ideas" (National Council of Teachers of Mathematics, 1989, p. 17). In general, reforms promote occasions where students can engage substantive content, develop higher order skills, and participate in active and shared learning experiences.

These reforms challenge modal practice. They call for teachers to know, think, and do very different things. This call is problematic in at least two ways, however, both of which help to explain why teachers' responses vary.

One problem is that these reforms do not prescribe all that teachers should know, what they should do, or how they should change their practices. Reforms provide direction. However, only rarely do they provide sufficient detail for teachers to engage the ideas deeply. Thus, the reforms themselves may contribute to teachers' varied interpretations because one can easily imagine teachers interpreting phrases like "constructing meaning" and "multiple representations" in very different ways.

Yet even if policies were more prescriptive, teachers would still construct varied responses. Teachers rarely encounter reforms directly (Cohen & Ball, 1990). They more often encounter representations of policy such as textbooks and tests. These representations are ubiquitous, but they do not necessarily reflect a coherent or astute sense of the reforms (Cohen & Ball, 1990; McDiarmid, Ball, & Anderson, 1989; Remillard, 1991).

Subject matter reforms present one other problem: They do not take into account the differential content knowledge teachers possess. Reformers demand that teachers know more about the subjects they teach because without that knowledge, changes may be thin and prone to misrepresentation (Heaton, 1994; McDiarmid, Ball, & Anderson, 1989) or quickly abandoned (Richardson, Anders, Tidwell, & Lloyd, 1991). However, not all teachers have the rich subject matter knowledge they need (Holmes

Group, 1986; Lanier & Little, 1986), and teachers' knowledge varies across subject matters. For example, most teachers are confident and competent readers. Reading reforms may challenge a teacher's extant practice, but teachers know how to read. Teachers are less sanguine about knowing how to do mathematics (Ball, 1988; Ball & McDiarmid, 1990b) or how to write (Calkins, 1986; Graves, 1983). Reforms in these areas ask teachers to know and do things they may have little knowledge of and many fears about.

These special problems of subject matter reforms promote, rather than curb, variation. Given few specifics, weak representations, and differential knowledge, teachers are more likely to fall back on individual knowledge and experience. Doing so helps them make sense of the reforms, but it also contributes to the cross-teacher and cross-reform variation.

Teacher Learning. If subject matter reforms provide only a general direction, they are even less specific about how to get there. Another category of explanations for teachers' varied responses emphasizes how teachers learn to make the changes reforms demand.

Professional development is frequently discussed among school reformers (Darling-Hammond & McLaughlin, 1996; Fullan, 1993; Guskey, 1996; Lieberman, 1995a). Yet, reformers might be excused for paying less attention to this issue than one would expect: Reeducating thousands of teachers is a huge challenge, there are few models worth emulating, and basic resources of time and money are rarely sufficient. Even if reformers knew what to do and had the resources to do it, the variation in teachers' responses would be scarcely decreased.

First, there is the matter of what teachers are to learn. Reforms represent a broad and expansive curriculum (Cohen & Barnes, 1993a, 1993b). Reading reforms, for example, promote new instructional goals, new kinds of text, new instructional strategies, and new forms of assessment. Confronted with a blast of new ideas, teachers are bound to attend more closely to some reforms than to others.

A second issue concerns the resources for learning. Teachers have numerous opportunities to learn about reforms (Grant, 1997a). Textbooks, tests, university courses, and professional development opportunities are common learning resources. They offer the advantages of accessibility, familiarity, and occasions to think and talk with peers.

At the same time, resources can contribute to teachers' varied responses by sending mixed messages. Textbooks are a good example. Although they are a common means of introducing new ideas (Grant, 1991), textbooks typically send messages that support both reform-minded and traditional views (Cohen & Ball, 1990; McDiarmid et al., 1989). For example, the state-approved textbooks that accompanied the 1985 California mathematics framework only modestly reflected new instructional approaches. Knowledgeable teachers used those textbooks, along with ancillary materials, to advance ambitious goals, but teachers who preferred conventional approaches found them equally usable. The typically superficial ways that textbooks treat ideas, then, offer teachers wide discretion in how they interpret reforms. This is not only the case with textbooks. Observers have noted that tests (Corbett & Wilson, 1990; Wise, 1988), university courses, (McKeatchie, 1980; Sarason, 1982), and professional development (Grant, 1997a) also send mixed messages about learning new ideas.

Mixed messages contribute to teachers' varied responses. Even if all teachers learned from a single resource, they would still take away different understandings because there are characteristic conditions of teaching and learning that inevitably contribute to multiple interpretations.

Subject matter reforms push in two directions—away from old traditional ideas and toward new constructivist ideas. For most teachers, learning new ideas means abandoning or unlearning old ideas.[7] This is no simple substitution, however, for new information is never perceived purely. Instead, it is understood through our prior knowledge, dispositions, and experiences (Fiske & Taylor, 1984; Resnick, 1987). This means that new learning will inevitably be shaped by old learning.

This condition has two implications. One is that the meanings each teacher constructs from reforms will reflect some measure of his or her past knowledge and practice. Thus, one develops new ways of teaching in a relative rather than in an absolute fashion. A second implication is related: If old learning shapes new learning, teachers may be disposed to conserve, rather than to change, their ideas and practices (Nisbet & Ross, 1980). Old knowledge and beliefs can be strongly held and may adhere even when challenged. This does not mean that teachers are unable to change their practices in important and fundamental ways, but it does mean that change in response to reforms is not guaranteed. Moreover, any changes that do result will be likely to occur in fits and starts, may look confused and inconsistent to observers, and will vary across teachers and reforms.

Individual Knowledge, Belief, and Experience. What teachers learn and how they learn are related to a larger category of explanations for their varied responses to reforms. That category centers on individual knowledge, beliefs, and experience (Eisenhart, Shrum, Harding, & Cuthbert, 1988; Elbaz, 1983; Fenstermacher, 1979).

In addition to knowledge, beliefs, and experiences, individual factors include dispositions (Buchmann, 1986; Zeichner, 1986), willingness to take risks (Meadows, 1990), personal and professional relationships (Little, 1982; Little & McLaughlin, 1993; Lortie, 1975; Rosenholtz, 1991), personal history or narrative (Carter, 1993; Connelly & Clandinin, 1990; Goodson, 1992), and capacity and will (Berman & McLaughlin, 1977; McDonnell & Elmore,

1987; McLaughlin, 1987, 1990). Richardson (1990) argues that such factors typically get short shrift in the policy implementation literature, but that stance may be changing. For example, Hargreaves (1994) observes that teachers' responses to reforms represent "not just to their *capacity* to change but also to their *desires* for change (and indeed for stability)" (p. 11).

Individual factors help explain both forms of variation. For example, it makes sense that what teachers know and are willing to do would be differentially distributed. Most elementary school teachers face reforms knowing more about reading than they do about mathematics or writing (Ball & Cohen, 1995), but this is not universally so. Moreover, what teachers know and believe about reading varies. For example, some are competent teachers of textbook-based reading skills, whereas others push toward more adventurous instruction by exploring both literature and students' ideas. What elementary school teachers know and believe about mathematics and writing also varies. Most know little about these subjects and may treat them in pedantic ways, emphasizing rote accumulation of discrete knowledge and skills. But not all do. These capacity differences undoubtedly contribute to the varied responses across teachers and across reforms.

Teachers' varied responses also owe something to factors such as disposition or will. Will can be an elusive construct because if one assumes any measure of human agency, will would seem to infuse all action and experience. Even a cursory look suggests that teachers are differentially disposed toward reforms. For example, Jones seems determined to reconstruct her current reading practices, whereas Jensen seems equally determined to maintain his. Differences in teachers' dispositions also help explain the cross-reform variation. For example, whereas she avoids mathematics and has been unwilling to change her mathematics practice, Irwin is interested in literacy reforms and willingly makes changes in her reading and writing practices.

I will leave the fine-grained distinctions among individual factors to others. My sense is that a teacher's differential responses to reading and mathematics reforms, for example, probably reflect a broad array of factors. My purpose is to suggest that individual factors help explain the cross-teacher and cross-reform variation in the ways teachers manage reforms.

Organizational Context. While individual factors would seem to explain much of the variation in teachers' reform responses, teachers do not work in vacuums. Another category of explanations takes this into account by highlighting the organizational contexts in which teachers work.

The organizational context of most of U.S. education is something of a paradox. On the one hand, there are clearly identifiable systems with levels and structures—schools, districts, and state departments of education. Each has identifiable functions and serves identifiable populations.

In these several senses, then, U.S. education looks like a run-of-the-mill bureaucracy. At the same time, schooling as an activity is characteristically decentralized (Cohen & Spillane, 1992). Organizational flowcharts and implementation schemes can be clearly delineated, but no serious observer of educational organizations puts much faith in these because structural and functional control over decision making often seem unrelated.

Michigan is a good example. There are identifiable units—schools, districts, and the state department of education—but these units operate in loosely jointed ways. The state education agency establishes curriculum and assessment policies, but has few tools to either induce or enforce compliance. Control over curriculum and instruction devolves to the approximately 600 local school districts.

Those districts may be as different as Hamilton and Derry, the districts represented in this study. Central office administrators in Hamilton exert considerable control over curriculum, instruction, and assessment. The district instructional guidance system emphasizes traditional skills-based goals, and administrators view recent reforms skeptically (Spillane, 1993). By contrast, central office administrators in Derry play a more circumspect role and provide more encouragement (at least in reading) for reform-minded practice (Jennings, 1996). This difference is important because the Derry teachers, Jones and Jensen, face considerably fewer institutional constraints than their Hamilton peers, Irwin and Goddard. The difference in organizational climates may not help explain the variation in their individual responses across reforms, but it seems to be an obvious factor in the cross-teacher variation.[8]

Teacher Autonomy. One last explanation focuses on the autonomous nature of teachers' work. Teachers work in bureaucratic systems, yet the influence of those systems does not reach evenly or consistently into each classroom (Meyer & Rowan, 1978; Rowan, 1990). Teaching, regardless of the district context, is a complex task generally performed in isolation (Cusick, 1983; Lortie, 1975). Teachers have little choice over some matters—the students they teach, the texts they receive, and the tests they use. Over other matters—how they group students, if and how they use texts, and what messages they draw from tests—they have considerable control (Lipsky, 1980; Lortie, 1975).

Autonomy helps explain both forms of variation in teachers' reform responses. The latitude each teacher has helps explain how teachers working in the same institutional climate could interpret reforms differently, and how an individual teacher might embrace one set of reforms while ignoring another. Teacher autonomy is not absolute in any sense, but as a key feature of teaching, it figures into the different ways teachers manage their classrooms and respond to reforms.

Each of these explanations permeates the teacher cases. The nature of policy—teachers' differential knowledge of subject matter, the vagaries of learning, individual differences in knowledge, beliefs, and experience, differences in organizational contexts, and classroom autonomy—all help explain the cross-teacher and cross-reform variation in teachers' reform responses.

As individual accounts, these explanations have considerable power; in interaction, they have even more. How a teacher responds to reforms—how he or she interprets reforms, if and how he or she learns about them, what changes (if any) he or she makes in his or her daily practice and in his or her assumptions about teaching and learning—is best understood through some mixture of these explanations. For example, a teacher who responds superficially to mathematics reforms may do so because he or she lacks the requisite knowledge, has few or weak resources for learning, or works in a district where traditional mathematics knowledge and skills are emphasized. Another teacher might also have little knowledge of mathematics and few district incentives to change his or her practice, but he or she embraces reforms by pushing himself or herself to confront those issues and work toward ambitious changes in his or her practice. Both examples show evidence of discrete factors, but more powerful insights emerge when one considers their interaction.

These examples illustrate the complexity both of teachers' reform responses and of the explanations for the variation in those responses. Examining those responses and how they vary deepens our understanding of the relationship between curriculum policy and classroom practice.

TEACHERS AND SYSTEMIC REFORM

Examining the variation in how teachers make sense of reforms also helps us understand the prospects for systemic reform. The systemic agenda is an ambitious one and this study cannot possibly address every aspect of it. Teachers are the key to that effort, however. By looking closely at how teachers manage multiple reforms in a state with an ostensible systemic initiative, we can begin to understand both the promises and problems of the systemic argument.

NOTES

1. Many observers borrow the metaphor of waves of reform, but not necessarily to represent the same phenomena. My use reflects that of Firestone, Fuhrman, and Kirst (1989). Others define the waves differently. See, for example, Hertert (1996) and Kirp and Driver (1995).

2. The basic skills reforms of the 1970s pushed academic standards downward, making minimum competency the goal. The subject matter reforms of the 1950s and 1960s pushed strong academic goals, but only for the nation's top students.
3. All proper names of teachers and the contexts in which they work are pseudonyms.
4. *Trade books* is a general term for fiction or non-fiction books written for school-aged children.
5. Kingdon (1984) notes that the ambiguity which becomes problematic for those enacting policy is a necessary condition for those trying to get policy through the political process.
6. This is also true in mathematics and writing. For example, teachers encountered the state mathematics policy and the revised mathematics section of the MEAP, proposals by the National Council of Teachers of Mathematics (1989, 1991), and local curriculum initiatives.
7. My colleague, Barry Shealy, reminds me that, though the notion of unlearning is widely used in the professional literature, it nevertheless ill-reflects current thinking about cognition, which suggests that prior knowledge shapes new knowledge development. Thus one can not really unlearn anything.
8. Whether the variation in teachers' responses is less in states with more centralized governance structures is an empirical question, which this study does not address.

Chapter 2

Michigan:
A Case of Systemic Reform

When advocates of systemic reform look at the problem with education in the United States they see a 900-pound boulder in the middle of the road. They see policy and textbooks and tests pushing in different directions. They see weak school governance, professional development, and certification standards. They see islands of success amidst an ocean of failures. Systemic reformers know they face a daunting task, but they also know that even the biggest rock can be moved with the right lever. They believe they have found that lever.

The lever is state policy. Systemic reformers argue that aligning state curriculum, assessment, licensure, and professional development policies will lead to a more coherent system, which profoundly changes the way teachers and students live their classroom lives.

It's a noble ambition. First, systemic reform represents a positive, active agenda. Whereas most policy analysts are content to snipe, advocates of systemic reform propose solutions, turning "not to despair but to invention" (Fuhrman, 1993a, p. 13). Those "inventions" may turn out to be problematic, but the impulse to do more than criticize is both noteworthy and admirable. Second, systemic reform represents a fundamentally new goal—high standards for all students. Reformers applaud those instances in which schools and districts have succeeded in transforming their educational programs. They argue, however, that these efforts are isolated and only rarely include students from the least advantaged settings. The reforms of the 1950s and 1960s aimed at higher academic standards, but they focused on the college-bound population. The argument that all students need access to rich ideas and instruction is new and powerful.

18

The systemic reform agenda has much to offer. The analysis of the problem is rational, insightful, and innovative. The solutions proposed make sense, offer a logical course of action, and address important needs. The systemic argument works well at the rhetorical level. As some observers note, however, it is built on a set of assumptions that are problematic in the real worlds of state governments, school districts, and classrooms (Clune, 1993; Cohen, 1995; Donmoyer, 1995; Fullan, 1996; Hertert, 1996; Kirp & Driver, 1995).

What are the prospects for systemic reform? In this chapter, I begin to address that question by looking in two directions. One direction is the systemic reform agenda. I describe how systemic reformers define the problem of education, the solutions they pose, and the assumptions that underlie their strategy. I then turn to Michigan as a case in point. The reform movement in that state, begun in the mid-1980s, continues today and offers an opportunity to explore the prospects for systemic reform on a living canvas.

THE ARGUMENT FOR SYSTEMIC REFORM

The problems of American education are daunting. Observers catalogue a litany of failures—bored and poorly prepared students, poorly prepared and burned-out teachers, vapid subject matter, and organizational inertia. Although far from new, these problems have baffled reformers for years.

Advocates of systemic reform acknowledge these concerns and the failure of past efforts to remedy them. They understand the radical nature of their proposals and the possibilities of failing. Systemic reformers believe, however, that the way they define the problem of American education and the solutions they propose offer a unique opportunity to reconstruct schooling in the United States.

The next three sections outline the systemic reform argument. In the first two, I describe how systemic reformers define the central problem of education and the multiple components of their solution. I then step back and consider the nest of assumptions that underlie the reformers' argument.

Defining the Problem

The problem of education, systemic reformers assert, is the system itself. Low test scores, poorly trained teachers, unequal resources, and the like are important issues. Reformers see these as symptoms, however, rather than as the illness itself. The illness is the "fragmented, complex, multi-layered educational policy system" (Smith & O'Day, 1991, p. 237).

From that vantage point, previous reforms tinkered with, rather than addressed, the real issue. Real change for all students will not come through piecemeal efforts. Instead, change must occur at the system level and it must be comprehensive. Hawley, Rosenholtz, Goodstein, and Hasselbring (1984) note, "No single variable, or even two or three variables, are likely to produce major change unless all the other interrelated characteristics change as well" (p. 9). Systemic reformers aim to promote high quality teaching and learning to all children. Previous reforms may have aimed similarly, but fell far short. Only a wholesale change will do.

This all-or-nothing assumption is problematic in a decentralized education system, yet there is a strong logic working here. Concerns about low test scores, underprepared teachers, and the needs of the least advantaged schools and children continue despite years of piecemeal reform. With this history, a radical overhaul of the education complex itself begins to make some sense. Fine-tuning will not suffice.

Proposing a Solution

All this, systemic reformers aver, speaks to the need to think big, to take on the system rather than its components, and to drive change from the top. To that end, they assign to states the chief responsibility for developing coherent and aligned policies that support a common vision for educational change.

The systemic solution begins with the state. Local educators have an important role in effecting systemic change. Education has always been a state responsibility, however, and reformers view the state as the "critical actor" (Smith & O'Day, 1991, p. 245). Three realities underscore this contention. First, states dominate the necessary resources. Local tax bases generally support local schools, but schooling is a tremendously expensive proposition and states play a large role in financing students' education. Money is not the only resource states control. Reformers believe it is a key one, however, because state monies influence local activity. Second, states govern the policy field. Policymaking has exploded since the early 1980s. Much policymaking goes on at the local level and much of this is in response to locally perceived needs. States have not been idle, however. Virtually every state has passed at least one version of a comprehensive school reform act. Such actions are important, because reformers believe that the wide-ranging policy power states hold can influence local efforts. Finally, states are uniquely positioned to provide the overarching vision for change. Reformers argue that systemic change must be vision driven. Resources and policies are important. For these tools to be effective, however, they must be supported by a consensus of thought. This consensus of thought must come from state leaders who create, build support for, and sustain a vision of change. Consensus, one reformer claims, is critical for it "reframes the problem from one of generating new support to one of maintaining support for an agreed-upon direction" (Fuhrman, 1993a, p. 26).

The vision a state creates, systemic reformers assert, should include three components: new and ambitious curriculum frameworks, the coordination of key policies, and restructured school guidance.

Improving teaching and learning is a key goal. Central to that effort, reformers argue, is the need for new subject matter frameworks. These frameworks should express high academic expectations of what students will know and be able to do. So important are these frameworks that Smith and O'Day (1991) call them the "basic drivers" of instructional guidance and they assert that developing new frameworks is the "first step" toward systemic change (p. 247).

As a necessary first step, frameworks should drive the linkage of resources and outcomes and the development of new opportunities for students to learn (O'Day & Smith, 1993). Frameworks will induce no real change, however, unless other policies are aligned with them. The second component of systemic reform, then, is the coordination of relevant state policies (e.g., curriculum materials, assessment, professional development, and licensure) such that they move in a common direction. Coordinating these policies with new frameworks brings together "two supremely logical notions: societal decisions about outcome goals and coordination of important policy instruments" (Fuhrman, 1993a, p. 3).

The third element of systemic reform focuses on restructuring school governance. Restructuring has two dimensions. One is the reduction or elimination of constraints on school practices. Reformers argue that the necessary school-level flexibility will only develop when local educators are freed from some of the state regulatory burden. The second dimension is the encouragement of new decision-making structures and procedures. This idea is perhaps best represented in the notion of site-based management in which key decisions are made at the school level by the various stakeholders—teachers, administrators, parents, and students.

Restructuring school governance is no less important than the first two components of the systemic agenda. In fact, O'Day and Smith (1993) argue that taken together these elements "marry the vision and guidance" of state-level policy with a "high degree of local responsibility and control" (p. 252).

Two concerns, coherence and alignment, guide the development of these components. Coherence, the need for policy to be "congruent, to send the same messages, and avoid contradiction" (Fuhrman, 1993b, p. xi), is the goal. The present system can be "very responsive" to pressures for change, but the results are not always "logical" (Fuhrman, 1993a, p.

15). To reach the goal of a logical and coherent system, systemic reformers argue for a strategy of policy alignment. The notion of alignment is to construct (or reconstruct) state policies about materials, assessment, professional development, and licensure such that they support and extend the academic goals expressed in new curriculum frameworks. In a state already well aligned, this could be as simple as adjusting one or more policies. In other states, however, alignment could mean a radical overhaul of the educational policy structure. In either case, the purpose of an alignment strategy is to reinvent policy relationships so that policies "build on one another in some way to form a larger whole" (Fuhrman, 1993b, p. xi). The "larger whole" is a coherent system which consciously directs resources toward improved teaching and learning.

The Assumptions Within the Systemic Argument

The logic of systemic reform is appealing, but logic is built on assumptions, and as a particularly rationalistic approach (O'Neil, 1993; Scheurich & Fuller, 1995), systemic reform rests on many suppositions. Some of those suppositions have already been mentioned. For example, systemic reformers assume that the problem is the system. They assume that aligning state policies will bring coherence to the system. Also, they assume that changing frameworks, coordinating key policies, and restructuring educational governance will transform schooling. These assumptions frame the systemic argument. There are more. In fact, a closer look suggests that each of these assumptions represents a complex of related assumptions, few of which are empirically grounded.

Systemic Reformers Assume That the Problem Is the System

Several assumptions support this premise. One is that there is an identifiable system and that it exists at the state level. Advocates of systemic reform do not define the term "system," a point observers often note (Clune, 1993; Cohen, 1995; Fullan, 1996).[1] Nevertheless, reformers clearly locate the system at the state level. They might have chosen the national level. National interest in education has certainly grown since World War II (Tyack & Cuban, 1995), and a national report, *A Nation at Risk* (National Commission on Excellence in Education, 1983), was the impetus for many current reforms. National education goals were proposed and a whole series of national curriculum frameworks were developed as part of Goals 2000. Systemic reformers do not ignore the national scene, but as noted previously, they argue that the relevant system lies at the state level (O'Day & Smith, 1993).[2]

A second assumption is that all educational issues in a state are linked and are equally amenable to change. Reformers assert that nothing less than wholesale system change will produce the desired effects. Their belief rests on two key premises. The first is that state and local policies and practices are linked so that change at the state level will induce change in local behavior. The second premise is that all policies and practices are tractable—that state and local actors will be willing and able to change whatever is necessary to effect new goals.

A third assumption is that the state system will remain stationary long enough to change the necessary components before new problems develop. Two points are important. One point relates to the view of the state system envisioned. According to one view, the system is static and reformers can take their time constructing and aligning new policies. According to another view, the system is dynamic; reformers will have small windows of opportunity and changes will have to come quickly and in massive doses. The second point relates to the relationship between state and national change agendas. Reformers assume either that national influences will coincide with state purposes, or if there are conflicts, that state actions will prevail over national efforts.

One last assumption is that the system can be reinvented by those who both created and hold the most stake in the current system. Many educators will be needed to effect the systemic change. The bulk of that work, however, will have to be done by insiders, the policymakers and practitioners who presumably constructed the system now so in need of change.

Systemic Reformers Assume That Aligning Policies Will Bring Coherence to the System

Building on the premises previously discussed, the key assumption here is that state government can and will assert itself as the prime agent of change. National activity may proceed apace, but it is only the state, as critical actor, that can build a coherent structure by aligning the necessary policies. This argument rests on two additional sets of assumptions.

First, reformers assume that state policymakers can come to consensus and that logic and reason are primary forces for change. Systemic reformers put the onus on state-level actors to construct a new and consensual vision for education and to develop policies that reflect that vision. Their critiques of the current system suggest that they understand the vague, political, and fleeting nature of policymaking. They presume, however, that the logic of their agenda will impel a group of state actors to put aside their preconceptions and coalesce around the necessary changes.

The second set of assumptions is that making policy and implementing policy are distinct processes and that these processes are institutionalized at different levels. Systemic reformers abjure movement toward a centralized, European-style educational system. They also reject radical decentralization schemes. Instead, reformers argue for a layered model based on the separation of policy making and implementation. The top layer is the state, the bottom is the local. State-level actors make policy by developing a state vision for schooling and the requisite policies that conceptualize that vision. Implementing that vision is then the responsibility of local actors (Fuhrman, 1993a).

Systemic Reformers Assume That Changing Frameworks, Coordinating Policies, and Restructuring Educational Governance Will Transform Schooling

This assertion also implies many assumptions. Some deal with the central role accorded to new curriculum frameworks. As O'Day and Smith (1993) note, "it may be relatively easy to make serious changes in an aligned system simply by changing the frameworks and allowing the alignment ripples to work throughout the system" (p. 303). This assertion presumes that people can agree on an ambitious framework, that state frameworks will take precedence over national and local efforts, that curriculum change will drive change in instruction and assessment, and that teachers will know and/or learn how to enact the changes envisioned.

Other assumptions deal with the effort to coordinate policies. Aligning curriculum, assessment, professional development, and certification policies should provide new ways of thinking about and identifying appropriate resources and practices, and should provide new bases for determining the worth of these resources and practices (O'Day & Smith, 1993). This contention rests on the assumptions that all policies can be changed and changed at the same time, that policies are interdependent and mutually supportive, that equal and adequate resources or both will be generated (and sustained) to support the new policy structure, and that policies matter to the work that teachers do.

One last set of assumptions deals with restructuring educational governance. The goal is to increase local flexibility by rethinking structures and relationships throughout the system hierarchy (Fuhrman, 1993b). Reformers assume that local actors will understand and support state goals more than local concerns, and that actors at all levels will be able to create the ideas and practices (with which they presumably have had no experience) which will transform schooling.

The systemic argument has a strong appeal: It is rational, it is all-encompassing, and it is activist. Like any grand theory, however, systemic reform is rooted in a complex of assumptions which may or may not accurately represent the realities actors at all levels face.

MICHIGAN: A CASE OF SYSTEMIC REFORM

It is often said that the devil is in the details. With systemic argument and assumptions in front of us, we can now grab the devil's tail through an examination of Michigan as a case of systemic reform.

Other states, notably California, Vermont, and Kentucky, garner most of the attention in the systemic reform literature.[3] Since the mid-1980s, however, state-level policymakers in Michigan have crafted a series of initiatives that echo elements of the systemic strategy. This is not to say that Michigan is a model case. A long tradition of local control over education has undercut state-level influence, and some elements of the systemic strategy such as control over textbook selection lie outside state influence. Still, policymakers have promoted state-level curriculum guides, they have taken steps to coordinate state policies, and they have encouraged the restructuring of local governance. These actions suggest that Michigan is a valuable site in which to study the prospects for systemic reform, because Michigan policymakers, like their peers in most other states, did not begin their reform efforts with the state-level context systemic reformers envision. Instead, Michigan policymakers have had to create both new policies and new contexts for those policies as they have gone along. Michigan might not be an ideal site for planting the systemic reform flag. Nevertheless, it is a useful site for exploring whether or not such a flag will stand and fly.

The State and the State of Reforms

State-level policymaking took off in the mid-1980s riding the wave of public interest in schools generated by *A Nation at Risk* (National Commission on Excellence in Education, 1983). Several states, most notably California, Florida, and Georgia (Firestone, Fuhrman, & Kirst, 1989), responded with ambitious, large-scale reform programs. The Michigan reform story also began in the mid-1980s, but in a far different manner.

In response to *A Nation at Risk*, the state superintendent called for a review of the existing state curriculum. In the 1970s, Michigan began developing state curricula in language arts, mathematics, science, and social studies. The superintendent's decision partially reflected the national call to reform, but it was also serendipitous: It was time for a routine curriculum review. The assistant superintendent in charge of curriculum called together the curriculum specialists and urged them "to get a vision" for their respective subject matters.

Three features of these Michigan Department of Education (MDE) actions are noteworthy. First, Michigan policymakers did not immediately push a comprehensive change agenda. Second, the initial reforms did not emphasize first-wave concerns, such as increasing certification and graduation standards and instituting new student assessments. And third, Michigan policymakers started right where systemic reformers said they should, with new curriculum frameworks. Comprehensive state policies did develop, but not until 1990. The initial state response, however, had an almost lackadaisical quality, a piecemeal effort that continued long-standing practices rather than bold new initiatives.

Systemic Reform Part I: Curriculum Frameworks, Tests, and Professional Development

In retrospect, the assistant superintendent's charge hardly seems like the stuff of systemic reform. Yet, education in Michigan changed dramatically afterwards. The ensuing revisions of the state curriculum frameworks and assessment tests were not radical, but they reflected the growing national mood toward more ambitious teaching and learning, and they acted as a precursor to the more comprehensive policy shifts that came later.

The curriculum specialists took their charge seriously. With limited state power and few available resources, however, their efforts varied considerably. In the following sections, I sketch the development of new reading, writing, and mathematics frameworks, the attendant changes in state assessment tests, and state efforts influencing professional development. Three points are important. First, the new frameworks reflected elements of national reform efforts and were quite different from their predecessors. Second, whereas the state tests were also revised, those changes did not necessarily reflect the scale of changes in the frameworks. Finally, state reformers understood the importance of professional development, but their efforts to help teachers learn about the reforms varied widely.

Reading Reforms.   Elaine Weber, the state reading consultant, was the first to respond to the call to "get a new vision." With the help of the state reading organization, Weber organized a committee and led it to conceptualize a new definition of reading in 1984, and 2 years later, to develop a new state policy, the *Essential Goals and Objectives for Reading Education* (Michigan State Board of Education, 1986). Weber then launched a limited, but ambitious, series of professional development conferences.

Developed in the late 1970s, the former state reading policy represented a traditional view, portraying reading as a series of isolated skills which students used to apprehend the "real" meaning of a text. Influenced by the emergence of cognitive psychology, Weber and her colleagues conceived of teaching and learning reading in different ways. They embodied their views in a new definition of reading:

> Reading is the process of constructing meaning through the dynamic interaction among: the reader's existing knowledge, the information suggested

by the written language, and the context of the reading situation. (Michigan State Board of Education, 1986, p. 1)

Reflecting a constructivist perspective, the new definition and the attendant goals and objectives state that comprehension, rather than skills development, is the fundamental goal of reading. In that light, the state policy emphasizes the interaction among students, texts, and the context of reading. It encourages use of various texts such as novels, poems, and magazine articles rather than sole dependence on reading basals. It promotes instruction in cognitive reading strategies such as predicting, summarizing, comparing and contrasting, and it concludes that students act as constructors of meaning.[4]

With a new conception of reading in hand, Weber and a small group of colleagues created a series of professional development opportunities. These reformers understood that their efforts called for profound changes in the way reading was taught in Michigan and that teachers would need to both learn to think and to act differently in their classrooms.

With some 90,000 teachers spread across some 600 school districts, Weber faced a daunting task. Compounding the problem was the fact that she had few state resources, financial or otherwise, to draw on. Her solution was to design a series of "training trainers" conferences. Teachers could attend, but Weber targeted district reading coordinators. She envisioned that training these coordinators in the new policy would pay off when, as trainers, they returned home and trained their teachers.

While Weber and her colleagues took the new reading policy to the field, another group began revising the reading portion of the state assessment test, the Michigan Educational Assessment Program (MEAP). The extant test looked like most standardized assessments: short reading selections; a few, largely literal, comprehension questions; and an abundance of skills-based questions (e.g., alphabetizing, identifying prefixes and suffixes, and identifying homonyms and antonyms).

The assessment committee worked for 2 years. The result is a test that maintains some features of the old (e.g., multiple-choice rather than open-ended questions), but in other ways reflects the view of reading promoted in the new state policy. The longer pieces of text, and selections from both narrative and informational sources, reflect more realistic reading contexts. The new forms of questions assess not only students' comprehension of the text, but also assess their familiarity with the topics of the selected texts, their knowledge about and attitudes toward reading, and their perceptions of themselves as readers. The comprehension questions look different from those on conventional standardized tests: Students must use their prior knowledge of the topic and must dig deeper into the selections for more sophisticated understanding.

The effort to reform reading in Michigan mirrored that across the nation. Other state policies (e.g., California Board of Education, 1987), national reports (e.g., Anderson et al., 1985; Goodman, Shannon, Freeman, & Murphy, 1988), and the professional literature pushed in roughly the same direction—toward using richer texts, teaching reading strategies, viewing students as constructors of meaning, and promoting reading for understanding. While promoting constructivist approaches to reading, reforms simultaneously pushed against traditional skills-based approaches. To talk about reading reforms, then, is to talk about a collection of ideas and practices that advanced in a common direction by addressing a set of shared concerns, by using a shared language, and by identifying past approaches as inadequate.

However, reforms and reformers are not univocal or all encompassing. Those who promote new views often emphasize different aspects. Some cognitive psychologists and reading researchers focus on the strategies students use (Baker & Brown, 1984; Paris, Cross, & Lipson, 1984; Paris, Wasik, & Turner, 1991). Others emphasize the kinds of texts students read (Goodman et al., 1988; Harris 1993; Hiebert & Colt, 1989). Still others advocate integrating reading with other language arts (e.g., writing and spelling) in what is known as "whole language" (Altwerger, Edelsky, & Flores, 1987; Cazden, 1992; Goodman, 1986). At the same time, proponents of conventional skills-based views continue to argue their points (Adams, 1989, 1990; Chall, 1983). Thus, while a new vision of teaching and learning reading emerges, that vision is neither singular nor unchallenged.

To put the point on this issue, consider one feature of the revised MEAP reading test. The Michigan reading policy places a premium on students as constructors of meaning. To that end, a "Constructing Meaning" section was developed for the new test. The questions in that section, however, are cast in a multiple-choice format. One could logically infer then, that while students might construct a range of meanings, there is still a right meaning for each question. This mix of messages—constructivist on the one side, traditional on the other—is not unique to reading (Grant, 1997b). It does raise, however, the potential for teachers to make very different sense of reforms.

Mathematics Reforms. Efforts to reform mathematics in Michigan shared some similarities with those in reading. Led by the state consultant, Charles Allan, a committee revised the state mathematics policy to advance constructivist notions of teaching and learning mathematics. Another committee revised the mathematics portion of the MEAP. As in reading, inconsistencies surfaced between the new policy and the new test. The major difference between reading and mathematics emerged in the way professional development was handled. Whereas Elaine Weber's ambitions were limited by an austere budget, Allan built a strong program using federal and state monies.

School mathematics has been the site of furious state and national activity since the early 1980s. Unlike the basic skills reforms of the 1970s, these initiatives advocate ambitious curriculum, instruction, and assessment standards. The National Council of Teachers of Mathematics (1989, 1991) captured much attention with its *Curriculum and Evaluation Standards for School Mathematics* and the *Professional Standards for School Mathematics.* The authors of the curriculum document argue that "all students need to learn more, and often different, mathematics and that instruction in mathematics must be significantly revised" (National Council of Teachers of Mathematics, 1989, p. 1). Reflecting this call, Michigan reformers constructed a sympathetic new state policy, the *Essential Goals and Objectives for Mathematics* (Michigan State Board of Education, 1990) and revised the mathematics portion of the state assessment test.

As in reading, mathematics reforms cover broad terrain. They challenge conventional approaches to teaching mathematics by offering new views of subject matter, learning, and teaching.

School mathematics is often perceived of as a collection of rules and routines and facts and procedures, which if correctly applied, yield the right answer. Multiplying a two-digit number by another two-digit number, for example, is presented as a substantively different skill than multiplying by a single-digit number. New views promote both conceptual and practical understandings of mathematics (Mathematical Sciences Educational Board, 1989; National Council of Teachers of Mathematics, 1989). As a conceptual field, mathematics involves the study of relationships, patterns, and regularities. Examples range from number sense (the notion that one has a feel for how numbers behave when variously manipulated), to probability (the chance that a given event will occur), to the search for pi. As a practical field, mathematics is concerned with real world applications such as deciding between a fixed or variable mortgage rate, determining the least amount of paint to buy for a household project, or understanding the effect of the prime interest rate on bank loans.

Conceptual and practical applications merge when mathematics is considered from a problem-solving perspective. The focus is on rich, complex problems which can be approached from multiple angles (National Council of Teachers of Mathematics, 1989; Peterson, 1990). Problems provide a context for learning rules and procedures as well as for learning problem-solving strategies such as estimation and mental math. Problems may have a correct solution, but more often than not, they are structured to support multiple solutions. Solving problems in this context emphasizes conjecture, inquiry, debate, and revision, as opposed to efficiency and accuracy in finding answers (Campbell & Bamberger, 1990; Lampert, 1990).

Perceived as a collection of rules and routines, mathematics teaching has focused on telling. With knowledge divided into small, sequential bits, teachers typically organized and delivered that knowledge in didactic fashion. New views of mathematics teaching promote alternative conceptions. Teaching moves from telling, to guiding or facilitating opportunities wherein students develop, test, and revise conjectures and share their thinking with others. Teachers, understanding that different constructions will emerge, should draw from a range of instructional representations (Ball, 1990a, 1990b; Wright, 1994).

Reforms also challenge traditional assumptions about learning. Those assumptions view learning as a reflex of teaching: Teachers organize continual practice in skills; students work to master those skills. Learning is demonstrated by swiftly and accurately applying skills to school-based tasks. New assumptions (Rabinowitz & Woolley, 1995; Smith, 1995) challenge the notion that practice leads to automaticity and that accumulating bits and pieces equals learning. Reformers do not ignore procedures like computation. Instead, they argue that procedures are best learned in the context of problems. They also hold that students actively build and revise mathematical theories (Kamii, 1993). Learners gain "mathematical power" through their ability to "explore, conjecture, and reason logically" (National Council of Teachers of Mathematics, 1989, p. 5).

Constructivist ideas are more easily represented in curriculum frameworks than in assessment tests, however. For a variety of reasons—the nature of testing, the past experience of test designers, and the cost of developing, administering, and scoring alternative assessments—the mathematics portion of the MEAP continues to reflect traditional views. The bulk of the questions focus on procedural knowledge and skills rather than on problem solving, and the multiple-choice format of the test emphasizes single, right answers. The authors of the new state mathematics policy assert that "conceptualization of mathematics and understanding of problems should be valued more highly than just correct solutions to routine exercises" (Michigan State Board of Education, 1990, p. 2). As in reading, then, translating new ideas into standardized tests proves difficult.

In one way, however, mathematics reformers in Michigan had a decided advantage over their reading counterparts. Although Allan described state-level professional development as "often unfocused . . . discrete activities presented in a disjoint manner," teachers had many more opportunities to learn about mathematics reforms than they did about reading reforms. In contrast to Weber's shoestring operation, Allan used a $7 million budget (most of it national monies) to develop the Michigan Mathematics Inservice Project (M2IP), a 4-year effort. One part of the first phase offered 17.5 days of introduction to new ideas in mathematics to some 5,000 K-8 teachers. A second part focused on another 260 teachers who received special training and encouragement to promote change in their schools and districts. Interestingly enough, though this effort easily eclipsed Weber's, Allan said he had no expectations of dramatically changing teachers' practices. Real change, he asserted, would take considerably longer.

Writing Reforms. Efforts to reform writing in Michigan were different from reforms in reading and mathematics. Department consultants, along with representatives from the Michigan Council of Teachers of English, developed a new, reform-minded writing policy (Michigan State Board of Education, 1985). There is no writing portion of the MEAP test, however, and no state-sponsored professional development around writing was scheduled. Although it is not clear why, the new state writing policy generated little controversy or interest. This seems odd because writing reformers were no less active than their reading and mathematics peers, and the nature of the proposals was no less radical.

The flurry of national reform activity related to reading and mathematics is matched in writing. Recent thinking abhors the fact that students spend a tiny fraction of their day writing, and that the writing they do is often pedantic and mind numbing (Applebee, Langer, & Mullis, 1987; Applebee, Lehr, & Auten, 1981). Reformers call for both more frequent and more engaging writing assignments (Atwell, 1987; Calkins, 1986; Graves, 1983; Kroll, 1990). More specifically, they call for writing opportunities that are more varied and have more connections with students' lives. Rather than limiting writing opportunities to end-of-chapter questions and occasional book reports, reformers advocate writing poems and stories and keeping journals and learning logs (Hancock, 1993; Walley, 1991). Reformers also promote writing as a cross-curricular activity, arguing that writing is a powerful learning tool to help students learn content.

Writing reforms also deal with instruction. Writing has traditionally been taught as discrete skills including identifying parts of speech, memorizing punctuation, and memorizing capitalization rules. Reformers challenge this approach. In the language of reforms, writing is a process. Though variously described (cf. Calkins, 1986; Courtland & Welsh, 1990; Graves, 1983), the steps of that process include brainstorming, in which one generates ideas; drafting, in which an idea is fleshed out with little attention to mechanics; revising, in which ideas, arguments, and examples are sharpened; and editing, in which mechanical problems such as spelling, grammar, and syntax are resolved. Two additional components of the writing process are conferencing and publishing. Conferences are opportunities for teacher and student to discuss a piece of the student's work. Conferences may cover a range of topics from elements of a story, to character development, to use of commas— whatever is the most pressing point at the time. When the final editing is done, students' work may be published by displaying it on a bulletin board, by reproducing copies for other students, or by binding it in book form.

Writing reforms push in these common directions. As in reading and mathematics, however, these proposals can be variously interpreted. The issue of when and how to teach mechanics is a prime example. Reformers urge an end to traditional decontextualized grammar and spelling exercises. They suggest that these elements be taught within the writing process and in the context of an active piece of student writing. The theory is that understanding when and how to use a comma, for example, will make more sense if students need to know about it for a piece of work about which they care. Teachers looking at new textbooks, for example, will see this view promoted, but those textbooks are typically divided into two sections. One features the writing process and teaching mechanics in context; the other offers traditional exercises in grammar, punctuation, and the like. Teachers may or may not view this as a problem, but it is likely to encourage various interpretations of what writing reforms are about.

One last issue is teachers' knowledge and inclinations. Few elementary school teachers are experienced and confident writers (Graves, 1983). In fact, many express fears similar to those they have about mathematics. With uncertain knowledge and private fears, teachers are likely to have various interpretations of reforms.

With no writing test on the MEAP and with virtually no funds for professional development, MDE specialists relied on the annual conferences of the Michigan Council of Teachers of English to provide most of the teacher training in the new state policy. Those sessions were well attended, but apparently little word got back to most teachers. In fact, while all four teachers in this study sensed that views of writing were changing, none have seen the new state policy.

Reading, writing, and mathematics reforms began taking hold in Michigan during the mid- to late 1980s. This fact is notable for two reasons. One is that some of it was reform on the cheap. Allan, the MDE mathematics specialist, could draw on federal monies, but his reading and writing colleagues were financially strapped. State-level reformers needed to develop resources at the same time they were developing policy.

The second reason Michigan's reform efforts are notable is that they preceded the systemic change movement. This is important because it means state policymakers and educators did not begin with a blank slate ready to be inscribed with the tenets of systemic reform. The education context was well established in Michigan, and when the reform movement began, no one was questioning the system itself.

Systemic Reform Part II: Public Act 25

The national concern with education showed no signs of abating as the 1990s began. Instead, interest developed in a new conception of educational policy—systemic reform. Michigan followed suit, for not only did state-level reforms continue, but state initiatives assumed systemic leanings. The result was a series of comprehensive state legislative acts beginning with Public Act 25.

In 1990, the piecemeal work of the MDE consultants was subsumed by a series of state-level actions that involved the state legislature, the state board of education, and the state department of education. These actions coalesced into Public Act 25 (PA 25), the first piece of state legislation aimed at causing wholesale change in the Michigan education system. Some of those changes were explicit because they directed state and local action. Others were more tacit, aimed at changing the policy context in the state.

PA 25 issued a host of directives. Among them, the MDE was charged with developing Model Core Curriculum Outcomes. Based on the recently developed subject matter policies, the Core Curriculum Outcomes were intended to guide the development of local curricula.[5] MDE was also charged with revising state tests to reflect the core curriculum objectives.

Other PA 25 directives aimed at local schools and districts. One was a mandated school improvement process. Local educators now had to form teams and develop improvement plans at both the school and district levels. These plans were to identify areas of concern and to propose solutions and timetables. Schools and districts were also required to publish annual performance reports, which among other things, had to include aggregate student test scores and suspension and dropout information.

The explicit messages of these directives aside, PA 25 also sent several tacit messages. One was that there would be no more piecemeal initiatives from the state. Revisions of curriculum frameworks and assessment tests, for example, would now be part of larger, more comprehensive state actions. The second message was that the state would no longer play a passive role. Local control was not dead in Michigan, but PA 25 signaled a shift toward a stronger state presence. All this suggested that Michigan policymakers were busy on two fronts. They were actively creating explicit new policies, and they were creating a new context in which those policies would be received.

The explicit and implicit messages sent by PA 25 correspond well to the systemic reform agenda. First, systemic reformers put great stock in new curricula as vehicles for change. Michigan policymakers may have sent confusing signals by first adopting the various state curriculum policies and then advocating a Model Core Curriculum. Nevertheless, local educators could not miss the point that the state was now firmly in the curriculum game. Second, systemic reformers promote the coordination of state policies. One way Michigan policymakers responded was by aligning new tests with the new curriculum frameworks. Another way was to elevate the importance of test scores by requiring their publication in school and district performance reports. A third dimension of the systemic agenda focused on local issues and actors. Michigan policymakers followed suit through a school improvement process designed to foster local flexibility and control by making school and district teams responsible for identifying problems and proposing solutions unique to their situations. Finally, systemic reformers support an activist state role. In and around PA 25, Michigan policymakers created a new context for educational change, part of which was a new and stronger role for state-level action.[6]

With PA 25, then, Michigan seemed poised to enact systemic change. Some elements of the systemic agenda were missing. For example, textbook adoption remained a local decision, and issues such as professional development and certification were not addressed in the state legislation at all. Those caveats aside, Michigan began the 1990s well on the road to systemic reform.

The State of Reforms and the Local Context

State-level policymakers were busy. As the national conversation about schooling developed, Michigan policymakers sensed an opportunity and, despite a tradition of local control, state-level activity reached new heights. Systemic reformers assume that local policymakers will sit on their hands until the state has spoken. Not so in Michigan: As state-level policymaking increased, so too did local policymaking. State-sponsored systemic reform had come to Michigan, but it would not get carte blanche treatment.

Local activity generally mirrored state interests, but not always (Cohen, Spillane, Jennings, & Grant, in press; Spillane, 1996). The long history of local control in Michigan meant that local policymakers were used to creating their own policy directions and approaches. As we will see in following chapters, local educators did not completely ignore state intrusions such as the MEAP, but they neither looked to the state for guidance nor did they get too worked up about state initiatives. From a state perspective, PA 25 transformed the educational landscape in Michigan. From a local perspective, however, it was business as usual. Instead of a single statewide vision for educational change, the education landscape was a crazy quilt of status quo and change. Instead of driving change, state-level policy had to compete with local interpretations and initiations as local policymaking continued as normal. Instead of a coherent statewide adoption of new curriculum policies, districts and schools differed widely in the degree and kind of reforms they encouraged and in the attempts they made to influence teaching and learning. And instead of a main course, Michigan teachers now faced a policy smorgasbord.

Not surprisingly, teachers' responses varied. As the chapter 1 vignettes described, teachers in the same district and even in the same school building viewed reforms quite differently. For example, Jones interprets reading reforms as a direct challenge to the way she has thought about and taught reading, but her colleague, Jensen, saw only confirmation of instructional approaches he has long used. This variation across teachers suggests that the same reform may face a very different future depending on how each teacher reads it. Uneven responses across teachers is only one form of variation. A similar range of responses can be seen across reforms in each teacher's classroom. Jones' ambitious response to reading reforms contrasts sharply with her more modest response to writing reforms.

The classroom is often viewed as the last stop on the policy train, but observers increasingly note that teachers play a powerful "street-level" policymaking role (McLaughlin, 1990; Schwille, Porter, Belli, Floden, Freeman, Knappen, Kuhs, & Schmidt, 1983; Weatherly & Lipsky, 1977). Kirst and Walker (1971) blur the clear distinctions many analysts hold between making and enacting policy. Capping their critique is the observation that new policies inevitably face the potential "pocket veto" of classroom teachers (p. 505). The implications are profound. Taken to its logical conclusion, this assertion implies that policy power ultimately rests in the classroom decisions of the very people identified by most reformers as the problem (Warren, 1989).

MICHIGAN AND THE PROSPECTS
FOR SYSTEMIC REFORM

Does all this variation mean that systemic reform is misguided and doomed and that Michigan is a poor site for the systemic agenda? I think the answer is no on both counts, but this conclusion does not mean that the systemic argument is unproblematic, nor does it mean that Michigan policymakers will eventually get it right. It does mean, however, that the efforts and experiences of Michigan policymakers and educators offer a lens for viewing the real prospects for systemic reform.

I discuss those prospects more fully in chapter 8. For now, consider four instances wherein the Michigan experience exposes tensions within the systemic change initiative.

One tension is about how to define the state. Reformers argue that the state is the critical actor in reforming the education system and they assign to the state a complex of new and challenging responsibilities—creating and building support for a vision of change, developing and disseminating new and revised policies that are ambitious and aligned, and promoting the restructuring of educational guidance at the local level. The case of Michigan suggests, however, that a key question is who represents the state? Compelling arguments could be made for the state education department, the state Board of Education, or the state legislature. Yet, given the history of local decision making, one might argue that the state is no more than the collective action of local educators. With a range of potentially relevant contexts, systemic reformers are probably wise to leave open the definition of state. Moving from rhetoric to reality, however, the Michigan experience highlights the tension likely to develop about who controls the reform agenda and what the message(s) of reform will be.

A second tension involves the proliferation of policy. The systemic argument presumes that as state policymaking increases, local policymaking will decrease. The Michigan experience refutes this assumption. State-level policymaking increased, but local policymaking continued as strong as ever. As a consequence, disjunctures developed between state and local reform directions. Local administrators gave state policies some attention, but only as those policies fit district interests. Teachers received mixed messages from this confusion of state and district interests.

A third tension surfaces in the hard distinctions drawn between making and enacting policy. Systemic reformers assume that locals will defer to state actions and that they will understand, support, and enact state goals more than local initiatives. As we have seen, however, local realities matter, and state actions are neither the only, nor the most profound, sources of influence. Local actors listen to and act on state policy talk, but they may also listen to and act on talk at both the national and coffee shop levels. This suggests a tension in the systemic argument that institutionalizes policy making and enactment at different levels. Reformers see a clear role for local educators, but it is a clearly defined role and one that differs sharply from that of the state. Simply put, the state makes and the locals enact. The Michigan experience, however, exposes a hard reality: Locals make policy too. While local policies and the enactment of them may reflect state initiatives, there is no guarantee. Moreover, questions arise about whether districts have the resources to help teachers change their practices in substantive ways.

One last tension involves the role teachers play in the systemic agenda. Teachers are not much mentioned in the systemic reform literature, and when they are, the presumption is that they will understand and enact the state reform program. The teachers in this study have changed some of their practices based on ideas represented in state policies (though not exclusively). The nature of those changes and variations among them, however, raise serious questions about the systemic goal of driving coherence downward from the state to the classroom.

That tensions surface between the rhetoric of systemic reform and the reality of schooling is no particular surprise. No comprehensive plan is immune from the vagaries of the real world. We must be careful, therefore, not to nit-pick. That said, systemic reform is sufficiently problematic to make me believe that the prospects for real change are dim. The systemic argument offers an insightful analysis of the endemic problems in U.S. education and a sweeping strategy to solve those problems. One need not follow the other, however, because the systemic solution of policy alignment and coherence is based on a particular reading of the problems. One can agree with the systemic reformers' definition of the problems without agreeing with their solution. In short, if the problem is systemic, is the solution?

NOTES

1. Holzman (1993) suggests that "systemic" can be defined at least five different ways: a) working with school systems—e.g., school districts and state departments of education or both, b) working with every school in a system, c) working with every aspect within a system, d) working across both horizontal and vertical structures, and, e) working to change the nature of the entire system.
2. It's worth noting, however, that Marshall Smith and Jennifer O'Day wrote an article in the *American Educator* (with David Cohen) that argued for a national curriculum (Smith, O'Day, & Cohen, 1990).
3. Studies of California include Grant, Peterson, and Shojgreen-Downer (1996), Kirp and Driver (1995), and Scheurich and Fuller (1995). See also Volume 12 of *Educational Evaluation and Policy Analysis*, and Volume 93 of *Elementary School Journal*. Vermont is the focus of studies by Murname and Levy (1996) and Lusi (1997). Lusi also examines the Kentucky reforms. Hertert (1996) draws on data from nine states and some 30 districts for her comparative study.
4. For a detailed description of Weber's work to create the new state reading policy and a deeper analysis of the difference between old and new policies, see Cohen, Spillane, Jennings, and Grant (in press).
5. School districts were required to develop core curricula, but were not required to adopt the MDE outcomes.
6. That role, as we will see in chapter 8, grows over time. For example, state legislation in 1991 mandated the development of a state-endorsed diploma tied to a new state high school proficiency test. Legislation in 1993 and 1995 further expanded the state role in education. Some of that legislation introduced changes in new areas such as certification and the length of the school year. Other portions of the new laws, however, revoked parts of earlier state acts. For example, PA 289, passed in 1995, overturned the requirement expressed in PA 25 that schools submit a school improvement plan to the state.

Part II

CASES OF TEACHERS, SCHOOLS, AND REFORMS

Prologue

The Derry School District and Donnelly-King Elementary School

Bonnie Jones and Frank Jensen teach in Donnelly-King Elementary, a small K-6 school located in the farming community of Lewis. Both are teachers of considerable experience. Jones, a fifth-grade teacher, has taught for more than 20 years. Jensen, who teaches a combination class of third and fourth graders, has also been in education for more than 20 years. Although Jones and Jensen teach but 40 feet from one another, their individual responses to reading, writing, and mathematics reforms reveal that they are teachers of very different styles.

Lewis is an idle little town. Quiet streets lie at right angles to the county road which bisects the town. Modest, single-family homes and marginal farms dot the flat landscape. The business district is a single street dominated by a large grain elevator on one end and two bars on the other. The few other establishments are nondescript and are economically borderline. Inhabitants who do not work the land drive to larger area communities for jobs in durable goods industries. The Donnelly-King principal, no fan of small town life, likes to tell a story about one of the school's original teachers. This woman, born and raised in Lewis, rarely left the town limits. After visiting a friend in New York City, she stopped at the principal's office. "Mr. Adams," she announced, "I've discovered the most amazing thing. Lewis is just a piss ant little town!"

Donnelly-King Elementary is located just off the main street. The school's odd appearance reflects the joining of the original section, a one-story, gable-roofed structure, with a new, two-story, flat-roofed gymnasium. The visual incongruities continue inside. The institutional greens and blues of most schools are absent here. Instead, orange-red walls and red-orange carpeting outfit the long corridors. The gymnasium is decorated in shades of turquoise. Classroom walls, generally beige, provide a welcome respite.

The 300 students sit in 16 classrooms, two classrooms for each grade K-6 and two classrooms for special needs students bussed in from other towns in the Derry district. Class sizes are moderate; Jones and Jensen each have fewer than 25 students. Those students are virtually all Eastern European Caucasians from working-class families. As a group, they are bright eyed, cheery, and cooperative. Parents tend to support teachers' efforts, the district superintendent reported, but have low expectations of their children's abilities.

Donnelly-King is a small school by Michigan standards. Nevertheless, the air in and around the school is filled with reforms. State, district, and school-level initiatives all vie for teachers' attention. Some reforms come directly from the state. Each teacher, for example, received a copy of the new state health education policy, the Michigan Model. Most other state reforms are mediated by district actions with varying degrees of enthusiasm. Teresa Jensen, the district reading consultant, introduced the new state reading policy and the changes in the state assessment test to district teachers. Active in the development and dissemination of the policy across the state, Jensen organized a week-long summer inservice for all district teachers in 1987. In 1989, she began organizing the selection of a new reading textbook series and a publisher-sponsored workshop. To select the textbook series, Jensen convened a committee of teachers and administrators who chose a slate of textbooks to be piloted, reviewed the results of the pilots, and adopted a single series by Harcourt, Brace, and Jovanovich (McCandless-Simmons, 1990) to be used in all district classrooms. After the adoption, Jensen hosted a workshop at each of the district elementary schools. During each session, a representative from the publisher introduced the text, demonstrated lessons, and answered teachers' questions.

District administrators gave less attention to the new state mathematics and writing policies. There is no district-level consultant in mathematics, and the district's primary response to the new state policy was to assemble another committee of teachers and administrators to adopt a new Addison-Wesley mathematics textbook series (Eicholz & Young, 1991). Publisher-sponsored workshops followed the adoption, but no other inservice opportunities were scheduled. District administrators did even less with the state writing policy. Jensen was working with a few individual teachers on classroom writing projects when this study ended. She had no plans, however, to do anything at the district level. Moreover, although the district

English language arts series was almost 10 years old, there were no plans to adopt a new series.

Although district administrators embraced state curriculum reforms with various levels of enthusiasm, they wholeheartedly adopted PA 25. Parts of this act (e.g., creating annual school performance reports) are largely administrative in nature. Other parts, however, deal with issues closer to schooling. District administrators were particularly drawn to the school improvement process. PA 25 calls for the organization of a school improvement team at each school site along with a district-level team. Teams are to be broadly representative of the school and community stakeholders. Their primary task is to create a 5-year school improvement plan which details intended changes in any of several areas (e.g., facilities, curriculum, and professional development).

Derry administrators moved quickly to set up school improvement teams and to get the process of goal-setting underway. They did not stop there. Working with colleagues in other Sheridan county districts, the Derry superintendent imported the Outcomes Driven Developmental Model (ODDM) developed by William Glasser. ODDM is a complex professional change program which consists of four components: cooperative learning, self-esteem, responsibility training, and mastery learning. A committee met during the 1991 to 1992 school year to plan an on-going series of workshops and inservices.

Beyond these district-level efforts, the Donnelly-King staff has developed several schoolwide initiatives, though virtually all center on reading. For example, several teachers were upset by state assessment test results in reading, which indicated that students had trouble answering questions about nonfiction or informational text. The teachers responded by inviting Teresa Jensen to meet with them and discuss ways to address the problem. Other teachers run the school-wide book program. Introduced 7 years ago to promote reading, this program uses a series of local fundraisers to purchase classroom sets of trade books. Students read and vote for their favorite books in a schoolwide referendum. The winners are announced in an all-school assembly and the titles are inscribed on plaques. To further promote student reading, the faculty voted a year ago to devote 1 week each term to a DEAR (Drop Everything and Read) program. Each day of that week an announcement from the office alerts students, teachers, and school staff that it is DEAR time. All activity stops and everyone reads from a selection of his or her choice for 30 minutes.

As Bonnie Jones and Frank Jensen construct their reading, writing, and mathematics practices, they face a blizzard of state, district, and school-level initiatives. Jones and Jensen attend to these initiatives, but they do so neither equally nor consistently. Not only does Jones approach reading reforms differently from Jensen, but she also approaches them differently than she does writing and mathematics reforms. There are some similarities across the two teachers and there are some similarities in how each teacher responds to the various initiatives. Still, it is the differences or the variation in their responses which stands out and speaks most clearly about the prospects for systemic change.

Going It Alone:
The Case of Bonnie Jones

Bonnie Jones is a reformer's dream: She hears the call to reform and she is changing her teaching in profound ways. As the vignette in chapter 1 suggests, Jones asks hard questions of her reading and mathematics practice. She learns about and tries new instructional approaches. She risks failing. Her response to writing reforms, however, is more modest. Changes are less obvious and more fragile, but rather than a failure, this example illustrates the complex variation in teachers' responses to reforms.

If Jones represents the success of reforms, her story also illustrates the difficult road teachers travel. She has learned a lot, yet she is unsure of what she knows and what more she needs to learn. She is convinced reforms offer powerful possibilities, yet she worries about realizing them. She has considerable classroom autonomy, yet she feels her efforts go misunderstood and unsupported. Jones pushes on, but she does so feeling alone and uncertain.

Bonnie Jones is a middle-aged, European American whose dress is stylish, but comfortable—slacks, blouses, and sweaters in conservative colors. Her eyes, however, command attention. Magnified by the convex lenses in her designer frames, they dance with energy and animation. Her talk is just as animated. Delivered at a staccato pace, it comes both in one word answers and in multiple paragraph expositions. She masks no feelings, taking pride in delivering honest (often dramatic) assessments of herself and of others.

Jones lives the life of her eyes and her talk. She pushes the school day in both directions, starting earlier and staying later than many of her peers. She often returns on Sundays to prepare for the coming week. Before and after school, she negotiates the blizzard of activities—locating and preparing materials for class, participating in school and district meetings, talking to and counseling students and their parents—that define the less obvious aspects of teaching. In class, Jones is constantly on the move. She teaches from all points of the room, sitting at her desk only when taking attendance and recording lunch counts.

Jones is also active outside her school and district. She belongs to state and national professional organizations and regularly attends regional and state workshops and conferences, usually at her own expense. Moreover, she has taken a steady diet of college courses over the past 2 years in pursuit of an advanced teaching credential. Going home is often like going to a second job. Jones manages the home lives of two young children and the bookkeeping chores of her husband's carpentry business.

Her classroom walls testify to Jones' interest in reforms. Hand-lettered posters represent workshop ideas she liked. From sessions entitled "Keys to Motivation" and "Positive Reactions to Hostile Situations," she made a series of posters: "It takes courage to take a risk." "We are free to make mistakes." "It is intelligent to ask for help." "Everything is hard before it is easy." "You are valuable." "You are unique." Other posters are commercially produced. One, "Problem-Solving Strategies," offers this rubric: "understand the problem, solve the problem, answer the problem, evaluate the answer." Fix-Up Strategies urge students to slow down, to continue reading, to re-read, to use maps and other aids, to use glossary/dictionary, to ask another student, and to ask the teacher. "Progress Charts" log the number of books students read.

The geography of Jones' interest in reforms continues on the floor of her classroom. Cupboards overflowing with battered classroom sets of trade books testify to her interest in reading. A small but growing pile of science models, equipment, and books supports her interest in hands-on science and in the Michigan Model, the state health curriculum. Her interest in mathematics is evidenced by the stacked crates of mathematics manipulatives, calculators, and the like in every corner. Everywhere are collections of students' work—timelines Civil War events hang from the ceiling, tessellation drawings sit on a table waiting to be displayed, and graphs of students' heights and weights, number of siblings, average hours of television watched hang behind Jones' desk.[1]

From these observations, one might imagine that Jones has always taught in ambitious ways. Not so. Jones reports being a very different sort of teacher before her self-described "cycle of change" which began with her introduction to the new state reading policy in the mid-1980s.

"I used to be known as 'the ditto queen,' " Jones explained.[2] Then, she spent her time assigning, collecting, and correcting pages of skills-based exercises. "I was only doing what I was taught and what the research said," she said, "In those days, it was all skills and I really got into those skills." Then, Jones was the acknowledged expert, "the almighty teacher." She took pride in her smooth ability to manage a wide array of routines. Students were quiet and on-task, papers moved efficiently from her to the students and back. The accumulating evidence, piles of completed work and record books filled with grades, testified to her teaching and to her students' learning.

When reading coordinator Teresa Jensen began promoting the new state definition of reading, Jones reached a personal and professional flash point. A string of difficult family circumstances including separation and divorce from an abusive husband, a new marriage, and the death of her middle child had left her shaken:

> I guess maybe the biggest thing is 9 years ago my son died. The night before he died, the doctor told me there was nothing wrong with him. I said there is something wrong and he said it was all in my head. And the next day, when I was holding a dead baby in the emergency room and the doctor saw it, I said to the doctor, "I told you there was something wrong." He said, "I should have believed you." And it was then that I started to think that you can't always trust the experts. . . . So I guess I started questioning everything. I started questioning my faith, my teaching, the experts, and it just seemed like the world started to change. Things just took on a different perspective.

Jones' struggles continued as her marriage broke up. "When I separated from my husband," she said, "I just started backing away from classes, conferences, and everything as my life fell apart." Her retrenchment took two forms. Professionally, she pulled back, closing the classroom door and maintaining her familiar and safe skills-based instruction. She pulled back socially as well, distancing herself from her colleagues and retreating into her family.

As her personal life gained some normalcy, Jones examined her teaching. She was not happy with what she saw:

> My career was falling apart; the kids weren't achieving and I didn't care. . . . I was burned out. I was frustrated. I knew something had to change, but I didn't know what. . . . Then I thought maybe this [new reading policy] was something I could try. It was there and what I was doing was shit.

Personal and professional needs drive Jones' current interest in reforms. Today, Jones is a teacher driven to ask big questions of herself and her teaching and to undertake big changes. Some of those changes are in her daily instruction (e.g., new curriculum materials, new teaching strategies, and new ways of organizing students). Others lie deeper, because Jones is changing not only her daily practice, but also her underlying assumptions about subject matter, teaching, and learning. These changes cost time, energy, and money. They also cost comfort and certainty. Jones embraces the vision that reforms offer. Pursuing that vision, however, is no mean feat.

RESPONDING TO REFORMS

The geography of Bonnie Jones' classroom maps her interest in reforms. Trade books, mathematical manipulatives, and science models figure prominently in the physical and intellectual environment of her classroom. New ideas about writing, classroom organization, cooperative learning, and outcomes-based education also figure into her practice.

Jones does not attend to every reform. Although it seems she never met an idea she didn't like, Jones' appetite is bounded. She gives no attention, for example, to using student portfolios for assessment, to plans to develop a state-wide proficiency test, or to the district and school improvement plans. This observation does not obviate her future interest in these issues. It only means that her current interests are but a subset of those possible.

I offer explanations for why Jones responds to reforms as she does in chapter 7. Here I focus on how she responds. In sections of this chapter, I examine Jones' responses to reforms in reading, mathematics, and writing. More specifically, I look at how she views reforms in relation to her past practice, I seek evidence of reform-minded ideas in her daily instruction, and I note changes in her conceptions of subject matter, teaching, and learning. I concentrate on reading, writing, and mathematics for three reasons. First, Jones invests considerable effort attending to these reforms. Second, these are subjects common to school classrooms and, as such, are targets of recent state and national reforms and are central to systemic change efforts. Finally, as basic subjects, these areas provide good sites for comparing teachers' responses.

Embracing the Possibilities of Reading Reforms

Bonnie Jones ignores the new district reading textbook in favor of trade books. Most reading reformers would applaud this act, but is this decision an act of pique because her choice was voted down, a superficial change in an otherwise conventional practice, or a piece of a larger effort to transform her reading practice? I argue for the last. Abandoning textbooks and adopting trade books reflects a key element of Jones' interpretation of reading reforms and has important implications both for her daily instruction and for deeper questions of subject matter, teaching, and learning.

Learning New Ideas About Reading.   Bonnie Jones dates her current interest in reforms from the onset of the state's effort in reading. Encountering the new Michigan reading policy during the district inservice led by Teresa Jensen, Jones remembers being struck by the notion of a dynamic interaction between students and text:

> It made sense because when I read, I subconsciously put myself in that character's place. And when I read, I live that character. I cry in the middle of the book or I laugh or I personally experience it. And if that's the way I read and the way I enjoy it, then this is what these kids should be having. They should be having this experience.

Connecting her own experience as an adult reader with those her students "should be having" made a powerful impression. For years, Jones taught reading through drill and practice, focusing on the word recognition and literal comprehension skills she found in her basal and student reading workbooks. She interprets the new state policy as a radical departure from such practices.

Jones' talk echoes the language of reforms. She learned to talk about reading strategies, trade books, text structures, helping students access their prior knowledge, and the ideas behind them through several sources.

Two of those sources were local. One was the week-long district inservice, Reading Update, led by district reading coordinator, Teresa Jensen. There Jones learned about the new state policy, strategy instruction, narrative and expository text, and the debate over textbooks and trade books. Another source was the Harcourt, Brace & Jovanovich (HBJ) textbook the district adopted 2 years later. Jones refuses to use the textbook, but she attended the publisher-sponsored inservices. She reports learning some new reading strategies. Overall, however, she thought the sessions were a "waste of time."

Jones also looks outside the district to learn about reading. She holds membership in the Michigan Reading Association and the International Reading Association and she attends a spate of yearly state-level conferences and workshops. This extra effort is necessary, Jones feels, as school and district interest in reading dwindles. "It's died down," she said wryly, "ODDM and science are hot now."

Reading Reconsidered.   Every fall Bonnie Jones distributes the district reading textbooks to her students. The bindings remain uncracked. Jones will not use the texts even though she admits they are better than the former series. Instead, she uses classroom novels which she purchases with the school book program funds. Substituting trade books for textbooks represents a change in curriculum materials. In Jones' case, it also represents her changing view of reading.

Before encountering reforms, Jones held a familiar view of reading. Her "skills/word" perspective (Richardson et al., 1991, p. 560) emphasized practice in discrete skills and extracting a literal interpretation of text. This traditional view carries several assumptions about the nature of reading and the roles of teacher, student, and textbooks. For example, reading is understood to be a function of identifying individual words which carry meaning as they accumulate (Goodman et al., 1988). The process of identifying words can be decomposed into a seemingly endless list of discrete skills such as identifying prefixes and suffixes, locating root words, and using phonetic rules. These skills can be taught within rich and meaningful pieces of text. The assumption, however, is that they are more efficiently taught through decontextualized exercises and basal readers which highlight individual skills. Thus, reading is more a function of knowing how to identify individual words than of constructing rich and varied meanings. The skills-based view also holds assumptions for teachers, students, and textbooks. It presumes, for example, that students act as passive receivers of knowledge, that textbooks serve as the source of knowledge, and that teachers function as expert technicians able to match students' needs with textbook prescriptions.

Reading reforms question this view (Anderson et al., 1985; Michigan State Board of Education, 1986). Jones agrees: "What I heard was that everything was changing and that all the things I had been doing for the last 16 years were rotten. And I agreed."

Jones identifies several "rotten" elements in her past practice. One is the idea of grounding reading in discrete skills. Whereas she once saw learning to read as a process of decoding and identifying words, Jones now embraces the reform emphasis on comprehension and the process of constructing meaning. The keys to building comprehension are reading strategies. In the constructivist view, strategies are approaches readers use to make sense of text or, as Smith (1979) notes, to read "directly for meaning" (p. 111). These strategies include predicting and summarizing, using contextual clues, understanding text types and structures, and accessing prior knowledge (Brenna, 1995; Paris et al., 1991; Yochum, 1991). Good readers use strategies as ways of asking and answering questions of text, of checking their understanding, and of comparing new ideas with previous experience (Anderson et al., 1985; Michigan State Board of Education, 1986).[3] Strategic readers can identify words, but their purpose is understanding text.

Another "rotten" element is the text students read. This is also a prominent theme in the reading reform literature (Anderson et al., 1985; Harris, 1993; Hiebert & Colt, 1989; McGee, 1992). Reformers appear of mixed minds about the role of textbook programs, but they agree on the need to include more and more interesting texts. Students' understanding of story structures develops at an early age; they need rich and meaningful texts to facilitate that understanding (Anderson et al., 1985).

The HBJ textbook adopted by the district represents a change in that direction. It is advertised as a literature-based series and explicitly refers to reading strategies. Jones acknowledges this improvement, although she questions whether the texts really represent a new view of reading. She argues that the few references to reading strategies still look like the discrete and isolated skills in her old basal textbook. Jones' criticism of the text's literature-based approach is even sharper. District administrators and many of her colleagues believe HBJ's abridged stories reflect the call to enrich the text students read. Jones is unconvinced: "To them it was literature based. To me, that's not my interpretation of literature-based." She interprets reforms as a call for students to read and discuss real literature (Goodman et al., 1988; Pearson, 1989). The selections in the textbook, she asserts, are "watered down" and read like "basals." She said, "I mean, sure it's [the HBJ text] literature-based; all the stories come from literature, but the book I wanted had full books in it." Jones contends that using "full books" is important to students' understanding. Jones asserts that textbook selections of any sort are neither sufficiently rich nor complex to engage students' interest. "When you talk about plot, subplots, character development, resolution, conclusion . . . you can take a story that's only maybe 10 pages, but that seems to me superficial. I mean you're not really getting into the real meat of it." Here, Jones is reacting to the bland, vocabulary-controlled stories written by textbook editors that she found in her basal readers. Created to emphasize one or more discrete skills, these stories offer little depth or richness from which to explore elements such as plot and subplot. One might argue that length alone is a poor indication of whether or not there is any meat to a text, but if she is to promote a new view of reading, Jones believes she needs powerful texts. Her past experience with basal reading textbooks suggests they are a "rotten" resource.

Jones also takes aim at the traditional division between reading and other subject matters. Although it is not mentioned in the Michigan reading policy, teaching reading across the school day is a theme in the larger reading literature (Anderson, et al., 1985; Applebee et al., 1987). Jones had always viewed reading as a separate subject, unrelated to any other part of the curriculum. She now embraces a reform perspective: Reading is a cross-disciplinary subject wherein students are taught how reading a content area textbook differs from reading other types of text, and they are given opportunities to read books other than textbooks.

In identifying what is "rotten," Jones illustrates her developing view of reading. Much of that view is centered in a new sense of purpose. Before encountering the reforms, she held a largely utilitarian view: One learned to read in order to identify the words and to understand the literal meaning of text. Jones' reading of reforms, however, encourages her to think about her own experiences as a reader and about the notion of constructing meaning. She concludes, among other things, that learning to read has multiple purposes. Some of those purposes are technical. Learning reading strategies, for example, helps a reader to understand and make sense of a piece of text. Other purposes are motivational. Reforms suggest that good readers are motivated to read and do so frequently (Anderson et al., 1985; Michigan State Board of Education, 1986). Jones accepts this premise. "I realized that kids weren't reading books," she said, "And I wanted to bring out the joy and love and enthusiasm I have for reading."

Still other purposes concern the notion that reading is a way of connecting one's own life experiences with others'. Recall Jones' realization that students would benefit from experiences with books similar to her own. She had powerful experiences as a reader, but she never considered teaching reading to that end. Reforms convince her that students profit when they "bring their own experiences from their lives and their pasts and relate them to the material."

One consequence is that Jones now sees a role for interpretation in reading. Although this idea is central to the notion of constructing meaning, Jones has found it only recently. As a skills teacher, she was a textual fundamentalist: Texts had real, authorial meanings and the purpose of reading was to apprehend them. The notion that one interprets text might have meant something to Jones, the adult reader. As a teacher, however, she took extracting the right meaning as primary. After learning that students need to connect their experiences with the texts they are reading, Jones acknowledges that students, in effect, interpret text. "For [students] to understand those books [texts, reference books], they have to think and interpret. The books are there to give the information. . . . But you have to interpret the information." It is not entirely clear what this means. The idea that students interpret text, and perhaps interpret it differently, is foreign to the kind of reading instruction Jones knows. It raises profound questions about her past practice, and if she continues to pursue it, may mean even more profound changes in her future practice.

Jones is responding to reading reforms by radically overhauling her conception of reading as a school subject. Rejecting a skills-based view, she is headed toward a conception that emphasizes a constructivist view of knowledge. She makes comprehension the goal of reading. She believes students need to learn reading strategies through substantive texts that go beyond worksheets and vocabulary-controlled basals. She avers that students may construct meanings different from hers or from those of their peers. Such beliefs stand in stark contrast to the skills-based approaches she once held.

A Look at Current Practice. Bonnie Jones talks about a new view of reading and much of her classroom reading instruction looks like the reforms, but both her talk and her practice have the feel of changes still in the making because one senses that both Jones and her students are still learning new ways of interacting with one another and with text.

It was not always this way. For 20 years, Jones taught reading in the prevailing skills-based fashion like most of her elementary school peers. Discrete reading skills dominated her instruction; managing the flow of skills sheets occupied much of her attention. Students alternated between two work settings, individual seatwork and ability-based reading groups. They read little and what they did read came from basal readers. They talked little, and when they did talk it occurred during round-robin reading and in their questions at the beginning of each new lesson. Textbooks and teacher's guides determined Jones' practice. They defined the content to be taught, the instructional methods used, and the tools of evaluation. They assured her she was teaching the right things and that students were learning. Jones explained, "I had always done things exactly as the basal said . . . I just assumed that if the kid got an A, then he learned something."

Elements of traditional practice remain, but as the following lesson suggests, Jones' reading practice looks much different today:

> Just before lunch, Jones asked the class to take out their copies of *Midnight Fox* (Byars, 1968). After directing them to turn to the chapter entitled, "One Fear," Jones stopped and asked the students to take out their writing folders. Her instructions were, "Please write a summary of what we've read so far." Several audible moans arose. She paused and said, "Okay, let's summarize it together; let's start at the beginning." A quick series of storyline questions followed: "Why does Tom have to go to his aunt and uncle's farm? What does he think the farm will be like? What changed his mind?" Students flocked to volunteer short, confident answers. Affirming their responses, Jones said, "All right, you've got 5 minutes to write what the story is about."

Two reforms surface here. One is that the students read and discuss a piece of literature instead of a textbook. Jones takes the call to use richer and more challenging texts seriously. Although she uses textbooks to teach content area reading strategies, she uses only children's literature like *The Midnight Fox* during her reading instruction. Jones knows that some students struggle with these texts and she worries about the few students who do not contribute much during class, but she believes that richer reading selections and more opportunities to talk about their ideas will elevate everyone's understanding.

A second reform is evident in the use of whole-class instruction rather than ability-based reading groups. Reforms such as *Becoming a Nation of Readers* (Anderson, et al., 1985) challenge the practice of grouping students by ability. Accumulating evidence suggests that students in the slow groups not only read less challenging materials, but that they also receive less instructional time. Classifying students as poor readers appears to seal their fate; students in low groups rarely break out of that categorization (Allington, 1980; Barr & Dreeben, 1983). Jones knows this literature and she accepts its conclusions, so when she abandoned the district textbook in favor of trade books, she also abandoned ability-based reading groups in favor of whole-class instruction.

A third reform, attention to reading strategies, is evident when Jones asks students to summarize the story and, in this vignette from later in the same lesson, to predict what the "tragedy" will be:

> Jones directed students to the last page of the previous chapter. "I want to get you back into the story," she explained, "Why would I have you turn to the last page of this chapter?" Jamie offered a prophetic response: "There is something there that will make you want to go on reading." Nodding, Jones read the sentence, "That night, the tragedy of the black fox began."
>
> "Okay," she said, "turn your papers over and write what you think that tragedy is going to be." Students quickly engaged the task and offered several possibilities: the fox is shot by the uncle, the uncle traps the fox and her baby, the uncle finds the den and kills the black fox. "Is this the setting, the character, the problem, or the solution?" Jones asked. Lisa asked if it was the problem. Jones nodded and turned to the chapter at hand.

Summarizing and predicting are two reading strategies used for making sense of text. Others include story mapping (i.e., understanding story elements such as setting, character, problem, solution) and using context clues (i.e., determining the meaning of a word by understanding the larger meaning around it). Although they have different functions, the purpose of reading strategies is to facilitate comprehension. In the first vignette, Jones asks students to summarize the story to check their understanding of the principal characters and events, and to rekindle their interest in the story. In the second vignette, she asks students to predict the tragedy to encourage speculation about possible outcomes which could then be checked by reading. Still another strategy, accessing prior knowledge, is apparent in this vignette:

> Jones read the sentence, "It was like my food passage had suddenly shrunk to the size of a rubber band." She looked up from the book, asked the class what the term was for such a literary device, and smiled when a student answered, "a simile." Jones asked if anyone had ever felt as though he or she could not swallow. Students readily offered examples: when about to throw up, when people tell jokes while you have food in your mouth, after finding a dead rabbit beside the road. Laughter, groans, and exclamations

exploded throughout the room. Jones eventually pulled the students back to the text, reading with enthusiasm and spirit; students followed intently.

Here, Jones forges a connection between students' prior knowledge and experience and the lives of the characters. Doing so facilitates students' understanding of the story and enlarges the role they play in their own learning. Jones could probably teach these strategies even faster using a series of worksheets. One learns reading strategies, however, not to know how the strategy works, but to use it to construct meaning from the text.

The end of this particular lesson provided one additional insight into Jones' embrace of reading reforms—teaching reading across subject matters:

> As the lesson ended, Jones asked, "Would you study for a science test in a different way than for a test on *Midnight Fox*?" Several students chorused, "Yes." Smiling, she continued, "Okay, what's SQ3R?" Jody answered: "Survey, question, read, reflect, respond." Jones nodded and said, "Good. Please take out your science books. We're going to do a little surveying and questioning."

Here, Jones suggests that a different type of text, an informational text like a science textbook, calls for a different reading strategy, SQ3R. This point reinforces the notion of reading as a cross-disciplinary subject. Hard distinctions between learning to read and reading to learn (Sawyer, 1987) dissolve as Jones makes explicit references to reading strategies during her content area instruction and uses trade books to supplement textbooks. Until recently, Jones' instruction in mathematics, science, and social studies centered exclusively on textbooks. She still uses them, but increasingly she draws from a growing trade-book library.

The approach to reading evident in these vignettes contrasts with the skills-based focus that once defined Jones' reading practice. Compared to her past practice, it seems a revolution is occurring. If so, it is a revolution colored by past practice, because as rich as Jones' reading instruction is, elements of traditional instruction remain.

In another lesson from *Midnight Fox*, for instance, Jones distributed a conventional worksheet focused on recalling literal information. Many of the questions had the skills-based feel of a basal textbook. For example,

- In Chapter 12, why was Aunt Millie so mad?
- How did this event affect Tom?
- On p. 104, why was Tom's nose all of a sudden running?

In the review that followed, Jones concentrated on extracting right answers. There was no call for discussion or for alternative ideas when, for example,

Melissa answered the first question, "Because the fox killed the turkey eggs," and the second, "He was worried about the black fox." There was no discussion around Peter's answer to the question about Tom's runny nose, "It always ran when he was scared." Jones accepted these responses and moved on. Questions and answers were fixed, no discussion ensued.

The second part of the worksheet looked even more conventional with 11 fill-in-the-blank sentences and 11 vocabulary words to choose from. The words came from *Midnight Fox*, yet the sentences were unrelated to the text:

- Without a word we _____ the fence and walked along the sidewalk. (skirted)
- The baby was very _____ because he was cutting teeth. (displeased)
- At camp, the campers were told about an old Indian _____. (legend)

This exercise mimics textbook vocabulary lessons. Students need no knowledge of the story to answer the questions. Instead, a rudimentary understanding of the listed words is sufficient because each sentence is tailored for only one answer.

Constructing a New Reading Practice. How should we interpret Bonnie Jones' practice? What are we to think about a mix of practices that might be interpreted variously as inconsistent, transitory, or revolutionary?

Several possibilities emerge. One is that Jones is experimenting, trying out new ideas and practices without committing fully to any. Another possibility is that Jones is making real changes, but that these changes represent additions at the margins of her practice. A third possibility is that Jones is modifying aspects of her teaching while her underlying assumptions about teaching and learning reading remain unaffected. One other possibility is that Jones is transforming her daily practice, and along the way, is raising questions that go to the core of her beliefs about teaching and learning. Depending on where and when one looks at Jones' instruction, one or another of these possibilities might seem more accurate. Her reading instruction is complex and is continually changing. Three years of watching her teach and listening to her talk about her practice convince me, however, that she is transforming both her daily practice and her conceptions of teaching and learning reading.

This is a hard conjecture to substantiate. Jones' talk is about texts and strategies and comprehension. She does not talk about conceptions of knowledge and underlying assumptions about teaching and learning. Such things must be inferred. Nevertheless, there are indications that something more than day-to-day changes are occurring.

First, Jones interprets reading reforms much as reformers do, as challenges to skills-based instruction. She reads the reforms as distinctly different from her past practice and she resolves to make changes in the directions reformers prescribe. Moreover, Jones continues to learn. She is satisfied neither with her understanding of the reforms nor with the changes she has made. She continues to seek out conferences and workshops about reading, even though the pressure to learn about reforms in other areas makes this difficult. What seems especially interesting is that she attends these sessions as a learner rather than as a presenter. Rather than viewing herself as an expert who will now tell others how to do as she does, Jones views herself as someone who needs to learn more.

Second, Jones manages an ambitious set of changes in her daily instruction including new texts, new instructional strategies, and new grouping arrangements. These support a new set of purposes. Whereas she previously held a purely technical purpose for reading, Jones now believes reading instruction should reflect the constructivist goal of reading for comprehension. Lessons focus on ideas and constructing meaning rather than on accumulating expertise in isolated skills. Her new purposes speak to the new roles she and her students are learning to play. As the vignettes imply, Jones is no longer a teacher who delivers instruction in discrete portions through worksheet and basal reader assignments. Instead, she sees her role as helping students engage with text in various ways (e.g., summarizing, predicting, and accessing prior knowledge). Students, too, have different roles. Instead of passively completing their reading lessons, they are expected to play a more active role in learning.

These changes suggest that Jones is reconceptualizing her views of teaching and learning reading. The norms of interaction between Jones and her students are changing. Lessons look increasingly like discussions rather than recitations. Students talk more and more often with one another. Their talk is more about the ideas and events in the text and the connections to their own ideas and experiences. Finally, the parameters of reading are changing. No longer a discrete subject taught with a specific set of materials and strategies, reading is now a part of the entire school day. While bundling these indications together does not prove that a revolution is brewing, it does suggest a rumble far below the surface.

Negotiating Between Old and New Practices in Mathematics

The cycle of change in Bonnie Jones' teaching began with reforms in reading. It now includes mathematics. Two years after her first encounter with reading reforms, Jones began exploring mathematics, and here too, she is after big changes in her practice. But there are differences. In contrast to reading, Jones' mathematics practice reflects a stronger conventional element and her efforts at reexamining her core beliefs seem more tentative.

Learning About Mathematics Reforms. Bonnie Jones embraces the directions advocated in the mathematics reform literature. She reads the new state math goals and objectives, the revised MEAP mathematics assessment, and the NCTM *Standards* as a challenge to her long-held view of mathematics teaching. She takes that challenge seriously and her talk suggests that she is after big changes.

Jones once viewed mathematics as a series of rules and procedures. Practicing addition, subtraction, multiplication, and division algorithms of whole numbers, fractions, and decimals comprised virtually her entire math program. Like many elementary school teachers, Jones has no background beyond introductory mathematics. An elementary education major, she took only a few mathematics courses and the mathematics education courses she took prepared her to teach mathematics in algorithmic fashion.

Perhaps bolstered by her efforts in reading, Jones did not resist learning about mathematics reforms. She soon discovered, however, that she needed to learn about both mathematics and mathematics teaching. Unlike reading, which many teachers see as a school subject without any particular disciplinary roots (Ball & Cohen, 1995), Jones brought far fewer resources to her mathematics teaching. Embracing mathematics reforms meant confronting both her weak subject matter knowledge and radical new approaches to teaching and learning. Jones did not flinch, even when she realized that district resources were sparse. Instead, she enrolled in university courses in both mathematics and mathematics education. She also joined the state math teachers' association, began reading journals, and started attending conferences and workshops. Through these venues, Jones learned about state and national efforts to reform mathematics curriculum and instruction, and about the revision of the math portion of the MEAP. She learned about mathematical manipulatives, estimation, and problem solving. She also learned some things about mathematics. Jones came away from these experiences with two thoughts: There was much more to reforming mathematics instruction than introducing an occasional manipulatives activity or a few story problems, and the gulf between the kind of teaching advocated in the reforms and her extant practice was wide.

Mathematics Reconsidered. Bonnie Jones approaches mathematics reforms much as she does reading reforms. She seeks out a wide range of ideas and practices. She uses these to make changes on a number of fronts. The changes she attempts cut deeply into issues of what it means to know, teach, and learn mathematics. Here, as in reading, Jones is after big changes.

Some evidence for this claim comes from Jones' changing view of what mathematics is and what students should know. That view has a number of components. One is the notion of mathematics as a conceptual field. Jones always assumed that learning algorithms and doing computations quickly and accurately was the heart of mathematics. Reforms, she understands, promote a different view of mathematics and what students should know about it. That view stresses the conceptual nature of mathematics (Michigan State Board of Education, 1990; National Council of Teachers of Mathematics, 1989). "Students need to understand the concept of things," she said, "And be able to think through a problem, and to have different strategies to work on problems."

A conceptual view of mathematics, in Jones' interpretation, has two parts: Students need to understand the concept of things and have different strategies to work on problems. An example of a mathematical concept is "number." "Number sense" or the "effective use and understanding of numbers in applications as well as in other mathematical contexts" (Michigan State Board of Education, 1990, p. 2) is frequently cited as one of the big or unifying ideas in a conceptual view of mathematics (Greeno, 1991; National Council of Teachers of Mathematics, 1989; Sowder & Schappelle, 1994). Jones learned about number sense in a summer workshop. She reports being amazed that students might have different interpretations of what a number is. The impact of this realization was profound. Rather than starting the next school year with the traditional review of whole number computation, Jones began with an exploration of numbers. "I started out with number sense," she said, "What do numbers mean to us? Where do we find them in our world? How do we use numbers in our world?" Aligning herself with reformers, Jones hopes that by emphasizing the concept of number, students will be able to think about what numbers represent and to use them sensibly in all mathematical contexts.

Another part of her changing view is teaching mathematical processes or strategies. Jones understands that strategies such as estimation and mental math help students understand that problems may be solved in various ways and may yield various answers (Michigan State Board of Education, 1990; National Council of Teachers of Mathematics, 1989). Finding a right answer is less important, however, than understanding how one approaches and solves problems. Now Jones has not eliminated all evidence of computation or procedure from her practice, nor does she intend to. She echoes the argument that computation has a role, albeit reduced, in learning mathematics (National Council of Teachers of Mathematics, 1989; Putnam, 1992). Knowing how to compute is important and some memorization (e.g., times tables) is useful, but, Jones now wonders, "Is it really important for them to practice for hours doing long division when they've got a calculator right there that could do it for them?"

One other aspect of Jones' new view of mathematics involves purpose. As in reading, the change in Jones' sense of mathematics as a school subject has meant a change in what she sees as the purpose of learning mathematics. She once held a largely pedantic view: One learned mathematics in order to compute answers to textbook and test problems swiftly and accurately. Any connection between what students learned in their mathematics lessons and what might be valuable in the real world was tenuous at best. Jones agrees with the reform literature that challenges this perspective:

> [Students] have to have a purpose to learn. Not to learn for the sake of learning or because you told them to do it. . . . There has to be some connection to the real world. And if there isn't a connection, if you can't convince them, then why are they going to learn it?

What once passed as a rationale for learning mathematics, learning for the sake of learning or because a teacher demanded it, no longer holds. In its place, Jones is constructing purposes that relate to the real-world lives of her students.[4]

Because Jones holds a conceptual view of mathematics, teaches problem-solving strategies, and promotes real-world applications, one might consider questions about her former view of mathematics and mathematics pedagogy. Her weak background in mathematics makes this problematic because she must learn as much about the subject matter of mathematics as about teaching and learning mathematics. Finding the time and energy to learn these things and to plan and deliver a different kind of mathematics instruction is also difficult. There is a lot on Jones' plate already, but the determination that marks her response to reading reforms is equally strong in mathematics.

A Look at Current Practice. As with reading, reform-minded ideas are evident in Bonnie Jones' mathematics practice, but there are differences. Jones is a more confident and certain teacher of reading than of mathematics. The changes are still fresh, but reading lessons exhibit a coherent flow. Mathematics lessons, by contrast, are often awkward. Evidence of reforms is strong, but so too is evidence of traditional practice. The two coexist, but as parallel rather than as blended activities.

Mathematics lessons have a pattern. Pages of practice homework problems are reviewed at the beginning and assigned at the end of each class. These familiar elements bracket mathematics of a different sort. This lesson on rounding decimals is illustrative:

Class begins with a review of the previous night's homework. Jones turned to the appropriate pages in the textbook and said, "All right, I'll take questions first." "Taking questions" cued students to ask her for answers to specific problems. For example, for problem number 20, Ryan asked, "Would number 20 be 0.601, 0.559, 0.441, and 0.438?" "Right," said Jones. (The question asked students to list these numbers from greatest to least.) At the end of class, Jones assigned another set of problems based on the day's work and announced:

> "In the first section on rounding decimals to the nearest whole number, there are 15 problems. I want you to pick seven. In the second section on rounding to the nearest tenth, there are 15 problems, pick seven, and in the last section on rounding to the nearest hundredth, pick seven."

Jones has changed some aspects of her homework assignments. In a summer workshop, she learned that simply running down a list of correct answers "wastes time and doesn't really answer the questions the kids have." She also learned that students need to "have choices and feel empowered." Jones is attracted to these ideas because they fit with another of her current interests in reframing teacher-student relationships. Jones feels that "taking questions" and giving students a choice about which problems they will do encourages them to feel more involved in their learning.

Perhaps this is so. In some ways, however, this seems like a gloss on a practice that remains fundamentally unchanged. Students do fewer problems, but the emphasis on drill and practice and getting right answers remains. Moreover, interactions seldom go beyond a student question and a teacher answer. On this day, neither Jones nor the students wondered about the nature of the assignment or why one particular answer was best.

Not long ago, Jones defined her entire mathematics practice this way. Lessons consisted of reviewing the previous night's homework and demonstrating the next procedure or algorithm listed in the textbook. She worked through a few problems on the board and asked for questions. If there were none, she assigned a raft of problems for seatwork. Students worked silently and individually, asking for and receiving help only from Jones. At the end of the period, students who had completed the assignment turned it in; the others finished it for homework. The textbook (and teacher's guide) defined instruction and Jones used it exclusively and deliberately. She took pride in starting school with the first page, proceeding through the units in order, and finishing the book by the end of the year. Such teaching represents standard fare in elementary school classrooms across the country. Mathematics means rules and procedures; teaching mathematics means efficiently organizing students, materials, and assessments; and learning mathematics means constant drill and practice and frequent demonstrations of skill.

Elements of traditional practice still bracket her mathematics lessons, but in between, Jones introduces a range of reform-minded activities. A lesson about rounding decimals, for example, provided a site to emphasize place value, use mathematical manipulatives, and connect mathematics to the real world:

> As Jones collected the homework, Scott and Gina passed out base 10 blocks.[5] Jones said, "Today we are going to work on rounding decimals. Who can tell me what rounding is? [Hands go up] I see one, two, three . . . hands. Some of you know and some don't. Okay, well, I want you to build this number." She turned to the board and wrote, "0.61." Students immediately began work manipulating the assorted pieces. Jones scanned the students' work (all seemed to be successful) before writing the number on the board in the following notation:

$$. \; | \; | \; | \; | \; | \; | \; \square$$

> Jones continued, "Sometimes when we work with decimals, we don't always want the exact number. So we need to round decimals." She said, "I'm going into the A&P and I see this price [0.61]. I want to round it so I can remember it. I want to round it to the tenths place. Please show me your answer." Students removed the 1 hundredths cube. Satisfied, Jones turned to the board and wrote "0.236" both in Arabic numerals and in the block notation.

$$. \; | \; | \; \square \; \square \; \square \; \bar{-} \; \bar{-} \; \bar{-}$$

> Jones: [after the students finished] Now I wouldn't see this number [0.236] in a grocery store, so I want to find a number that would be easier to use. For example, what place value might you want to round to, Scott?
>
> Scott: Tenths.
>
> Jones: Good. Kelly, what might be another one?
>
> Kelly: Hundredths.
>
> Jones: Good. [to the class] Show me what to do to round to hundredths. [The students work quickly and quietly.] Can you tell me what you did?

This vignette illustrates several changes. The lesson is ostensibly about a conventional procedure—rounding decimals. Rounding decimals is a common topic in fifth-grade mathematics texts and Jones is concerned that her students understand and master it. Rather than teach the procedure as a tool in and of itself, however, this lesson is an opportunity to reinforce the concept of place value. Place value is a key concept in the reform literature. The authors of the NCTM *Standards* (National Council of Teachers of Mathematics, 1989) state, "Understanding place value is [another] critical step in the development of children's comprehension of number concepts" (p. 39). Yet students are frequently confused (Boulton-Lewis & Halford, 1992). Using mathematical manipulatives such as base 10 blocks help students see the effect of rounding a decimal. Jones concludes that number lines displayed in the textbook might be "okay for some kids, but if they're still having problems, then you still have to go back to the blocks."

Reforms are also evident when Jones explicitly connects school lessons and the real world. Once, she would have taught the rounding decimals algorithm from the textbook alone, considering only how it fit into the sequence of lessons in that chapter. Today, she stops to consider other purposes. That one learns to round decimals because it is useful for shopping in grocery stores may seem to be no big leap, but from the view of mathematics instruction Jones once held, it is a leap of some distance.

Another leap is toward problem solving. On another day, Jones introduced an activity emphasizing the problem-solving strategy of estimation:

> The problem-solving exercise involved estimating the number of "Teddy-Grams" (small graham cracker cookies shaped like teddy bears) in a sealed clear plastic box. Jones explained:
>
>> Okay, between now and May we'll be using the guessing box quite a bit. And I'll always try to make it edible. Now this is a liter box, like a liter bottle of pop. You'll have to guess how many TeddyGrams there are in the box. Now there are lots of ways, but I'm not going to tell you. You have to come up with some ways to decide. But I want you to discuss strategies before you start predicting because predicting is better than guessing. Guessing means you have no method at all. In predicting, you have some knowledge, some idea of method.
>
> Jones passed the box around the class for inspection. Some of the discussion follows:
>
>> Jones: Can someone tell me some strategies (to estimate the number of TeddyGrams)?
>>
>> Jason: Well, you can tell there's more than 20 or 30 so you know you have to guess more than 20 or 30.
>>
>> Jones: So your prediction is 20 to 30? (Jason shrugs in agreement.)
>>
>> Jane: You could buy another box of TeddyGrams.
>>
>> John: You could call the makers of TeddyGrams and see how many are in a box.
>>
>> Chris: Or you could look on the side of the box to see if it says.

Jones: Do you think that would be helpful? (Chris nods. Jones gives him the box. The number of cookies is not listed, but the weight of the product in ounces and grams is.)

Jones asked the students what they would do if she gave them a centicube and a scale. There was much discussion about what to weigh and with what to compare different weights. Students talked both with Jones and one another. The talk was interrupted when Ralph got Jones' attention. After checking with him, Jones announced, "News flash! We've got some more information." Ralph said, "It says on the package that 11 pieces equals one-half an ounce." Jared volunteered, "So if you read on the box to see how many ounces, then you just keep adding 11 pieces to get the number." Jones nodded, "Good. So you can see the difference between what Jason said about 20 to 30 pieces and getting more information."

Jones sent around a package of Post-It Notes and asked students to record their predictions. She told them they could use any of the strategies discussed and that she would make a variety of weights and scales available to them. Students then posted their predictions on the front board.

During this activity, Jones talks explicitly about problem-solving strategies and pushes students to construct a wide range of them. There are no right answers here. Instead, Jones is open to any approach short of guessing. This, she believes, helps students understand that problems "may have more than one answer and may have many strategies to solve the problem." Her goal is to ease students' concerns about working through problems and to see that, as she said, "Yes, there is a problem, but there are different ways to approach the problem. There's not always one way. And that you can have more than one way of expressing an answer." If students know that multiple responses are possible, Jones contends, they will be more confident in approaching problem-solving situations and more willing to offer inventive solutions.

Behind the rounding and problem-solving activities are two other changes of note. One is the changing dynamic between Jones and her students; the other is her newly conceived role as curriculum planner.

Reflecting a position common in the reform literature (National Council of Teachers of Mathematics, 1989, 1991), Jones reasons that students benefit not only from their texts and assignments, but also from their interaction with her and with one another. Consequently there is much talk in her classroom. Whole-class discussions like that in the problem-solving vignette are routine. So too are opportunities for students to talk in pairs or in small groups. In the lesson about rounding decimals, for example, she encouraged students to confer as they manipulated the base 10 blocks:

There has to be more to [changing her practice] than just bringing in the manipulatives. There has to be more to it. The kids have to interact with each other. . . . They have to be able to talk to each other, to teach each other, to basically verbalize their thinking and what's going on. Now that can't go on if I'm saying, "You do this, you do that."

Changing the way she and her students talk is related to other role changes. Until recently, Jones was the undisputed knowledge authority in her classroom. "I was the teacher," she said, "I was supposed to have all the answers." She often did not, however, and thus felt threatened when students asked questions. In a summer workshop highlighting new ideas about teacher and student relationships, Jones began questioning her need to feel "the almighty teacher" and her sense that students depended on her for all that they learned.

Those questions took root in another change. Until recently, Jones taught mathematics exclusively from her teachers' guide and student textbooks. Rules and procedures defined mathematics, and textbooks delivered them in tight, easily managed sequences. Like many elementary school teachers, Jones did not question the centrality of the text to her practice.

The new district-adopted mathematics textbook continues to center much of her instruction. Unlike the reading textbook, she feels the Addison-Wesley text represents reforms fairly; she cites the emphasis on problem-solving strategies like estimation and mental math, and on alternative representations of some concepts and processes. A few topics or activities pose problems (e.g., using number lines alone to illustrate decimals), but she is willing to use the textbook as an important piece of her mathematics instruction.

But only as a piece. Jones refuses to give up control to the textbook as she once did. "I'm not going to let a textbook drive my lesson plans," she said. As evidence, she cites a willingness to skip around the textbook. Rather than starting on page one and marching lockstep through the text, Jones rearranges the order of topics. She began this past year, for example, with units on number sense, metrics, and decimals (all of which she tied into her first units in science), rather than with the initial textbook chapters on computation with whole numbers. Sometimes she skips entire sections. For example, after observing that students could perform simple calculations during a unit on metrics and decimals, she decided to skip the entire set of chapters devoted to whole-number computation.

Supplementing the textbook is a growing array of ancillary activities and materials such as base 10 blocks and the guessing box. Jones collects and uses these materials because she believes the textbook places too much emphasis on abstractions and too often fails to provide concrete illustrations of concepts. "It doesn't carry through," she said, "After it introduces a concept, it goes right back to the abstract." Jones understands that reforms promote student experiences with concrete materials. As a result, she frequently uses manipulatives to supplement textbook lessons. She capped a recent textbook unit on fractions, for example, with an activity from *Fractions with Pattern Blocks* (Zullie, 1988). Students were given *tangrams* (plastic shapes in the form of squares, triangles, parallelograms) and worksheets of figures, parts of which were shaded. The task was to cover the unshaded section of each figure with the designated shapes (e.g., triangles) and to write a fraction which expressed the ratio of shaded to unshaded space.

So convinced is Jones that the textbook no longer holds the key to all her instructional needs, that on occasion, she abandons the textbook altogether. She then substitutes ancillary materials for entire textbook units. For example, she recently concluded that the measurement unit in the textbook was inadequate. Once unthinkable, Jones replaced the entire unit with materials from Project AIMS[6] without hesitation.

Constructing a New Mathematics Practice? Managing these changes has not been easy. Bonnie Jones' mathematics instruction was as strongly rooted in traditional skills-based approaches as was her reading instruction. Unlike reading, however, Jones finds she needs to learn as much about the subject matter of mathematics as she does about new instructional approaches. She is nevertheless determined to make big changes in her teaching. The incorporation of a conceptual perspective, problem solving, real-world applications, and a range of new representations suggests that she is changing her day-to-day instruction in fundamental ways. Those changes coexist with a still strong element of traditional practice. As a result, it is too early to tell whether or not Jones is reconceptualizing her views of teaching and learning mathematics.

Jones' efforts can be read in various ways. One might be tempted to dismiss her changes in light of the firm evidence of skills-based practice. A slightly more generous interpretation suggests that these changes are real, but tenuous, and are susceptible to being undercut without more, and more substantial, changes. A third possibility, however, is that Jones is turning a corner in reframing her mathematics practice because of reforms.

This third possibility seems the most viable. As in reading, Jones' view of mathematics mirrors the common themes of the reforms. Jones pursues opportunities to learn about new ideas and practices, and she endorses what she hears. She describes sharp distinctions between her past practice and the vision of practice advanced in reforms, and she works to change her teaching. The many changes evident in her daily instruction testify to her successes. Jones is using new and different curriculum materials and methods, and students are having new and different experiences in learning mathematics.

These changes in daily practice imply changes at deeper levels. As she does in reading, Jones teaches to new purposes. Technical competence and skill in computation are no longer the sole purposes of learning mathematics. New purposes such as conceptual understanding and real-world applications now vie for attention. Jones also seems to be redefining the roles of teacher and student, encouraging a more active role for students and a less directive role for herself. Finally, interaction patterns are changing. Mathematics is no longer a silent, individual activity. Students talk about their ideas with Jones and with one another.

These changes aim deeply and seem to be on the same order as those in reading, but they also seem fresher and much more tentative. Moreover, they are colored by traditional elements which seem both stronger and more persistent than those in reading. What are we to make, for example, of the homework assignments, which other than a gloss of student choice, seem little changed from the convergent, drill and practice approach she describes as her former practice? Students do fewer problems, but neither the type of problem, the purpose problems serve, nor the press for a single right answer have changed.

That old and new practices appear, however, tells little in and of itself. The point is not that Jones refuses to reexamine her beliefs about teaching and learning. In fact, she seems to be doing just that, but it is less clear here than in reading. A better conjecture, then, might be that the appearance of parallel skills and reform-minded approaches implies that Jones is still negotiating between old and new practices.

Ignoring Reforms in Writing

To this point, Bonnie Jones seems like a reformer's dream. She responds vigorously to reading and mathematics reforms, embracing multiple new ideas and making a host of changes. Yet not only does Jones not embrace every reform, in some cases, she simply ignores them. Until a year ago, writing reforms were a case in point.

Learning About Writing Reforms. Although Michigan has a new state writing policy (Michigan State Board of Education, 1985), Bonnie Jones has not seen it.[7] She learns about new approaches to writing through conference sessions and journal articles. But knowing about them does not mean that Jones will do anything with them.

In contrast to the efforts on behalf of reading and mathematics, there have been no district writing workshops or inservices, and no new textbook series has been adopted. Teresa Jensen is promoting writing reforms, but she works with only a few teachers individually.[8] This does not mean Derry teachers are oblivious to writing. These reforms have been circulating for over a decade and some teachers have embraced them. But if teachers know about or do anything with writing, they do so in spite of district efforts rather than because of them.

Like the district, Jones has ignored writing reforms. Asked why, Jones does not cite district ambivalence because, given her earlier experience with the reading textbooks, she no longer counts on district guidance or assistance. Instead, Jones claims that a long-standing personal discomfort with her own writing underlies her response. "[Writing] is a weak area of mine," she said, "I always have to push myself to do it. I avoid it because I'm not very good at it. I have to get better, but it's a conscious effort." She contends this lack of confidence in her own writing caused her to be reluctant to promote writing among her students.[9]

A Changing View of Writing? For many years, Bonnie Jones held a traditional view of writing instruction: Writing decomposed into a series of discrete grammar skills—identifying parts of speech, parsing sentences, and memorizing rules for capitalization and punctuation. Students learned these skills by circling the appropriate noun, verb, or adjective on pages of decontextualized sentences. They applied these skills in short responses to textbook questions and in occasional book or research reports.

There are several parallels between this view of writing and the skills-based view of reading Jones held. Both view knowledge as dissected into small bits that can be easily organized into sequential lessons. Similarly, they suggest that knowledge is cumulative—that is, what one knows are the individual bits built up over time and practice. Finally, practice is seen as essential, because the goal is the accurate and adept use of the skills learned. According to these views, correctly identifying the words in a piece of text appears to count as much as understanding the different ways the text might be interpreted, and correctly identifying the parts of speech in a sentence is as important as being able to write with clarity and grace.

During the past year, Jones decided to confront her discomfort with both writing and with her skills-based writing practice. She said, "I'm trying to push myself to do more writing this year: more expository, more poetry, more writing in general." Jones' unease with teaching writing is palpable because this assertion seemed designed more to convince herself than me. Changing the way one talks about reforms may indicate changing practice,[10] but talk is an inexact measure of change. Jones may be transforming her writing practice, but now this is speculative at best.

A Look at Current Practice. Bonnie Jones' writing instruction looks more like her mathematics instruction than her reading instruction. Elements of old and new coexist, in effect, as parallel curricula. There is a different balance here, however. Reform-minded instruction increasingly defines her mathematics practice. Her writing practice, by contrast, is defined by the traditional study of grammar. Consider a typical English lesson about parts of speech:

After reviewing the previous night's homework, Jones handed out the next set of worksheets. The first, mirroring the homework, asked students to identify the underlined word as a noun, verb, or adjective in each of 15 sentences. The second asked them to identify the adverb in each of 28 sentences. Jones reviewed the first two items on the first sheet.

Jones: Who can tell us number 1? ("You can roller-skate best on a *level* sidewalk.") Mary?

Mary: Adjective?

Jones: Why? You're right, but you have to know why. (No response) Thomas?

Thomas: Because it describes the sidewalk.

Jones: Right. Number 2? ("The river rose to a *level* of 60 feet during the flood.") Randy?

Randy: A verb?

Jones: Why? (No response)

Sherry: It's an adjective because it's describing the river.

Jones: Okay. Put "level" next to "river."

Eric: It's a noun.

Jones: Why?

Eric: Because it's not an adjective or a verb!

Jones: All right. But notice that it's also preceded by an "a."

Jones then asked students to turn to the second sheet. She did not review any of these items. Eric asked if they had to do all 28 items. Jones looked at him and said, "Okay, I'll compromise at 20."

This lesson illustrates Jones' skills-based view of teaching and learning writing. First, writing consists of mechanics—parts of speech, grammar, and punctuation. The assumption is that one writes either well or poorly based on one's knowledge of the elements of writing. In this lesson, the activity devolves into correctly identifying the underlined word. Jones does not ask students to consider the function a word plays within a sentence. She does not ask students to consider alternative sentence constructions. Words are treated literally; there are no shades of meaning. Second, writing is taught as a discrete exercise apart from any particular context; teaching is about introducing, reinforcing, and remediating discrete skills. Jones' grammar lessons frequently take the form of individual worksheets highlighting one or more skill. The sentences are unrelated to one another other than through use of the same identified word, and there is no effort to extend the lesson beyond the confines of the worksheet. Finally, learning to write means acquiring knowledge of mechanics through continual drill and practice. The assumption is that students' ability to write depends on their mastery of mechanics. Students neither learn about crafting plots, developing characters, or making arguments, nor do they learn how to use mechanics within a piece on which they are working. Instead, learning to write means learning to identify and correct mechanical errors.

Jones recognizes that such lessons are some distance from reforms. "[They're] something weak in my program," she explained. Jones takes seriously the reformers' contention that students learn to write by writing. Consequently, she is providing more opportunities for students to write. Asking students to summarize the story and to record their predictions as in the *Midnight Fox* vignette is one example.

Another aspect of the writing reforms Jones is beginning to attend to is the writing process. This conception of writing suggests that students' writing improves through a process of brainstorming ideas, writing and editing a series of drafts, and conferencing with a teacher or peer. As Graves (1983) notes, however, the writing process only works if students have opportunities to write:

> The writing process is discovered by doing it. . . . Students can be lectured on the components of the process, but they still only know the process by actually doing the writing, making words fulfill their intentions. (p. 250)

Jones does not believe students need to follow the entire process with every piece of writing. Even if she did, she observes that time constraints would prevent it. Increasingly Jones develops assignments where students can work on a piece of text over a period of time. For example, Jones recently assigned the writing of a cinquain poem.[11] Using Halloween as the theme, she urged students to work through the writing process stages. At various points, she met with each student, sometimes individually, sometimes in pairs. She encouraged students to discuss, critique, and edit their work with one another.

If Jones adopts some elements of reforms, she ignores others. One is the connection between opportunities to write and learning mechanics. Calkins (1986) makes a point common among reformers: "The single most important thing we can do for students' syntax, spelling, penmanship, and use of mechanics is to have them write often and with confidence" (p. 197). Jones provides more opportunities for students to write. She may understand that their knowledge and use of mechanics will improve as a result. At this point, however, she seems unwilling to trust that connection. Jones continues her direct instruction lessons in grammar, punctuation, and parts of speech.

Writing reforms promote a far different view of teaching than the skills-based approach Jones practices. Reforms emphasize opportunities for students to write and rewrite, to think, and to talk about writing. Mechanics are important. If teachers never get beyond correcting spelling and grammar mistakes, however, students will not either (Graves, 1983). The notion that systematic direct instruction may not be the best way to teach writing or mechanics, however, is undoubtedly difficult to accept. It runs counter to the way most teachers were taught, and to the periodic rebirth of direct instruction initiatives such as the Instructional Theory Into Practice (ITIP) program proposed by Madeline Hunter (1983).

A Changing View of Teaching and Learning Writing? The question of whether Bonnie Jones' views of teaching and learning writing are changing is even less clear than in mathematics. Indications in both in her talk and in her teaching hint that Jones is attempting to make her current practice look more like the reforms. At the same time, however, she acknowledges that her practice remains largely conventional. Her classroom practices confirm this. If Jones' views of teaching and learning writing are changing, it is a change still in its infancy.

RESPONDING TO REFORMS IN THE CONTEXT OF SCHOOLING

The discussion thus far has considered Bonnie Jones' response to reforms in the context of her preexisting practice. Changes are occurring in both her day-to-day instruction and in her conceptions of subject matter, teaching, and learning. In making these changes, however, Jones must manage factors inside and outside her classroom that are not benign: Some support the changes Jones is working toward; others do not. In either event, understanding how Jones responds to reforms requires an accounting of these factors.

Managing the Regularities of Schooling

One set of factors are the regularities of school (Sarason, 1982). These factors—time constraints, content coverage, and assessment pressures—tend to be common concerns across teachers and are part of the context of teaching school.

Time is a perennial concern. At the height of her skills-based practice, Bonnie Jones' textbooks and teachers' guides cookie cut lessons into readily manageable chunks. She always felt pressed for time, but she managed to finish each of the texts.

Compared with many teachers, Jones is fortunate. Neither her school nor her district imposes guidelines on instructional time. Jones may always need more time, but she has a great deal of discretion in how she schedules her instructional day. This discretion is critical now because Jones discovered that by adopting new practices she can no longer plan her lessons with the precision she once did. Introducing more complex and engaging assignments, opening up discussion, and providing opportunities to write just takes more time than skills-based lessons:

> The more time I allow them to [discuss ideas] the less teaching time I have, so now I'm really struggling within myself. I'm not where I should be in the textbooks right now. Do I cut back on that and say, "Well, I don't have time to do this. I don't have time to allow you to do this because I have to be on this chapter? We have to get through so much material and we are behind."

Jones feels caught. She senses the value of allowing students time to discuss their ideas. She rarely cuts off promising activities or discussions, but that means she must compromise in some other fashion, by taking time away from, postponing, or even eliminating subsequent lessons. Jones has the flexibility to make these decisions, but the constant negotiation of time wears on her.

A second regularity involves content coverage. By abandoning the new reading text and vowing not to let the new math text drive her lesson plans, Jones assumed a large measure of control over her teaching. What she teaches and how she teaches it are now decisions she will no longer cede to teachers' guides and textbooks.

This new authority does little to relieve Jones' worries about what content to cover and how deeply to cover it. Textbooks and teachers' guides once provided ready answers. She now faces decisions about what to teach without her familiar tools. Jones rejects the superficial view of subject matter that defined her teaching for more than 20 years, but reforms which offer a panoply of ideas and generalizations about doing less is more are seldom accompanied by specific recommendations about what to do in practice.

Some of the difficulties Jones faces are evident in the story she tells of an encounter with a sixth-grade teaching colleague:

> I had a sixth-grade teacher last year say, "You didn't cover multiplication and division of decimals. Now I have to go back and start from the beginning. It was your job, you should have covered them. It was in your textbook. Why didn't you?" My answer was, "I spent more time on the concepts with manipulatives."
>
> [She said] "Well, that's fine, but you should have covered multiplication and division of decimals." And my answer was that I didn't think that they were ready to handle it because they were still having problems with the

concept of a decimal and place value. [She said] "Well, just go back and teach them the algorithm."

Jones knows that students must demonstrate the division of decimals on a district test, and she worries about students' scores dropping as a result of her curricular decisions. She wonders, "Which is more important? Knowing that the kids have the concept or [being] able to do the algorithm?"

Time pressures exacerbate the rub between covering content and teaching in new ways. Jones embraces reforms that stress substance more than coverage. Yet as a fifth-grade teacher, she knows that her sixth-grade colleague expects Jones' students will know certain content. The unwritten expectation, Jones explained, is that she "cover at least three fourths of [any] textbook" before the end of the school year. As lessons take longer and longer and she gets further behind, and Jones anticipates her colleague's dismay.

Concerns about what to teach are tied to a third regularity—assessment. While Jones is committed to fundamental changes in her teaching practice, she knows the kind of teaching that reforms espouse is not well measured by skills-based assessments like the district-administered Abbreviated Stanford Achievement Test (ASAT):

I have the Stanford Achievement coming up. . . . Do I cut back on the manipulatives? Do I cut back on the thinking process? Do I cut back on the questioning? Do I now take more control and give less to them [students] because I have . . . this test coming up and the administrators and the parents will all look at the scores? And judge you by the scores?

Not all tests are hostile to the kind of teaching and learning Jones wants. The revised MEAP advances many of the ideas she finds appealing: The reading test measures comprehension rather than skill acquisition and promotes use of rich and substantive text; the mathematics test gives more attention to problem situations. Jones might cite the new goals of the MEAP as justification for her ambitious response to reforms. The potentially positive force of the MEAP is undercut, however, by the fact that Jones' fifth-grade students do not take it. They take the more conventional ASAT.

To date, students' scores on the ASAT have shown little change. Jones' students may end up outperforming their peers even though standardized assessments like the ASAT do not reflect the kind of content and instruction they receive. But what if they don't? Jones might redouble her efforts at effecting changes in her teaching, but she might also be pressured to abandon some of the changes she has made. In the end, she may decide the effort necessary to continue reforming her practice is simply not worth the cost.[12]

Managing Relationships

Donnelly-King Elementary has a reputation as a progressive school. Jones disputes that label. She finds little explicit support from teachers, parents, or administrators for the ambitious changes she wants to make.

Those changes have gone neither unnoticed nor uncriticized. Bonnie Jones faces no formal sanctions. In fact, the laissez-faire attitude of the school and of district administrators appears to guarantee significant classroom autonomy. But unpleasant exchanges with colleagues occur and this resistance increases as Jones dives deeper into reforms. She describes another conversation with a peer at an inservice for the new Addison-Wesley mathematics text:

> She asked me . . . what page I was on. I said, "I'm skipping around in the book." She said, "You can't do that." Now this woman has been teaching math [but] she hasn't taken any classes . . . she has her Masters and she knows it all!
>
> She said, "Well, you can't do that." And I said, "Why not?" She said, "It's a brand new book. You have to go chapter by chapter and go in sequence." I said, "Why can't I skip around?"
>
> "Because it's a new book. You won't find out; math is built upon all these prior skills. You just can't do that. You have to go page by page, chapter by chapter," [she said].
>
> And I said, "Well, I'm not doing that." So she said, "Well, you're not doing it right. You shouldn't be teaching math this year."

These incidents are discouraging. "I'm kind of pulling back," Jones said, "Not talking, not wanting people in my room anymore." Ironically, reforms aimed at encouraging students to talk more result in Jones feeling more isolated. The starkness of her choice—ignoring reforms and the attendant changes in her practice for the comfort of her peers' approval, versus embracing reforms and change and braving the fallout—is as discomforting as it is illuminating about the difficulties of changing teaching.

Parents also raise questions about Jones' response to reforms. Beginning the school year with the unit on number sense, Jones used a variety of materials and activities. Her textbook does not cover this concept so she did not distribute it until the 2-week unit ended. One parent complained to the principal. Another objected to his child choosing which mathematics problems he worked on. "[The parent] wanted to know why they just didn't do them all," Jones said, "He thinks the more they do, the more they'll know. I tried to explain it to him, but I don't think he got it." There has been no organized parent outcry, but administrators heed these reports. Both her principal and superintendent have stopped by to observe her classroom. Neither said much, but Jones feels she is now being watched. She is angry and feels that her professional judgment is being questioned. As she manages this complex array of reforms and changes in her practice, she increasingly feels that she does so on her own.[13]

This last point raises an important issue. Jones must negotiate these difficult issues of regularities and relationships because she's trying to make big changes in her practice. Those changes are stressful in and of themselves because in embracing reforms, Jones must learn whole new approaches to subject matter, teaching, and learning at the same time she unlearns all that she came to know and count on. Complicating that effort are regularities and relationships which seem designed to maintain the status quo. In her willingness to think hard about reforms and act in ambitious ways to enact them, Jones encounters more problems than if she simply closed her classroom door to reforms. Rather than make life easier, attending to reforms opens a Pandora's box.

Conclusion

Bonnie Jones is a teacher with a mission. She embraces reforms, seeks opportunities to learn, pushes changes in her daily practice, and reexamines her basic beliefs. However, she does not manage all reforms in the same ways. Variations emerge and those variations have two implications. One is that teachers' reform responses are unpredictable. For example, the cycle of change claim aside, one should not assume the deep changes in Jones' reading practice will be replicated in writing. These subjects might seem related, but as this case illustrates, a teacher's knowledge, experience, and motivation can differ across subjects.

Responses are unpredictable across reforms, and are also unpredictable over time. It may be no accident that the biggest changes arise in areas Jones has dealt with the longest. There is no guarantee, however, that she will eventually make big changes in all areas. Moreover, there is no guarantee that her current responses will hold into the future. Jones' world is much too complex and dynamic to expect changes will occur predictably or regularly.

The second conclusion is that, although outside influences are obvious, Jones' inner resources guide her responses. I deal more fully with this point in chapter 6. For now, however, I want to emphasize the point that Jones' determined efforts demand considerable knowledge and determination. As she moves from traditional to constructivist approaches, Jones faces the enormous challenge of unlearning what she was taught and learning something quite new. It would be one thing if the difference was limited to new materials or to new instructional techniques. In Jones' view, it isn't. Instead, constructivist approaches involve changes in her basic beliefs about teaching and learning. Meeting these demands head-on requires a strong will because not only does Jones feel the uncertainty and doubt associated with learning new things and trying new practices, she does so in an environment that is ambivalent at best.

NOTES

1. Besides this fire marshal's nightmare, Jones' classroom is populated with a plague of frogs—frog drawings, frog planters, frog balloons, posters, wall-hangings, and figurines. Jones' predilection for frogs is well known and well supported; she claims not to have purchased any of the dozens in her classroom or in the boxes catalogued and stored in her attic. "People just know that I really like them," she said, "so they give them to me all the time."
2. Unless otherwise indicated, all quotes come from interviews with Bonnie Jones conducted from 1991 to 1993.
3. Though this view is widely accepted, it is not universally so. See Carver (1992) who argues that prediction, prior knowledge, and text type are generally irrelevant to the way most readers make sense of text.
4. Mathematics reforms such as the NCTM *Standards* support Jones' assertion that students need to see real-world purposes in their study of mathematics, but they also underscore the purpose of introducing students to the intellectual discipline of mathematics. These two purposes are not mutually exclusive. In Jones' classroom, however, the former takes precedence.
5. Base 10 blocks are manipulatives used to demonstrate the concept of place value. A set consists of *flats* which represent ones, *rods* which represent tenths, *cubes* which represent hundredths, and *chips* which represent thousandths. Bingo chips act as decimal points.
6. Project AIMS (Activities to Integrate Mathematics and Science) materials are teacher resource books. Mathematics activities include estimation, measuring, sequencing, probability, and computing scale. Science activities include observing, classifying, collecting, and interpreting data. Jones saw these materials demonstrated in a workshop and purchased them with her own money.
7. Interestingly enough, while all four teachers in this study have seen the state reading policy, none has seen the state writing policy, and only Frank Jensen has heard of it.
8. Jones counted Teresa Jensen as an early and helpful advocate of the changes she attempted. After Jones rejected the district reading textbook, however, the two had a falling out. Although she is now interested in writing reforms, Jones does not ask for Jensen's assistance.
9. Unfortunate personal experiences are frequently cited for teachers' reluctance to embrace mathematics. Graves (1983) argues that a similar phenomenon exists with regard to writing.
10. Some would argue that using new language signals a change in belief, a prerequisite for changing practice (Eisenhart et al., 1988; Fenstermacher, 1986). Others (Cohen et al., in press) argue that this relationship is murkier, but that change in the language teachers use is nonetheless an important feature of responding to reforms.
11. A cinquain poem is a five-line stanza with a standard format. The first line is one word which identifies the subject of the poem. The second line describes the subject. The

third line describes an action. The fourth expresses a feeling or observation. The last line renames the subject. Lines two through five have no prescribed length.

12. Some observers (Corbett & Wilson, 1990; Wise, 1988) suggest this is not an unreasonable conclusion. They claim standardized testing distorts the curriculum in ways that may make it impossible for reform-minded teachers to continue.

13. One of the interesting stories to be told from this study is that of the relationship between teachers and administrators in the context of reforms. Conventional wisdom contends that administrators play a central role in how teachers respond to reforms. For example, Applebee and colleagues (1987) claim, "Administrators are the key to successful implementation of new instructional approaches" (p. 46). The case of Jones undercuts the sweep of such generalizations.

Chapter 4

A Paradox of Talk and Practice:
The Case of Frank Jensen

Forty feet away from Bonnie Jones, Frank Jensen also hears the call to reform. What Jensen hears and how he responds, however, stand in stark relief. While these two teachers work in the same school, receive the same textbooks, and attend the same district inservices, their responses to reforms vary greatly. Jones wants big changes in her teaching and reforms provide her with a vehicle. Jensen responds more modestly because he believes reforms generally confirm ideas and practices he has long maintained. Jensen's talk echoes the language of reforms, but his classroom practice preserves, rather than transforms, his extant practice.

Frank Jensen is a European American in his late forties. If clothing defines the man, Jensen is aptly dressed. His casual, often rumpled, clothing and well-worn sneakers contrast with the crisp shirts and ties of the Donnelly-King principal and three other male teachers. His dress reflects, however, his intentional informality and disinterest in "doing things the regular way."[1]

Jensen has not followed the regular way for some time. After 5 years as a fifth-grade teacher and 13 years as an elementary school principal,[2] he became increasingly dissatisfied with regular school. Concerned about students who, while bright, were not succeeding in school, Jensen resigned his principalship and helped design a district program for underachieving gifted learners.[3]

The effort produced the Challenger program, now in its eighth year.[4] Jensen terms his 16 third and fourth graders "academically interested and talented" with "above average potential."[5] They are "right-brained, holistic learners" and "non-linear thinkers," Jensen explains, whose needs are not met due to a "mismatch between their learning styles and the basic curriculum."

More important than students' cognitive development, however, are their affective needs. "The kids' affective development is really the most important thing," said Jensen:

> There were gifted and talented students who were not making it in the regular school program. . . . We figured that there was an affective reason . . . [so] we decided we had to work with the affective area before we could get into the academic area. We thought it was an attitude thing . . . that maybe it had to do with attitude and perception, self-esteem, and all of that kind of stuff.

Challenger students fail, Jensen contends, not because they lack intellectual capacity, but because of a range of affective deficiencies—poor self-concept, low self-esteem, inability to work alone or in groups, and poor organizational skills.

Jensen senses his students' needs from personal experience. "I was a Challenger-type kid as an elementary student," he explained, "I was a good reader except I was nontraditional." Jensen recalls few teachers who understood his cognitive needs as a "global learner, very much right brain" and his affective needs to be "praised for the things I did right."

He intends to be different. Jensen teaches a "holistic curriculum," one in which a lesson in self-concept is as important as a lesson in multiplication.[6] "We're trying," he said, "to adapt a traditional curriculum to meet their needs. . . . It's like a traditional curriculum in non-traditional ways. . . . With these kids, you need to try a lot of different things." Asked to describe his teaching, Jensen said, "I use a shotgun approach."

Jensen's efforts seem admirable, but what this talk means is not clear, because Jensen also takes a shotgun approach to ideas. His talk is peppered with references to "non-linear thinkers," "affective needs," and "holistic curriculum." His talk is also sprayed with references to reforms. Jensen talks confidently and at length about "reading strategies," "whole language," "mental math," "problem-solving," and "the writing process." However, neither his talk nor his teaching explains what these terms mean. Jensen's talk is in broad, sweeping generalities whereas his teaching, particularly in reading and mathematics, is quite conventional. His mathematics instruction, for example, looks neither non-traditional nor rooted in problem-solving. Instead, it is skills based and focuses primarily on drill and practice of algorithms. By contrast, his reading instruction is a mix of old and new. On any given day, one is as likely to observe students working on a decontextualized phonics worksheet or practicing reading aloud as participating in an in-depth discussion about a character in a story.

A self-described "pack rat" with a "cocktail party mind," Jensen's classroom reflects his ideas and instruction. It bursts with all manner of odds and ends. There are the usual classroom accoutrements of textbooks, bulletin boards, desks, and chairs, but these things compete for space with a hodgepodge Jensen has collected through the years. One corner houses the first in-class computer in the school. Disks, manuals, and printouts spill onto the floor. In the opposite corner is the reading area, a large, two-story structure made from scrap two-by-fours and plywood. During free-reading time, students take books and crawl underneath and on top, lounging against the assorted pillows. Dominating a third corner is Jensen's self-described junk pile. Cardboard boxes overflow with metal, wooden, and plastic doodads. Heaps of partially disassembled devices including radios, typewriters, and telephones cover shelf and floor space. Spools of wire, trays of nuts and bolts, and boxes of tubes and transistors lie scattered about. This collection became the fodder for a recent unit on inventions. The hallway door, in the fourth corner of the room, is the only unobstructed area in the classroom. Classroom walls function as gathering places for sets of old encyclopedias, an extensive collection of *National Geographic*, bookcases of trade books and cut-up magazines. Squeezed into the middle are students' desks and the podium from which Jensen occasionally teaches. Jensen's desk, near the back of the room, flows over with a sample of all of the above. This classroom jumble is more or less permanent, though at different times of the year, class projects take over the room.

The look and feel of Jensen's room reflects his "cocktail party mind" and his shotgun approach to teaching. It also reflects what he terms the "bubble of privacy" that surrounds the Challenger program and the "special dispensation" he has to run it with minimal interference. Describing the program and the classroom in which it resides also says much about how Jensen responds to reforms: Frank Jensen collects ideas just as he collects things—in large, loosely connected piles. Like the stuff in his classroom, however, Jensen takes more interest in collecting ideas than in their use. He has much to say, but it is not clear that he thinks deeply about ideas or teaching. Jensen claims his teaching reflects the reforms, but if so, it is mostly in bits and pieces scattered across the school day. His talk about reforms and non-traditional approaches aside, Jensen's instruction is largely conventional.

RESPONDING TO REFORMS

There are some commonalties between Frank Jensen and Bonnie Jones. First, neither teacher attends to every reform. Like his colleague, Jensen attends to more than reading, writing, and mathematics reforms, but much of the national education conversation passes by him. A second similarity is that both teachers have considerable autonomy. Jones claims no "special dispensation" or "bubble of privacy," but neither teacher's actions demonstrate any particular constraint.

In most ways, Jensen's responses differ sharply from Jones'. Jones sees yawning gaps between reforms and her skills-based instruction and she is pushing for ambitious changes. Jensen, by contrast, generally believes reforms support and justify his extant thinking and practice.

The differences between these teachers will develop as this case unfolds. So too will another form of difference because like his colleague, Jensen's reform reponses are textured and varied rather than singular.

Blurring the Distinctions I: Reading Reforms

From his talk alone, one might accept Frank Jensen's claim to embrace reading reforms. He talks easily and at length about reading strategies, literature-based instruction, comprehension, and prior knowledge. Looking beyond the talk, however, is illuminating, because while Bonnie Jones interprets reading reform as a serious challenge, Jensen believes they simply reify ideas and practices he has long held. Thus, while Jones pushes ambitious changes throughout her practice, Jensen is more ambivalent, adding a few pieces, but leaving the bulk of his practice intact.

Learning the Language of Reading Reforms. Frank Jensen learned the new reading language from state and local sources. One source was the state reading policy. Jensen encountered the state policy and the revised reading section of the MEAP at a state conference in the mid-1980s. He also encountered it at home. Teresa Jensen, the district reading coordinator and also his wife, served on a state-level committee charged with reviewing the fledging policy and disseminating the final version throughout the state. He read early drafts and later volunteered to pilot the revised MEAP with his students.

District sources provided additional opportunities to learn. Frank Jensen attended several sessions of the district-sponsored Reading Update inservice. He reports learning little new, however. More important, in his eyes, is the new HBJ reading textbook. Jensen expresses none of Jones' concerns, however. An "excellent representation" of the state policy, he uses it regularly.

From these sources, Jensen reports learning the language of reform, but little more. Other than "picking up a few little tidbits," most of what he learned was a new way to talk about ideas and practices he claims to have already held. Jones and many other Michigan teachers interpret the reforms as revolutionary (Cohen et al., in press). Jensen does not. As he said, "It all fit my orientation and justified what I'd been thinking all along." Since the initial state and district activity, Jensen's interest in reading reforms has faded. He pursues no other opportunities to learn about reading, and reports that he is currently occupied with new science and outcomes-based initiatives.

   A Blurred View of Reading.   Frank Jensen's orientation toward reading is difficult to interpret. Researchers differ in characterizing the range of approaches teachers take toward reading (cf. Harste & Burke, 1977; Hiebert & Colt, 1989; Richardson et al., 1991), but most believe that teachers follow a predominant line. Richardson and her colleagues, for example, characterize teachers as taking one of three stances toward reading: skills/word, literary structuralist, or whole language. Of the 39 teachers in their study, all but 4 fit into one of these three categories. Those 4 teachers are characterized as holding a view that "does not represent an extant approach" (p. 571). The researchers conclude that this view represents "either extreme theoretical complexity or confusion" (p. 583). Jensen's view of reading fits this category.

   If we accept Jensen's contention that reforms mirror his extant view, then that view reflects his shotgun approach and his sense that reading is a potpourri. In effect, Jensen takes eclecticism to its logical extreme. He may see some distinctions among various views of reading. He avers, however, that all are entirely compatible and are equally useful. As a result, Jensen's view of reading runs in several directions at once: skills-based instruction (emphasizing phonics, oral fluency, and discrete skills), strategy instruction (which focuses on the structure of text and the construction of meaning), literature-based instruction (which highlights the reading of good stories), and whole-language instruction (which emphasizes integrating reading and writing across the curriculum). So wide is Jensen's view that he understands there to be no apparent inconsistency in statements he has made, such as "phonics is part of whole language. It's just one of the skills" and "oral fluency is a good measure of comprehension."

   Reading reformers might cringe. Phonics and oral fluency each reflect a traditional view, which emphasizes the sequential accumulation of decontextualized skills. Whole language and comprehension reflect constructivist views by emphasizing meaning and context. Reforms make much of the distinction between traditional and constructivist views (Anderson et al., 1985; Michigan State Board of Education, 1986). When Jensen claims to embrace the reforms, then, he embraces an interpretation which blurs all the distinctions reformers hold dear.

   An example involves the purposes for reading. Jensen recognizes that reading has cognitive purposes. His interest in reforms, however, is less cognitive than affective. In short, he believes that reading is primarily a means of fostering affective growth. "We always deal with the affective side [of reading] first," he said, "because we consider that of primary importance."

Jensen's view of reading and his interpretation of recent reforms contrasts with Jones'. Whereas Jones interprets the reforms primarily in pedagogical terms, Jensen interprets them largely in terms of his long-standing affective agenda. Unconcerned about cognitive and pedagogical debates and distinctions, and with an eye on affective goals, all approaches to reading appear to him to be equally viable.

Such comparisons highlight the point that teachers interpret reforms in many ways. The different knowledge and experience each teacher brings, as well as the different purposes each holds for reading, play out in their varied interpretations of the meaning and importance of reforms. However, the Michigan reading policy may sanction such differences: If students construct meaning and if those meanings vary according to prior experience, then one should not be surprised to learn that teachers, too, interpret reforms differently.

A Look at Current Practice. Frank Jensen's blurred view of reading surfaces in his teaching because there is no pattern to his instruction. On any given day, one is equally likely to observe him reading from a trade book, assigning textbook questions, or distributing a phonics worksheet. This is the essence of Jensen's shotgun approach—doing whatever he thinks will be instructive at the time.

Some lessons do have the look and feel of reforms. A reading lesson, for example, became a site to reward and motivate a student's interest in reading:

> The day's reading lesson began with Jensen asking, "Donny, who is Wayne Gretsky?" The boy answered, "A famous player . . . a millionaire. He just kept on practicing and didn't give up."
>
> "Well, Donny," Jensen continued, "because you were so interested in the story yesterday, I'm going to use you for a demonstration." He called the class to the front of the class and dragged over two large canvas bags full of hockey equipment. Jensen, an avid amateur hockey player, later said he wanted to reward Donny's interest in the story by dressing him up in hockey equipment.
>
> With the students gathered around, and Donny standing awkwardly in front of them, Jensen explained the purpose of each piece of equipment as he dressed the boy. There are a lot of pieces to a hockey uniform, so Jensen had ample opportunity to describe the equipment and tell stories about his college playing days. Students were attentive, calling out questions related to the different components—why the thumb on the glove moves, why the puck has bumps on the side—and to aspects of the game—why

players take off their gloves when they fight. Jensen answered each question in great detail, though students did not always seem to listen.

Motivation is a key to reading (Anderson et al., 1985). With his affinity for all things affective, Jensen agrees. Donny is a reluctant reader and Jensen takes every opportunity to encourage him. The chance to dress in hockey equipment was Jensen's reward for showing interest in the previous day's reading.

Later in the lesson, Jensen pulled the fourth graders aside to discuss parts of the story. Again evidence of reading reforms surfaced:

Jensen: Dan, what did you find interesting in the story?

Dan: He had a hockey rink in his back yard.

Jensen: Where is that in the story?

Dan: I don't know.

Jensen: Will it be in the beginning or in the end?

Dan: The beginning?

Jensen: How do you know that?

Dan: Because he was just a boy then.

Jensen: Good. Donny, what else did you find interesting?

Donny: The whole thing.

Jensen: Chris, what did you think was interesting?

Chris: He got to be a millionaire.

Accessing prior knowledge is frequently cited as an important reading strategy (Langer, 1984; Paris et al., 1991; Yochum, 1991). In asking what students find interesting, Jensen tries to enlist their prior knowledge in order to engage them in the story. Another hint of reform can be seen in his question to Dan about where a piece of information might be found. Understanding that stories represent sequences of events is a piece of becoming a knowledgeable reader (Michigan State Board of Education, 1986). Through his questions, Jensen helps the boy connect information across the text to determine when the event occurred.

One other example of reforms is Jensen's occasional use of trade books. Although he likes and uses the new HBJ reading textbook, he drops the textbook from time to time to use a trade book as the primary reading text. His reasoning, however, has less to do with reformers' arguments about richer text than about promoting affective issues. "The kids can see themselves in the characters and they can learn about themselves through the characters," he said.

Examples of reform-minded practice are notable but rare; the bulk of Jensen's instruction is skills based. For example, phonics instruction is commonplace. Reformers suggest that phonics, if done at all, should be completed by the end of second grade (Anderson et al., 1985). Jensen is either unaware of, or chooses to ignore, this advice. In his view, phonics is "an efficient way of reading" and "all kids need some." Consequently, he regularly distributes worksheet exercises covering the "44 sounds of the English language."

Traditional reading practice also surfaces in the literal-level questions Jensen routinely asks of students. Consider two examples from the discussion about the Wayne Gretsky story:

Jensen: Donny, what can you tell us about Gretsky?

Donny: Like I said before, he's a famous hockey player and he practices a lot. Oh and it told about when he scored his first goal.

Tom: At the age of 18 he was a millionaire.

Jensen: Can we find the year he did that?

Tom: (locating the reference) Nineteen seventy-eight.

Jensen: Katie, yesterday you were talking about the Lady Byng trophy. Where in the book does it talk about it? (She appears not to understand the question.) What page is it on?

Katie: (looks through the section) 109.

Jensen: What does it say? (She stiffly reads the passage and stops at the word, "phenomenal.") What is that word? Break it down into parts. (Jensen helps her sound out the word. He did not ask if she understands its meaning.)

Encouraging students to find evidence for their ideas is part of constructing meaning. In these examples though, Jensen's questions are all at the literal or the factual level. Asking students to support their answers in that context seems less an example of constructing meaning than of checking whether or not students can remember and locate small details of the story.

One last example of skills-based practice can be seen in a month-long unit about reference books. Reading lessons consisted of worksheet exercises for looking up and identifying words from dictionaries, thesauri, and encyclopedias. One worksheet directed students to take out dictionaries, look up words, and write down page numbers, guide words, and pronunciations. The activity was purportedly connected to a pioneer unit the students were doing in social studies. The ten words assigned in the pioneer unit, however—aerobic, complain, flail, haze, metronome, pleat, sari, stegosaurus, tapir, yeti—were unrelated to the pioneer project or to anything else. "I just thought they'd be interesting for the kids," Jensen explained.

This lesson and others have the look and feel of a traditional skills assignment. Students look up a series of unrelated, decontextualized words and record the appropriate guide words. Why? There is no obvious connection among these words or between these words and any other work they are doing. The meagerness of the lesson is underscored when Jensen brushed off students' inquiries about whether they should record definitions of the words. "That's not our purpose," he answered. Jensen saw this lesson as part of a larger instructional whole, but it is not clear that students understood this. Their responses suggested it was just one more school assignment. Though the task seemed relatively straightforward, students dawdled; most had not finished more than 1 hour later.

Reforms offer a vision of teaching and learning that calls for students to read, think, and share the meanings they construct. When Jensen talks about reforms, much of what he says sounds sympathetic. His practice, however, suggests a different story. In virtually all of his lessons, the instruction is didactic—teaching as telling. The learning is passive and often rooted in repetitive practice. Much attention is aimed at eliciting right answers. Students are occasionally encouraged to offer their ideas and opinions, but they often resist. His talk about holistic and nontraditional approaches aside, Jensen seems to hold a traditional view of teaching and learning reading.

A Traditional View of Teaching and Learning Reading. Frank Jensen's reading practice is stuck. Reform-like activities appear, but there is no indication that he is pushing his practice farther in that direction. Instead, Jensen adds a few new pieces onto a practice that remains skills centered.

Jensen claims to be making no substantive changes because he sees little to change. Blurring the distinctions between old and new approaches, he avers that he already knows what he needs and argues that reformers, in effect, have finally caught up to what he has thought and done all along.

I also observed Jensen's insistence that his interest centers on student affect. Affective lessons occur frequently. What these efforts mean, however, is difficult to understand because the effect seems fairly diffuse. This is a typical example:

> During a reading lesson, Jensen delivered two pointed and lengthy affective messages. Reading the play, "The Price of Eggs" (McCandless-Simmons, 1990), Tanya read the line, "I have little enough to eat. I'm a poor widow." Jensen seized the opportunity to label this a "poor me" statement, noting that it served as a means of "putting yourself down."[7] A few minutes later, Jensen again stopped the student reading. "What is the good mistake you just made, Carl?" he asked. The boy looked puzzled. "You said, 'littler in purse' instead of 'lighter in purse,'" Jensen said, "That's a good mistake. It means the same thing." Jensen then spoke for several minutes extolling the virtues of good mistakes.

Jensen often puts content aside to make an affective point, but as in this example and in the hockey equipment vignette, the result is unclear. Asides about "poor me" statements and "good mistakes," and events like the hockey demonstration appear to have a negligible effect. Students frequently seem disengaged and oblivious to both affective and content lessons. A telling example came as a coda to the hockey lesson. Donny, the boy Jensen hoped to reward, misbehaved the rest of the morning and ended up being kept after school.

Blurring the Distinctions II: Mathematics Reforms

As in reading, Frank Jensen knows the language of mathematics reform and he talks in ways consistent with it. For example, he explains that reforms are about "[c]hanging the whole structure of mathematics and understanding that there is more than just the skills of arithmetic. It's more the reading of graphs and charts and teaching problem-solving methods." Such statements echo the reform literature. The NCTM *Standards* (National Council of Teachers of Mathematics, 1989), for example, recognize that "mathematics [is] more than a collection of concepts and skills to be mastered; it includes methods of investigating and reasoning . . ." (p. 5). Jensen agrees with this notion, yet asserts that it does not apply to him; for he interprets mathematics reforms as he does those in reading: nothing new here. Jensen contends that his teaching reflects new ideas about mathematics and always has. Observations of his instruction, however, suggest otherwise.

Learning the Language of Mathematics Reforms. It is difficult to tell why Jensen talks so confidently about reforms in mathematics. Although he remembers hearing about the revised MEAP mathematics test, he is unaware of the new Michigan mathematics policy and the NCTM *Standards*, he neither belongs to professional organizations devoted to mathematics, nor does he attend conferences, workshops, or take university courses. The prime source of his talk appears to be the newly adopted district mathematics textbook and the publisher-sponsored inservice. Here, Jensen apparently picked up the vocabulary of reforms including patterns, mental math, estimation, and problem solving.

Jensen appropriated this language, but he terms it "educational jargon." He taught such things as supplements using the previous textbook. "I just called them something else," he explained. If Jensen supplemented the previous mathematics series, he rarely does so now. Today, he relies exclusively on the new Addison-Wesley textbook. He believes the text embodies the direction reforms advocate and he is willing to follow its lead:

I really haven't changed much [due to the] new textbook. I was doing the
same sorts of things before. Now they're just built into the textbook. . . .
My math teaching is much more orderly now. I hate to say it, but it's driven
by the textbook. I'm following that structure.

It is not altogether clear what Jensen thinks is "built into" the textbook
or why he "hate[s] to say" that he follows it,[8] for in spite of his talk about
reforms, Jensen's mathematics practice looks very conventional. If the new
textbook reflects current thinking about mathematics, that message is lost
in his presentation.

A Mixed View of Mathematics.   Two themes permeate Frank Jensen's talk
about mathematics. One reflects constructivist notions about problem solving and doing mathematics. The other is rooted in a more conventional
view of mathematics as rules and routines, computation and math facts.

As he does with reading, Jensen uses the language of reforms with
confidence and ease. Terms like mental math and estimation percolate
throughout his talk. The term problem solving occurs most frequently,
however, and it is in this direction that Jensen says the mathematics reforms
point. He is right. The reform literature proposes problem solving as central to a new view of mathematics:

> Problem-solving should be the central focus of the mathematics curriculum.
> As such it is a primary goal of all mathematics instruction and an integral
> part of all mathematical activity. Problem-solving is not a distinct topic but
> a process that should permeate the entire program and provide the context
> in which concepts and skills can be learned. (National Council of Teachers
> of Mathematics, 1989, p. 23)

Jensen believes that problem solving should permeate instruction, but
not mathematics instruction alone. In fact, when asked to define the term,
he balks at any specific reference to mathematics. "Problem solving is
generic," he said, "You need to do problem finding first. Then you need
to identify the situation and isolate the problem. It's a totally generic
process." Jensen claims this view of problem solving reflects the scientific
method and that it can be broadly applied. Problem solving not only
applies to mathematics, then, but the problem-solving process applies
equally well across subject matters:

> [It's] the same process to get kids to draw out what a story problem is that
> is asked for in a problem within a math context. . . . If a learner goes into
> a situation with an attitude or methodology or process in mind, what's going
> to come out is going to fit math as well as reading as well as it fits science
> and so on.

This view raises a complex issue. Curriculum reforms make much of teachers' need for deep subject matter knowledge. Considerable attention is also given to thinking skills. The research base on thinking skills, however, is of two schools. Some researchers hold that thinking is done only in context and is subject matter specific (Brown, Collins, & Duguid, 1989; Resnick, 1987). Others promote the notion that thinking or problem solving is a generic activity (Glaser, 1984; Perkins & Salomon, 1989). The complication comes when reforms might be read to endorse either subject-specific or generic problem solving. For example, the Michigan mathematics policy (Michigan State Board of Education, 1990) states:

> Problem-solving permeates all content strands.[9] Because of their central purpose in mathematics and in practical situations, problem-solving and logical thought are viewed as threads that run through all content areas. Beyond [that], there are problem-solving strategies in a separate strand that can help students be better problem-solvers. (p. 5)

This statement establishes problem solving as fundamental to mathematical reasoning and to all aspects of mathematics content. At the same time, however, it suggests that some set of problem-solving strategies can be separated out and taught independently of any particular mathematical context.

Whether or not Jensen recognizes these disparate views is difficult to say. He has read neither the Michigan policy nor the NCTM Standards and one wonders what sense he might make of all this if he did. Would he focus on the generic view and feel justified in his perspective, or would he zero in on the notion that problem solving needs to be a contextual matter that makes sense only within a mathematical setting? It's a good question. Jensen talks about mathematics, but as in reading, he disregards distinctions among ideas and focuses instead on broad generalizations. If he were to read the Michigan policy, he might reconsider his view. Now, however, Jensen takes the position that the problem-solving process he teaches in mathematics is the same process he might teach in a reading or science lesson. The "basic framework [of all subject matter] is the same," he said, "And it's easier to use one than to make up a bunch of new ones."

Problem solving, however defined, is one aspect of Jensen's view of mathematics. Equally important is an emphasis on mathematical rules and procedures. He states that reforms call for "changing the whole structure of mathematics" and that his view of mathematics reflects this push. Like his view of reading, Jensen's view of mathematics cuts a wide swath, and within that view is the traditional conception of mathematics as computation.

Reforms challenge the primacy of computation. "Conceptualization of mathematics and understanding of problems should be valued more highly than just correct solutions to routine exercises" (Michigan State Board of

Education, 1990, p. 3). Reformers do not dismiss computation, but they do challenge the notion that mastering computation is a necessary precursor to problem solving. The proper approach, then, is to contextualize computation by centering it within problem situations (Rabinowitz & Woolley, 1995).

When he observes that reforms downplay the skills of arithmetic, Jensen implies that he understands this argument. Much of his talk, however, has a different cast. Jensen holds that while computation is "pretty unexciting," it nevertheless "is a very necessary phase. . . . Being able to perform the calculations is still terribly important." So too is memorization. "[Memorizing multiplication tables] is one of those unfortunate things. It's one of the building blocks of mathematics. . . . There's no new ideas about teaching the times tables. It's just something you have to learn," he said.

Though drilling students in computation and on the multiplication tables is "every teacher's bane," Jensen questions neither of these practices nor the conception of mathematics they represent. In fact, when pressed about the relationship between computation and new views of mathematics, Jensen makes an astounding connection. Just as he blurs distinctions between subject-specific and generic ideas about problem solving, he also blurs the distinction between problem solving and computation. "It's [problem solving and computation] really the same thing," he said, "You start with What are the facts? Then you figure out what you're being asked to do. And then you decide what operations to use."

This statement reflects Jensen's propensity to speak in generalities and to make large and loose connections between ideas. He may see a deep connection between computation and problem solving, but his breezy acquaintance with such ideas makes this unclear. As in reading, then, Jensen's view of mathematics and his interpretation of the mathematics reforms are a stew of ideas in which the identifiable pieces take on the flavor of whatever is around them.

A Look at Current Practice.   The parallels between Frank Jensen's reading and mathematics practices are strong. There is one difference between his reading and mathematics instruction, however. Whereas he takes a shotgun approach to reading, Jensen's mathematics lessons are drawn almost exclusively from one source, his mathematics textbook, and aim at essentially only one goal, mastery of computational rules and procedures. A lesson in division of whole numbers is representative:

Jensen wrote this problem on the board: $3 \overline{)246}$. He covered the 4 and 6 with a piece of paper.

Jensen: William, what's the first step?
William: Three divided into two?

Jensen:	That can't happen, right? Will 3 go into 24? (Jensen moves the paper to reveal 24. William nods.) How many times?
William:	Eight.
Jensen:	Where does it go? (William points at the board. Jensen interprets this as above the 4.) Up top? (William nods.) What is 8 times 3?
William:	24. (Jensen writes "24" under the 24 in the dividend.)
Jensen:	What's the next step?
William:	Subtract. (Jensen does this.)
Jensen:	What's the next step?
William:	Bring down the 6?
Jensen:	Okay, what's the next step?
William:	Three goes into 6. (Jensen does this.)
Jensen:	How many times?
William:	Two. (Jensen writes "2" over the 6.)
Jensen:	What is 3 times 2?
William:	Six. (Jensen writes "6" under the 6 in the dividend.)
Jensen:	Then what do we do?
William:	Subtract. (Jensen subtracts 6 from 6 and records "0" underneath.)
Jensen:	(to the class) When you have a pattern like that, do you know what it is called? (No response.) An algorithm. That's a big word that you don't have to remember. (pause) If you remember the steps, it's sort of like a song.

Jensen then set the third-grade assignment—a textbook page of 20 division problems. To the rest of the class, he announced, "Fourth graders will need to go one step further today."[10] He wrote the problem:

$$4 \overline{)\ 556}$$

on the board and said, "It's the same process, a few more steps. It's the same series, just keep going."[11] He quickly reviewed the "steps" of solving the problem and assigned a number of textbook problems. As students turned to their work, Jensen circled the room. In response to numerous questions, Jensen repeated one of two refrains—"Remember to go step-by-step" and "You forgot the pattern, didn't you?"

Jensen claims reforms mean that students need more than the skills of arithmetic, yet his instruction is rooted in just that. He demonstrates the division procedure, focuses on the correct steps to take, and assigns a sheet of practice problems. Consistent with a skills-based approach, the emphasis is on doing the procedure correctly and getting the right answer. The interaction between Jensen and the student is also typical. There is virtually no discussion; most students sit passively, disengaged from the lesson and from each other.

Ironically, in this most traditional lesson, Jensen uses a term central to reforms, *pattern*. Although its use and interpretation varies,[12] pattern generally refers to a relationship characterized by regularity and predictability (National Council of Teachers of Mathematics, 1989). Jensen, however, equates pattern with a routine or procedure, as in the steps of solving a division problem. He uses the term frequently, but he does so in ways outside any common mathematical use.

Jensen's instruction is at odds with reforms in other ways as well. First, there is the issue of computation. Reformers argue that computation should be taught in a problem-solving setting and with an eye toward conceptual understanding. Neither this lesson nor any of the others I observed reflects these ideas. Jensen makes no attempt to connect the division lesson with any particular problem or issue, nor does he attempt to connect the lesson with larger concepts like grouping, partitioning, or naming and renaming. Instead, working the procedure and getting the right answer are emphasized. Second, there is the issue of instructional representations. The Michigan mathematics policy urges teachers to "identify and use models and thinking strategies for basic facts . . . to use models [for example] to show the multiplication algorithm" (Michigan State Board of Education, 1990, p. 9). The NCTM *Standards* (National Council of Teachers of Mathematics, 1989) support that view:

> By emphasizing underlying concepts, using physical materials to model procedures, linking the manipulation of materials to the steps of the procedures, and developing thinking patterns, teachers can help children master basic facts and algorithms and understand their usefulness and relevance to daily situations. (p. 44)

If Jensen is concerned about his students' conceptual understanding of division, one wonders why he does not use mathematical manipulatives, for example, to provide alternative representations of the division algorithm. This seems ironic given his attention to students' learning styles. Jensen is determined students will learn to divide, but there appears to be only one right means to that end.

While skills-based instruction prevails, reform-minded ideas are not completely absent. The reference to patterns, weak though it might it be, is one example. Another is the problem-solving activity Jensen schedules each Friday. Fridays, Jensen explains, are game days. On game days, he said, "We do about a half a lesson out of the regular math and then we do that [problem-solving] kind of thing." A typical activity follows:

Jensen distributed a handout and asked Louise to read the problem:

> Kevin, David, Julie, and Tom contributed a praying mantis, a katydid, a ladybug, and a wasp to their class insect collection. Don't let the clues BUG you as you sort through the puzzle.
>
> 1. Kevin, David, and the boy with the wasp brought their specimens to school in jars with holes poked in the lids.
> 2. Julie lives next door to the boy who brought the katydid and down the street from Kevin.
> 3. The boy bringing the ladybug to school carried it in a baby food jar lined with grass.

The handout showed drawings of the four characters, the insects in labeled jars, and a matrix with the insects listed across the top and the children's names along the side. As he reproduced the matrix on the board, Jensen said, "This one will take a lot of thinking, so if you get a headache, then that's good." He added, "Remember, this is math, but it's also reading. You've got to remember that."

As about half of the students worked the problem, Jensen exhorted them to "read the clues and think . . . you can't do this one quick and dirty, this one's hard . . . all the clues are there, just think about it." Noticing that two boys and one girl had finished, Jensen called the class back to order and said, "Okay, let's see if we got it right."

Jensen read the first clue, "Kevin, David, and the boy with the wasp brought their specimens to school in jars with holes poked in the lids," and asked Bryan, "What does this tell us?" No response. "Who brought the wasp?" he continued. Several students call out, "Tom." "Right," said Jensen. He wrote "yes" at the intersection of Tom and wasp, and "no" in the rest of the row. He also filled the wasp column, beside the other characters' names, with "no." Then Jensen read the second clue ("Julie lives next door to the boy who brought the katydid and down the street from Kevin."). Talking aloud, he concluded, "So David must have brought the katydid." He wrote "yes" at the intersection of David and katydid, and "no" in the remaining places.

Joey said, "Wait, Mr. Jensen, I don't get the first one [clue]." Jensen paused, "Joey, you are to be commended for asking that question. The only dumb question is the one you don't ask." He talked through the first clue until Joey said that he understood. Jensen then read the third clue and concluded aloud that Julie had brought the praying mantis and Kevin the ladybug. He completed the matrix and asked who among the students had arrived at the same answer. A couple of hands went up. Jensen called on Robert to explain how he had solved the problem. "I just figured out the clues and then it came easier," Robert said. Jensen accepted this without comment. He concluded the activity by asking if the task was a math or reading problem. William called out, "It's both!" "Right," Jensen said, "and both reading and math are important."

If the division lesson does not look much like the reforms, what about this activity? Reformers would undoubtedly object to the association of problem solving with games and to the partition between problem solving and regular math. On the surface at least, the activity offers potential. There is an opportunity for students to engage in logical reasoning and problem solving by drawing pictures and developing conjectures, and by sharing their ideas.

Apart from the problem-solving label, however, it is not clear how Jensen's treatment of this activity differs from the division lesson because both lessons have a traditional cast. The teaching is didactic. Jensen steers the discussion of the situation and clues in step-by-step fashion. He entertains no alternative conceptions of the clues or how to use them. He offers only one way to solve the problem, and he suggests there is only one right answer. The learning is passive and reflexive. In the division lesson, there is little sense that students understand what they are doing or why they are doing it. They follow Jensen's instructions and reproduce them. In the problem-solving lesson, they sit as Jensen solves the problems and then they mark their papers accordingly. In neither lesson do students have much opportunity to make their thinking public or to consider and critique each other's ideas. One can only wonder what students who arrived at answers different from Jensen's understand about this activity and their ability to do mathematics.

A Conventional View of Teaching and Learning Mathematics. Frank Jensen claims mathematics reforms merely confirm approaches he has held for some time. He sees no significant difference between his practice and reforms, and he senses no need for fundamental change.

Although his talk echoes reforms, there is little indication that Jensen is moving his practice in that direction. In fact, he seems generally content with his conventional approach to mathematics. He has made no major changes and plans none in the future. Any visible changes, then, have been added on to his traditional practice. Use of the word "patterns" is an example. Jensen undoubtedly teaches the division algorithm much as he did early in his career—as a step-by-step routine aimed at computing right answers. He now uses the word "patterns" frequently, but his conception of division, his approach to teaching it, and his expectations of learners seem highly conventional and little changed.

Jensen's response to mathematics reforms parallels his response to reading reforms. Reforms are more evident in reading, but in both subjects his daily instruction and his basic assumptions about teaching and learning reflect traditional approaches. By emphasizing procedures more than conceptual understanding, right answers more than multiple responses, single representations more than alternative representations, and individual learning more than group learning, Jensen's instruction is rooted in the very kind of pedagogy that reformers decry. Unlike Bonnie Jones, Jensen hears nothing that impels him to question his current practice, to learn more, or to make any substantive changes.[13]

Taking a Second Look at Writing Reforms

Until this year, Frank Jensen ignored writing reforms completely. He is now taking a second look, and his ambitious response contrasts sharply with his responses to reading and mathematics reforms.

Learning About Writing Reforms. Frank Jensen cites two sources for his current interest in writing. One is the state, which he heard is promoting student writing. "They're trying to encourage more free writing because the more [students] do it, the better they get at it," he explained. Not surprisingly, Jensen appends an affective justification: Free writing is "confidence-building" and is "good for students' self-esteem." It is not entirely clear, however, how Jensen reached these conclusions or what free writing means to him. He has attended no workshops or inservices about writing other than a single session during the Reading Update inservice 5 years ago, nor has he seen the state writing policy.

The most likely source is his wife. Although technically the district reading coordinator, Teresa Jensen is increasingly interested in connecting reading and writing. She supports and encourages writing as a regular part of the curriculum and in cross-disciplinary units. Whether the state or his wife holds sway, Frank Jensen is actively responding to the call of writing reforms.

Writing Reconsidered. Until this year, Frank Jensen not only ignored writing reforms, he ignored writing instruction all together. Nothing like writing or English ever appeared on his daily list of topics along with reading, spelling, and handwriting. He taught no lessons about identifying parts of speech, using punctuation marks, or parsing sentences. He did not offer students opportunities to write beyond worksheet exercises and end-of-the-chapter questions. Interview transcripts reveal that, although he holds a view on nearly every subject, there is virtually no talk about writing. In the single reference, Jensen notes that he increasingly uses video technology because "kids find the physical act of writing and rewriting off-putting." Evincing his considerable classroom discretion, Jensen apparently decided he would conduct no formal writing lessons.

Although his sources of change are few, Jensen appropriates the language of writing reforms. He talks about elements of the writing process such as brainstorming and revising. He talks about students' need to do more real world writing, and he talks about the need for writing across the curriculum. Jensen makes no connection between writing and mechanics. In fact, he does not talk about mechanics at all. His interpretation of writing reforms centers primarily on providing students more opportunities to write.

Interestingly enough, Jensen does not describe this as a big change. Although he gave virtually no writing practice before this year, adding writing caused neither any disruption to his daily schedule nor encouraged him to seek opportunities to learn about new approaches.

A Look at Classroom Practice. The first writing lessons I observed in Frank Jensen's classroom came during the third year of this study. From this perspective alone, one might argue that Jensen is transforming his practice. Not only is writing now an explicit part of his instruction, but there is much in these vignettes that looks like the reforms. From another perspective, however, this change looks much less radical, because it is not clear that Jensen sees this effort as an important change in either his daily practice or his prevailing assumptions about teaching and learning. Moreover, it remains to be seen if writing will continue to be a regular part of the school day. Those caveats aside, Jensen's efforts in writing seem substantively different from those in reading and in mathematics.

One reform evident in Jensen's classroom is journal writing:

> Fifteen minutes before science, Jensen announced that it was "journal time." Students pulled stenographer pads from their desks and flipped through to the first open page. Jensen said, "Today is absolutely free form. The only rule is you have to write."

Reformers believe that daily writing is critical to students becoming regular and competent writers (Calkins, 1986; Graves, 1983; Michigan State Board of Education, 1985). Journals provide one opportunity. Jensen creates the time for students to make daily journal entries. Students set their own agendas of writing and Jensen controls neither the topic nor the assessment of these entries. He requires only that students write. In these ways, Jensen helps "make writing seem possible" (Calkins, 1986, p. 4). In a classroom where virtually all content area instruction is teacher directed and tasks are closely defined, allowing students time to write in journals is a change of some note.

Reform-minded ideas can also be seen in the pioneer project Jensen organized with Teresa Jensen's assistance. Jensen describes it as an "integrated research unit" combining reading, writing, and computer skills around a social studies topic. Students, working with partners, write chapters for a *big book* for the school library. A big book is a large-format text written and illustrated for beginning readers. The project took approximately one month.

A number of reform-minded elements emerge here. One is the purpose for writing. Writing, as it is generally taught in elementary-school classrooms, focuses on discrete grammar exercises. The small amounts of writing most students do are confined to worksheet and textbook exercises which do not call for much thought or skill (Applebee et al., 1981). The pioneer unit, by contrast, gave students a real purpose—creating a book that younger children can read. Jensen's students collected information from a number of sources, decided how best to represent that information for younger readers, and constructed the text.

A second instance of reform is the interdisciplinary aspect of the unit. Writing reforms argue for teaching writing across the school day. The Michigan writing policy suggests, for example, "provid[ing] instruction and time . . . for students to practice their writing skills in all disciplines. . . . [Teachers should] not limit writing to the English composition classes" (Michigan State Board of Education, 1985, p. 5). With a book rather than a test as the product of the unit, students engage a number of writing tasks as part of the whole school day.

One other example is the writing process. Students spent some time brainstorming ideas about their topics. Later, they wrote early drafts and went through a series of revisions. Publishing their work as a book for the school library capped the process and rewarded the students' work.

Journal writing and the pioneer unit are bold steps, yet what kind of change is this? Remember, writing was virtually nonexistent in Jensen's classroom before this year. Against a barren background, almost any change might look significant. Looking further into Jensen's efforts suggests that he may be glossing over some key features of the reforms.

One example is the writing process. Jensen talks cogently about the process and its importance for student writing, but consider how he describes the actual process of writing the pioneer book:

> We started with facts and simple words like ax and tool. The kids looked them up in the dictionaries and created a data base[14] looking up things about pioneers. . . . We talked about how to look up facts. What different sources there are and how to use them, like how a dictionary is organized. . . . Then the kids categorized and organized this stuff—tools and weapons, health, travel, clothing. . . . They wrote one sentence for each word. Then we grouped the sentences together and discovered that they made paragraphs. And each group of paragraphs will become a chapter in the book.

Statements like this, combined with observations of Jensen's instruction, suggest that he holds a pedantic view of writing instruction. As he describes it, students paged through reference books looking for terms related to pioneer life. They wrote individual sentences, largely definitional, describing the terms. These sentences were then combined into paragraphs, which were further combined into chapters. The book is a compilation of the various chapters. Jensen talks about writing as a process, but there is little evidence of the rehearsal, drafting, revision, or editing phases advocated by researchers of writing. There is little sense that writing is a means of thinking about and expressing ideas. Instead, writing is taught as an additive process of accumulating more and more words and putting them into sentences and paragraphs until a book emerges.

Cast in this fashion, the pioneer unit seems at odds with the new views of writing. Calkins (1986) warns against the temptation of "interpret[ing] the stages of the writing process as discrete, linear steps" (p. 19). If writing is presented as a step-by-step procedure, students may develop a skewed idea of how text is constructed. Moreover, they do not have opportunities to revise or "re-see" their texts. This phase of the writing process as critical:

> The importance of *revision* is not the succession of drafts, but the act of "revision," of using one's text as a lens to resee one's emerging subject. When children merely add on and on and on, they do not stop to hear and see what their writing is saying. (Calkins, 1986, p. 86; emphasis in original)

Jensen's students create text, but because it is simply added together, they miss the important opportunities to revise or resee it while what they know and what they want to say evolves.

Another issue is student *voice*. Giving students a voice in their writing is a central feature of new visions of writing instruction (Atwell, 1987; Calkins, 1986; Michigan State Board of Education, 1985). Graves (1983) argues that voice is an essential dimension of writing. "The voice is the dynamo of the writing process, the reason for writing in the first place [and] the voice starts with the choice of the topic" (p. 31). Students exercise their voice at various points during the project. For example, Jensen asked each writing group to name its chapter and to suggest alternative organizations for the book. At other points, however, students' voice was muted. For example, they had little or no say in choosing the pioneer theme or selecting the topics about which they wrote. It also appears that it was Jensen who decided when the pieces were finished. In making these decisions, Jensen streamlines the book's production; left to their own resources, students might not have been able to complete the project. There are consequences, however, because Jensen may have displaced his students' interest in and commitment to the project. Students often had trouble settling down to their work and few seemed interested in the project or their piece of it. Although Jensen continually reminded them that the purpose was to produce a book for younger children, most students acted as though this was just one more school assignment to work on, hand in, and move on.

These and other observations cloud Jensen's effort. He has created space within the school day for writing. He gives students an opportunity to write freely and regularly in journals, and to write a substantive piece of text for the pioneer book. These efforts might have encouraged him to rethink not only his approach to writing, but also approaches to other subject matters. So far, they have not. The journal activity lasted for 6 weeks. Jensen discontinued it then, saying that he wasn't sure it was "all that beneficial." The big book activity was also a limited effort. Jensen thinks he might do a similar project next year, but he has made no plans to extend the idea of writing across subject matters any further.

A Mixed View of Teaching and Learning Writing. One wonders what this experience means to Frank Jensen. Does it signal a fundamental reordering of his attention to writing reforms? A gentle inclination? Isolated activities? What will his writing instruction look like in the future?

These are difficult questions. In Jensen's efforts there is some indication of new purposes, new roles, and new norms of interaction. At this point, however, these seem episodic at best. Trying something new occasions no discomfort or questions about what Jensen knows or can do. Instead, he pronounces himself satisfied. The pioneer unit went "very well" and, if he does it again, he will do it "exactly the same." Ironically, the journal activity, which might be the most direct challenge to Jensen's conventional views of teaching and learning, is of uncertain benefit and is unlikely to reappear. This response is ironic in another way. Given Jensen's strong affinity for affective things, one might suppose he would see journal writing as an invaluable piece which encourages student self-esteem. His willingness to drop it after a short run seems curious.

RESPONDING TO REFORMS IN THE CONTEXT OF SCHOOLING

The discussion thus far has focused on the relationship between reforms and Frank Jensen's current practice, and has been centered in his classroom, but Jensen, like Bonnie Jones, also works within a larger context. Despite the "bubble of privacy" and "special dispensation," he must negotiate an array of regularities and relationships. In contrast to Jones, however, Jensen feels very little pressure to respond to these factors. He structures the Challenger program, delivers instruction, and determines the results with little interference.

Managing the Regularities

Frank Jensen cannot completely ignore the regularities of content coverage, time, and testing, but neither is he much constrained by them. Like teachers everywhere, Jensen plans and delivers subject matter lessons. The difference is that concerns about covering a prescribed amount of content—a specified set of lessons or the "three fourths of the textbook" Bonnie Jones under-stands as the norm—do not arise. While Jensen may feel some compunction to cover as much content as possible, he holds firmly to the affective mission of the Challenger program and he feels no anxiety about allotting big chunks of the instructional day, as in the hockey vignette, to make an affective point. Other teachers might feel compelled to make up for lost time. Jensen does not. He claims the time given to affective exercises is as valuable as any other, so whatever content he does not teach one day is squeezed into a smaller time, pushed to the next day, or dropped.

Related to this point, the rushed feeling of many elementary school classrooms does not exist in Jensen's room. While teachers like Jones complain constantly of too much to do in too little time, Jensen makes no such complaint. He once noted "sometimes you just don't get through everything." During class, however, he rarely mentions time or the press to finish a lesson. Students and activities take a leisurely pace. The lesson allowing students more than 1 hour to identify guide words for 10 terms is not unusual.

Jensen also takes a casual attitude toward testing. Although his students were identified for the Challenger program by their scores on a standardized intelligence test, assessment does not figure prominently in Jensen's world. He administers the district-mandated ASAT test to all his students and the state-mandated MEAP to his fourth graders. He evades specifics about their performance, however, preferring generalities like "they did okay" or "they didn't do quite as well as last year." His students apparently do neither significantly better nor worse than their regular classroom peers. This condition has no appreciable effect on Jensen: He makes no obvious adjustments to his instruction in preparation for these tests or in response to the scores.

Managing Relationships

If managing the regularities of school causes Frank Jensen little concern, neither does managing relationships. Unlike Bonnie Jones, he rarely re-ceives any criticism from peers. His students can be difficult to deal with and Jensen claims few teachers would be anxious to have them in their charge. Consequently, he brooks no challenge from those who might criticize his methods. When a colleague questioned something about his program a few years ago, Jensen said he responded, "What, do you want your kids back?" The teacher demurred and no teacher has questioned him since.

The Donnelly-King principal also maintains a hands-off approach. Part of this reflects his belief that veteran teachers need little administrative oversight, but in Jensen's case other factors are at play. Jensen's students are more unruly than their peers in the hallways, in the cafeteria, and during assemblies. Principal Adams seems to accept this, perhaps trading off having them all in one classroom with Jensen taking responsibility for them. Jensen understands this and expects no questions of his practice from this quarter.

Jensen does not expect any questions or criticism from his students' parents either. He cultivates a positive relationship by sending home monthly newsletters, inviting parents to class, and calling them at home with good reports about their children. It is unclear what parents think about the program or about what their children might do in a regular classroom. Perhaps they understand and accept the Challenger program's emphasis on affective growth above cognitive development. Perhaps they are pleased that their children were identified for a special gifted program. In any event, parents rarely ask what students are learning and are unlikely influences on Jensen's plans and delivery of his instruction.

Frank Jensen ascribes his lack of constraint to the "special dispensation" and "bubble of privacy" surrounding the Challenger program. That may account for some of it. Also contributing are the norms of schooling because teaching is an insular job and teachers routinely operate with little interference from administrators or peers (Lortie, 1975).

Another factor may be Jensen's modest actions. Bonnie Jones finds herself renegotiating regularities and relationships largely because of her ambitious undertakings. Reading and discussing trade books and providing opportunities to build conceptual understanding by using manipulatives creates time, content, and assessment pressures; using textbooks in non-conventional ways creates problems with peers and parents. Jones felt some constraints during her skills-based days. Attending to reforms, however, exacerbates them. Jensen, by contrast, has a much easier time. Although his talk sounds like the reforms, his actions cause little dissonance. In fact, so loosely jointed is his teaching practice, that even his more ambitious response to writing reforms resulted in no particular attention. How Jensen responds to reforms, then, reflects the choices and decisions he arrives at largely on his own.

Conclusion

Frank Jensen is more receptive to reforms than to change. Talking to him, one senses his excitement with new ideas. Below the surface, however, a different image emerges. There ideas blur. Teaching is didactic, and learning is passive. Jensen is drawn to the bright light of reforms, but his interest fades in the classroom. Writing may be a different case, because the changes there seem dramatic. Where his initial effort will lead, however, is unclear.

In spite of his talk, Jensen takes few risks. One way he avoids risks is by blurring distinctions. In asserting that new ideas reflect those he already holds, Jensen glosses over differences between ideas and between reforms and his practice. Doing so buffers potential threats and permits him to maintain his reform patter and his conventional practice. His "special dispensation" and "bubble of privacy" provide a second means of protection. Whether these notions exist in any form outside Jensen's mind is debatable. What counts, however, is that he acts as if they do. He presumes the Challenger program carries special exemption from outside interference and the presumption works: He has considerable classroom latitude. The "special dispensation" and "bubble of privacy" allowed him to create an entirely new writing practice, but they also allowed him to avoid teaching writing for years and to avoid any standards or accountability now. Jensen's strong steps toward writing reforms are admirable. He could abandon them, however, and face no questions or sanctions. By blurring distinctions and asserting his autonomy, Jensen insulates himself and minimizes potential risks to his instruction. In so doing, he protects himself from deep and powerful change.

This last point suggests one other: Frank Jensen is satisfied. Bonnie Jones' dissatisfaction is apparent and it feeds her ambitions. By contrast, Jensen believes his efforts meet reformers' intentions. There are no open questions, no issues left unresolved. Jensen's pedagogical comfort provides no compelling reason either to question his views or to make profound changes in his practice.

NOTES

1. Unless otherwise indicated, all quotations come from interviews with Frank Jensen conducted from 1991 to 1993.
2. Jensen was principal of a school in the Derry district, but not Donnelly-King Elementary.
3. The construct "underachieving gifted" is not of Jensen's making, but he is unsure of its origin. He points out, however, that as he investigated the literature about gifted education, he found little that addressed the phenomenon of gifted children not reaching their potential. Finding little of value either in the literature or at the conferences he attended, Jensen decided to "follow [his] nose."
4. Jensen is fascinated with the U.S. space program. The "Challenger" label comes from the space shuttle of the same name.
5. Potential Challenger students can be recommended by a parent or teacher, but they must score in the top 5% on the Otis-Lennon test administered in the first and second grades. Students are placed for a 9 week trial period. Few students return to regular classrooms at that point or during the remainder of their years at Donnelly-King Elementary.

6. Jensen's belief in affective development has few bounds. He notes, "Whenever I give a piece of data to a student, the student's whole affect is going to determine how they [*sic*] perceive what it is that I see, I say, or do which is then going to powerfully determine what the outcome, the learned outcome is."

   That perception contrasts with reforms which urge greater emphasis on content. Applebee and colleagues (1987), using NAEP data, suggest, "There is a temptation to ask schools to do too many things, many of which have little to do with developing academic skills. When priorities are set and resources allocated, academic goals should be among the top priorities" (p. 45). Unlike the reforms of the 1950s which stressed only academics (Cohen & Barnes, 1993a), current reforms suggest that both content and social goals are important and that one reinforces the other (see, for example, National Council of Teachers of Mathematics, 1989, 1991).

7. On other occasions Jensen talked about "killer" statements (inappropriate comments which stop or kill discussion) and "vulture" statements (comments disparaging of others). Though Jensen uses this language extensively, students do not seem to adopt it, nor does the incidence of such statements seem to decrease.

8. One possible explanation for the latter statement is that Jensen is sufficiently savvy to know that instruction "driven by the textbook" is considered unenlightened.

9. Problem solving is one of six mathematical "processes" which the policy asserts should weave throughout the content. The content strands or areas are whole numbers and numeration; fractions, decimals, ratios, and percent; measurement; geometry; statistics and probability; algebraic ideas; problem solving and logical reasoning; and calculators. The other processes are conceptualization; mental arithmetic; estimation; computation; and calculators and computers.

10. With rare exceptions (e.g., the problem-solving vignette which follows), students are always divided at some point in their mathematics and reading lessons. Science and social studies lessons are taught across grade levels to the whole class.

11. After the lesson, Jensen explained that "one step further" meant that fourth graders would compute a product with three digits as opposed to the two-digit products in the third-grade assignment.

12. The California math policy (California Board of Education, 1992), for example, lists patterns as one of the central themes of a new view of mathematics. Heaton (1994) points out, however, that "What is a pattern?" is no mean question.

13. There is one interesting difference in the way Jensen responds to reading and mathematics reforms. In contrast to reading (and virtually every other subject), there is little mention of student affect in Jensen's talk about mathematics. Why this is so is not clear, but taken together with his solidly traditional approach to mathematics, it complicates Jensen's claim to be teaching in nontraditional ways.

14. The "data base" consisted of a form Jensen created on the in-class computer to keep track of the information students collected. An entry consisted of the group members' names, the topic category, a brief description (often only a word or phrase) of the item, and a place to indicate the source. The form listed three types: Reference Books (almanac, atlas, dictionary, encyclopedia, *Who's Who*), Books and Magazines, and Other Sources (family history, interview, letter, photograph, video or television). The several items I looked at all listed a dictionary as the sole source.

   Jensen talked at length about student use of a computer for this project, but most of the time, Jensen used the computer instead of the students. Their computer activity seemed limited to initially entering their text and using the spell-check program.

Epilogue

Variation in Teachers' Responses to Reforms: Bonnie Jones and Frank Jensen

They teach but 40 feet from one another, they attend many of the same inservices, they both speak the language of reform, yet it is hard to imagine two teachers more different than Bonnie Jones and Frank Jensen. Equally interesting, however, is the cross-reform variation because not only do Jones' reform responses in reading differ from Jensen's, but they also differ from her own responses in mathematics and writing.

In this section, I explore both cross-reform and cross-teacher responses. To illustrate these constructs, I focus on three dimensions: the relationship between reforms and past practice; daily instruction; and assumptions about subject matter, teaching, and learning.

Variation in Responses Across Reforms

Bonnie Jones is a teacher who sees both the promise and the uncertainty of embracing reform. Frank Jensen is a teacher who sees confirmation in reforms. While such generalizations illuminate the differences between the teachers' responses, they obscure the differences within each teacher's practice. The cross-reform variation within Jones' and Jensen's responses is complex and dynamic.

The Variation Within Bonnie Jones' Responses

There are similarities across Bonnie Jones' reform responses because she generally interprets reforms sympathetically. The differences across her responses, however, are distinct and bear explication.

Reforms and Past Practice. One point of comparison is Bonnie Jones' interpretation of the relationship between reforms and her past practice. Jones' interpretations of reforms suggest that she has appropriated the major themes. In reading, she echoes reformers' concerns for comprehension, for rich text, for reading strategies, and for students as constructors of meaning. Her interpretation of mathematics reforms is similarly agreeable. She talks easily about conceptual understanding, problem solving, and real-world applications.

The exception is writing. For while Jones talks about giving students more opportunities to write and about teaching the writing process, she misses the key point that mechanics are best taught through students' writing. Jones may be ignoring this point, or she may simply be unaware of it. In any case, Jones' interpretation does not match the intended reform well.

These interpretations relate to the relationship between reforms and Jones' past practice. Jones believes that reforms deeply challenge her extant reading and mathematics approaches. In reading, constructivist reforms offer new views of text, instruction, grouping, and purposes. The story is similar in mathematics. There, too, reforms advocate new purposes, curriculum materials, and instructional methods.

Writing is a different story. Though still uncomfortable as a writer, Jones acknowledges the gap between her practice and reforms and she is resolved to push herself to confront it. But only so far. Until Jones recognizes that reforms offer a very different view of mechanics, her practice is unlikely to change in profound ways.

Reforms and Daily Instruction. Bonnie Jones has made numerous reform-minded changes ranging from subtle to profound. Some general similarities appear. Students are more active. Instruction is more varied. Content is richer and more complex. Beneath these similarities, however, are notable differences. In reading, the changes are profound and suggest that a revolution is occurring. Big changes are also evident in mathematics, though how deep they run is unclear. Changes are fewest and most fragile in writing. There, Jones has added on a few new activities, but her practice centers on mechanics.

Jones is constructing a brand new reading practice. The changes, such as substituting trade books for textbooks, teaching reading strategies instead of discrete skills, abandoning reading groups for whole class instruction, and pushing reading instruction throughout the school day, are leaps away from her past practice. They are more than a series of discrete actions because in combination they suggest that Jones is reconceptualizing her reading instruction. Her purposes and practices work toward students constructing meaning, a fundamentally different end than the word recognition and skill acquisition ends of her past practice.

She is also constructing a new purpose, conceptual understanding, in mathematics. Jones provides multiple representations of concepts and procedures and the time to explore them. She makes real-world connections between the mathematics that students are learning and the lives they lead. She opens up the conversation about mathematical ideas and she challenges students to think beyond one right answer. These are dramatic changes from her silent, textbook-centered, school math practice. Coloring these changes, however, are persistent elements of the old, such as drill and practice assignments and an emphasis on efficient and accurate computation, which interweave with the new. That old and new coexist does not undercut Jones' commitment to or her actions toward powerful mathematics teaching, but the possibility that changes in mathematics may not run as deeply as they do in reading must be considered.

The relationship between old and new is even more different in writing. Evidence of reforms exists. Jones is providing more writing opportunities and is encouraging the writing process. Writing also seems more visible across the school day, but skills-based instruction in the mechanics is Jones' writing program. Reform-minded activities appear added on rather than integral.

Reforms and Assumptions About Teaching and Learning. One last site to compare Bonnie Jones' responses across reforms is her set of assumptions about teaching and learning. Again, there are broad similarities. First, Jones is receptive to reforms. Her interest, enthusiasm, and willingness to pursue new ideas is remarkable. Second, Jones is not satisfied. Though she has made what many teachers might consider a career's worth of changes, her commitment to learning and doing more continues even as new reforms (e.g., science, outcomes-based education) press her time and attention. Finally, Jones takes risks. Her eager and ambitious responses court uncertainty throughout her practice.

Despite all these similarities, it is the differences which stand out. Changes in Jones' beliefs about teaching and learning are most obvious in reading. One senses a teacher willing to shake her practice to its core and able to reconstruct it around a different set of assumptions. The case for fundamental change is less clear in mathematics and writing. The difference in Jones' daily mathematics instruction is palpable, but changes in her beliefs, especially in what it means to know mathematics, are not distinct. One senses a teacher negotiating the difficult relationships between content and pedagogy. Changes in Jones' assumptions about teaching and learning writing are less evident. Jones has added a few reform-minded exercises, but the bulk of her practice supports conventional approaches.

The Variation Within Frank Jensen's Responses

In general, Frank Jensen sees little new to learn about subject matter or pedagogy and he does not feel the need to question his basic beliefs. That said, notable differences, especially with writing, do arise.

Reforms and Past Practice.   Frank Jensen's talk recalls reading reforms. That talk, however, blurs distinctions between skills-based approaches and constructivist approaches: Reading is neither skills-based nor constructivist, but both. Moreover, Jensen believes reading reforms confirm and support his extant beliefs and practices. Reforms use new language, he contends, but they express ideas he has held for a long time. The immediate impact of this sense is that Jensen believes he already possesses all the knowledge and skills required by reforms.

Jensen's response to mathematics reforms parallels that in reading. First, he blurs distinctions between traditional views of mathematics as rules and procedures, and constructivist views of mathematics as problem solving. If mathematics reforms offer anything new, it is in addition to, rather than distinct from, his conventional approaches. Second, he believes reforms justify his current practice. Jensen has no quarrel with reforms; he simply believes he is already doing them. Third, Jensen sees as little new to learn in mathematics as he does in reading. He has attended fewer mathematics inservices than reading, though the sense that he already knows what he needs is common.

Reforms and Daily Instruction.   Frank Jensen's reading instruction modestly reflects reforms. New literature-based and strategy instruction practices are added on. Though notable, these actions signal no profound change in modal practice, because the dominant strains of skills instruction, text-based lessons, and single interpretations remain prominent.

Jensen's mathematics practice is even more conventional. New activities are fewer and appear even more tacked on. Jensen's talk about patterns and his game day problem-solving exercises, for example, seem more decorative than functional. Thus, if his efforts in reading have been modest, they are superficial at best in mathematics.

Reforms and Assumptions About Teaching and Learning.   Frank Jensen knows the language of reform, but he feels there is nothing new to learn. He acknowledges picking up some new language and activities, but he routinely dismisses these as significant influences. Given this stance, it is no surprise that Jensen is satisfied with his assumptions about teaching and learning reading and mathematics. Reforms induce no particular questions or concerns because Jensen believes he is already doing the reformers' work. Why would he question the assumptions that got him where he is?

And Then There Is Writing. . . . In writing, Frank Jensen acts as if reforms matter. Here, he makes no special claims about his knowledge or past practice. Instead, he adopts a measure of the writing reforms without question or qualification. He provides journal writing time, introduces the writing process, and includes writing in a cross-disciplinary project. Rather than adding pieces onto a preexisting practice, Jensen is creating a new practice in which he adopts key reform elements and a key stance toward writing, namely, that students need more and richer opportunities to write. Jensen handles some activities awkwardly and he completely misses the reformers' point about teaching mechanics in the context of students' work. Given that he ignored writing and writing reforms for years, however, Jensen has taken big strides.

This fact makes his lack of interest in learning more about writing puzzling. Jensen admits reforms differ from his past practice, but even in this new and unfamiliar territory, he avers no doubts. Consequently, it is no surprise to hear that Jensen entertains no questions about his basic beliefs about writing. The changes in his practice are palpable, yet those changes do not seem to have inspired Jensen to dig deeply into his assumptions about teaching and learning writing. Instead, he manages writing reforms largely in the same breezy manner he does those in reading and mathematics.

Variation in Responses Across Teachers

Frank Jensen's generally modest efforts toward reading and mathematics reforms stand in stark contrast to Bonnie Jones' ambitious responses. This generalization reverses in writing, however, for there it is Jensen who is taking the biggest strides.

Differences in their responses to reading and mathematics reforms surface along several dimensions. First, Jensen and Jones view the relationship between reforms and their practice differently. To Jones, reforms represent new approaches she should try and old approaches she should abandon. To that end, Jones propels herself into new learning opportunities, attending workshops, inservices, and courses within and beyond the district. Jensen holds a different view. Distinctions between old and new are unimportant, because he contends that all approaches are part of a larger process and thus are equally useful. From his perspective, reforms simply provide more ammunition for his shotgun approach. Jensen attends the required district workshops and inservices, but does little beyond that.

A second difference emerges during daily instruction. Both teachers' practices reflect old and new elements. Though more true in reading than in mathematics, skills-based instruction in Jones' classroom is more exception than rule. The reverse is true in Jensen's classroom. There, conventional practices are well established and reform elements are the exception.

One last difference concerns assumptions about teaching and learning reading and mathematics. The disparity between reforms and her practice pushes Jones toward deep and difficult questions. This seems more apparent in reading than in mathematics, but in both cases, her determined efforts suggest she is not content with superficial changes. Jensen, by contrast, believes his reading and mathematics practice already reflect reforms. He has made some changes in his daily instruction, but those changes mount no challenge to his fundamental beliefs about teaching and learning.

The situation is reversed in writing. There, Jensen's ambitious response contrasts with Jones' more cautious efforts. Reforms do not stir any anxiety about what he knows and he seems confident that his existing beliefs about teaching and learning will suffice, but Jensen takes big steps toward a new writing practice. Jones, by contrast, doubts her abilities as a writer and as a teacher of writing. She is willing to confront those doubts and learn more. Her approach, however, is considerably more circumspect.

Prologue

The Hamilton School District, Sanford Heights Elementary School, and Sheldon Court Academic Center

Derry is a laissez-faire district. Textbook adoptions and standardized testing suggest a district presence, but a closer look shows that teachers like Frank Jensen and Bonnie Jones have considerable classroom autonomy. The two teachers in this second set of cases, Marie Irwin and Paula Goddard, work in very different school and district contexts.

Irwin and Goddard teach in Hamilton, a large metropolitan school district, though under very different circumstances. Irwin teaches 25 sixth graders at Sanford Heights Elementary, a sleek, modern building nestled into an attractive upscale neighborhood in the northwest corner of the city. Virtually all the 300 students are Caucasian and from middle- to upper-middle-income families. Goddard teaches at Sheldon Court Academic Center (SCAC), an alternative school with an almost exclusively African-American student body. SCAC is located in an old, but well-maintained building that formerly served as a Catholic school. The inner-city neighborhood around SCAC testifies to all of the problems of urban life. Abandoned houses and vehicles, homeless men and women, drugs, crime, and violence all compete for attention. Many of Goddard's 30 second graders come from this neighborhood; others are bussed in from other Hamilton neighborhoods. Whether from the immediate vicinity or not, the 350 SCAC students share a common lot in that they are from poor families.

Unlike many cities, Hamilton has managed to stay solvent throughout recent economic downturns. Industries are open and productive. Unemployment is low and the incomes of both skilled and professional workers are competitive. Yet all is not well in Hamilton, particularly for the schools.

110

A succession of superintendents left many unfulfilled promises and unrealized plans. Voters regularly turn down school funding increases. Plans for new construction and the expansion of programs have been shelved. Art, music, and gifted and talented programs were eliminated and those teachers were laid off. Finally, reductions in force are common, and though most are regularly rehired, each spring all Hamilton teachers receive pink slips.

Hamilton's problems began in the early 1980s when a financial scandal rocked the community. The school board, hoping to restore some order, hired a reputedly hard-nosed superintendent. He pursued an aggressive program designed to redress cumulative administrative and financial problems. He also directed a profound change in the district's instructional program.

The new superintendent believed as strongly in instructional accountability as he did in fiscal responsibility. He introduced and secured board approval for a sophisticated instructional guidance system. The several components included mandated use of district-adopted textbook series in core content areas along with required instructional time allotments, a pacing scheme for reading and mathematics instruction and assessment, a monitoring system whereby teachers had to keep and give to their principals detailed charts of the lessons they taught and how students performed on textbook chapter and unit tests, and a district-developed essential skills test in reading and mathematics for all students K-12.[1] The program emphasized basic skills instruction and held teachers accountable. Teachers accustomed to wide-ranging curriculum and instructional autonomy suddenly found themselves adjusting to new limits.

The superintendent left Hamilton, but the instructional guidance system and the basic skills orientation remained. Not surprisingly, Hamilton teachers and administrators ignored reforms calling for more adventurous instruction. State efforts to promote a new conception of reading, for example, fell on barren soil. Teachers taught from their skills-based textbooks, logged pacing chart data, tested frequently, and maintained an ever-increasing paper trail to the central office.

However, cracks are developing in the strong district presence. One set of cracks resulted in the creation of the Sheldon Court Academic Center. A coalition of African-American parents, concerned that their children were not being well served by city schools, petitioned the school board for an alternative school. Their efforts succeeded, and in the early 1980s SCAC opened through the combined energies of parents and a select teaching faculty. The school and staff are not bound by the district instructional guidance system. They can, and do, use district textbooks and tests, but they do so by choice. Interestingly enough, the SCAC curriculum is geared significantly more toward basic skill instruction than are other city schools.

That decision seems to have paid off: The scores of SCAC students on standardized tests are among the highest in the district.

If creating alternative schools is undercutting the district control, so too is a nascent attention to curriculum reform. As national interest in mathematics instruction grows, district administrators have scheduled inservice sessions and purchased kits of manipulatives. Teachers are still required to follow the pacing of their textbooks and to concentrate on computational skills, but they are also encouraged to attend the inservices and to use the manipulatives to supplement their textbook instruction. Although outside the instructional guidance scheme, district administrators also encourage teachers to learn about and to implement new ideas about writing. A recently adopted English textbook series promotes real writing assignments and use of the writing process.

What have been only fissures may be about to crack wide open. Until recently, district administrators largely ignored the new state reading policies. The basic skills curriculum and concern about the district Essential Skills test apparently undercut any serious effort to revamp the district reading program, until PA 25, that is. That policy's clear connection between improved MEAP scores and state funding is pushing a reluctant central office to revisit reading reforms. As a consequence, two new literature-based textbooks are being piloted in selected schools. (Irwin and Goddard are among the pilot teachers.) This single act may mean a profound change in reading instruction: During the 2-year pilot, there will be no pacing guidelines, no pacing and test score charts, and no Essential Skills test. Pilot teachers may teach the material, which includes a textbook, trade books, and student journals, and assess their students as they deem appropriate.

School principals generally follow the district lead. Under the instructional guidance system, principals play the enforcers, collecting and monitoring teachers' lesson plans and test scores. This is still the United States, however, and even in the most structured school districts, variation emerges. So while the Sanford Heights and Sheldon Court principals respect the district authority, each has also embraced some reform-minded changes.

The Sanford Heights principal, Tom Nettles, is a strong proponent of reading and writing reforms. Nettles takes seriously his role in administering the district instructional policy, yet he also led his faculty in creating an ambitious schoolwide literacy program, which emphasizes daily reading and writing. Nettles is less interested in mathematics reforms. In fact, despite reformers' call to deemphasize computation, Nettles instituted a building policy requiring timed computation tests in grades 4 through 6. Students must, by the end of sixth grade, correctly compute 100 problems in 4 minutes. These problems include individual addition, subtraction, multiplication, and division tests.

By contrast, Nettles' colleague at Sheldon Court, Natalie Simon, seems more interested in promoting new ideas in mathematics than in literacy. Simon leads a school with an explicitly basic-skills mission and she takes student performance on the district essential skills test very seriously. Yet, after a teacher returned from a conference session about a manipulatives-based mathematics program, *Mathematics Their Way* (Baratta-Lorton, 1976), Simon encouraged her primary-level teachers (including Paula Goddard) to use the program. Simon has been less interested in literacy reforms. She is allowing the piloting of the new literature-based reading textbook, but she remains committed to a basic skills approach to literacy.

Irwin has taught using the central office instructional plan since its inception. Goddard is under no obligation to attend to the district instructional plan, yet she teaches under an equally strong institutional mandate, the SCAC basic skills program. Given the organizational differences, one might expect Irwin and Goddard's responses to differ not only from one another, but also from the Derry teachers. The cases support that conjecture: Although there are similarities across all four teachers' responses, notable differences emerge. A second form of variation, the variation across an individual teacher's reform responses, also surfaces. Interestingly enough, the variation in the Hamilton teachers' individual responses to reading, writing, and mathematics reforms is as great as that in the Derry teachers. In the cases which follow, I describe how each teacher responds to reading, writing, and mathematics reforms and how her responses vary across teachers and across reforms.

NOTE

1. All Hamilton students take the district-developed Essential Skills test and the nationally normed California Achievement Test. Students at grades 4, 8, and 10 also take the state MEAP test.

Chapter 5

The Center Holds:
The Case of Marie Irwin

Given a different school and district context, one might expect Marie
Irwin's reform responses to differ from those of Bonnie Jones and Frank
Jensen. They do. For example, unlike Jones, who rejected a new reading
textbook, and Jensen, who uses it as part of a melange, Irwin centers her
practice in the textbook. At the same time, she regularly supplements
textbook lessons with classroom novels, to emphasize the power and grace
of a well-told story.

The approach of adding elements of reform (e.g., classroom novels) to
a strong, extant traditional practice generally characterizes Irwin's response
across her practice. New ideas, materials, and activities surface, but in small
doses as supplements to a practice rooted in conventional methods. Irwin
is no revolutionary; although she is not out to transform her practice as
Jones is, she is not as feckless as Jensen. Instead, Irwin is a solid, no-nonsense
teacher who views reforms cautiously and is willing to make small changes
once she is convinced students will benefit.

This dedication to do well by students drives what may become the most
profound change in Irwin's teaching. While Irwin generally takes an additive approach to reforms, she worries that her mathematics practice is
not meeting students' needs. She has made no dramatic changes. In contrast to her response to reading and writing reforms, Irwin views mathematics reforms as a challenge to her extant practice and she asserts an
interest in changing it.

A tall, European-American woman in her late forties, Marie Irwin exudes
a calm determination. Her deeply quiet voice is authoritative; her eyes are

quick to smile, though she rarely laughs aloud; her movements are fluid
and efficient. She never raises her voice, threatens, or cajoles. She is quiet
confidence, business with a kind face. Irwin enjoys the respect and support
of her principal and peers, but trusts her own instincts first and foremost.
"I learn a lot from my own teaching," she said, "I learn a lot from what I
do that is successful and what isn't, what I'd like to do again and what I
would change." "I teach myself a lot," she concludes.[1]

Irwin began teaching grade 6 at Sanford Heights Elementary in 1985
after an 18-year hiatus. She started as an upper-elementary teacher, leaving
after a couple of years to begin a family. Four years later, she returned to
education as a part-time teacher of adults. She taught basic skills in reading
and mathematics, advised students working on GED degrees, and directed
the city adult-education program. When the job at Sanford Heights came
up, she jumped. "I always knew I'd return to the classroom," she said, "I
always wanted to come back to elementary school." Irwin continues her
work with adults. Two days a week, she leaves her sixth graders to teach
evening classes in basic reading and mathematics skills to adult learners
at a local community college.

A tour of Irwin's classroom reveals a mix of old and new ideas. Reforms
are evident: Trade books line classroom shelves; a large box of mathematical manipulatives sits on the floor near her desk; posters outlining the
writing process are displayed on a classroom wall. These artifacts exist
within a landscape of tradition. Dwarfing the writing process posters is a
display of more than 30 small, handmade signs defining the parts of speech
(e.g., noun, helping verb, predicate adjective, and subject pronoun) and
sentence structures (e.g., declarative sentence, run-on sentence, and sentence fragment). Other posters detail phonics practices (e.g., dividing
words into syllables, vowel sounds, long vowels, accent marks, and schwa
sound). Also prominently displayed are charts listing the students who
passed the school-mandated math-facts tests.

This coexistence of old and new is telling. Irwin describes herself as a
"traditional" and "old-fashioned" teacher. Classroom observations support
that self-assessment: Each school subject is treated as a distinct entity,
instruction is didactic and rarely strays from textbook lessons, and learning
is an individual task. Both her talk and practice, however, suggest traces
of reforms across the school day. Trade books are used and reading strategies are presented. Students write in journals and author-publishable
pieces. Even in mathematics, reforms whisper: Students learn about estimation, they use manipulatives.

Irwin's teaching has changed in response to reforms. She manages that
change, however, in ways that neither threaten nor challenge her long-held
views of subject matter, teaching, and learning. Mathematics may prove

different. For now though, when change occurs, it's at the margins of her practice. The center holds.

RESPONDING TO REFORMS

The cross-teacher and cross-reform variation evident in the earlier cases re-emerges here. Marie Irwin represents a sort of middle ground between Bonnie Jones and Frank Jensen. She works toward less ambitious goals than does Jones, but unlike Jensen, she follows through on the commitments she makes.

Irwin's responses to reforms vary from other teachers, and they also vary across reforms. As we have seen in the previous cases, teachers do not attend to reforms in predictable or consistent ways. Thus, while Irwin tends to treat all reforms as add-ons, important differences emerge. For example, reforms are most obvious in reading, in which the line between reform-minded and traditional practices blurs as Irwin works toward a new set of instructional objectives. Irwin's additive approach to reforms is most obvious in writing, in which some reform-minded writing activities appear, but are segregated from formal English instruction. Irwin's responses to mathematics may ultimately prove to be the most interesting because she long avoided reworking her mathematics practice, but now reports a change of heart.

Although the case of Irwin provides another illustration of how teachers' responses vary, it is instructive in another way, for Irwin works in a much different organizational context than do Jones and Jensen. The district influence on regularities and relationships is stronger in character and effect than anything Jones or Jensen faces. Irwin could not substitute trade books for the basal as Jones does because textbook units are the basis for pacing charts. She could not give large amounts of time to affective lessons as Jensen does because she must pace her lessons. Unlike these teachers, Irwin must regularly administer and record the results of textbook and standardized assessments. The district system of texts, pacing charts, and tests constrains Irwin's actions in far more ways than those of her Derry peers.

The organizational constraints in Hamilton are powerful, but their influence is not absolute. Factors such as Irwin's knowledge and beliefs about teaching and learning, her disposition toward some reforms and not others, and her personal experiences figure into what she is willing and able to do, for as prescriptive as the Hamilton instructional system is, a measure of classroom autonomy is apparent.

In the next sections, I look at Irwin's response to reading, writing, and mathematics reforms. I explore how Irwin learned about the reforms, her view of the subject matters, illustrations from classroom practice, and what all this means for her view of teaching and learning.

Embracing Reading Reforms as Nothing New

Marie Irwin's reading practice is a complex mixture of old and new. Although skills-based instruction is central, Irwin adds on a layer of reform-minded practice. She uses new texts, instructional strategies, and grouping arrangements and she teaches toward purposes different from those commonly found in basal readers. Interestingly enough, however, Irwin contends that these practices are nothing new. Reforms offer no challenge because they represent long-held ideas.

Learning About Reading Reforms. Marie Irwin has had numerous opportunities to learn about reading reforms. She discounts those at the state level though, in favor of those opportunities closer at hand.

One of the least important influences is the state policy. Irwin learned about it from her school reading teacher. "I've seen it," Irwin said, "I'm aware that it's out there, but I don't think about it in terms of my planning. I teach reading from what I think is important." Irwin is similarly unaffected by the new MEAP reading test. She knows the revisions reflect more emphasis on comprehension than on discrete skills. She also knows that the results are taken seriously by her principal, district administrators, and many of her peers. Her sixth graders do not take the test, however, and Irwin feels no compunction to attend to test scores:

> As a building, we might just have some exposure to the fact that the fourth graders are taking the test, but generally, it will be the third-grade teacher who will hear if there's an area that needs to be focused on because they're the ones who are preparing these kids.

Irwin is concerned that her students score well on the district Essential Skills and California Achievement tests. Any influence state reformers hoped a new test would generate, however, is lost on Irwin.

More influential are those initiatives closer to home. District administrators have ignored reading reforms until recently (Spillane, 1993). Now, however, the district plans to adopt a literature-based textbook series. Two textbook programs, Silver Burdett & Ginn (Pearson & Johnson, 1991) and Houghton Mifflin (Pikulski & Cooper, 1991), are being reviewed. Both series address reform ideas. For example, reading selections are based on children's literature and reading strategies (e.g., SQ3R, classifying, and context clues) and are presented in the context of stories. Moreover, each series includes classroom sets of novels and encourages teachers to use them freely. Irwin attended the publisher-sponsored inservice sessions for the Silver Burdett and Ginn (SBG) text. The biggest benefit, however, is her own study of the textbook and teacher's guide.[2]

New ideas about reading are also part of the Sanford Heights Elementary School program. Principal Nettles urged the staff to adopt programs designed to promote a literate environment. One program is Stop Everything and Read. Teachers schedule a 20-minute period each day for silent reading. What students read is optional; the only requirement is that they read quietly. Another school initiative features book talks. Each fifth grader selects a book to read aloud and discuss with a K-2 classroom. The student must rehearse beforehand and must field questions during the session. The classroom teacher then writes an evaluation of the presentation, noting, for example, whether the student "spoke loudly and clearly," "read with expression," and "enjoyed the book." One other school reading program makes every fourth-grade student responsible for taking two to three kindergarten children to the library for an orientation tour.

Irwin might have interpreted the conceptions of reading embodied in the new state policies, the new reading series, and in programs such as Stop Everything and Read as a direct challenge to her view of reading because the old district reading series largely defined her reading practice. That practice centered on discrete skills, bland reading passages, and ability-based reading groups. Irwin had taught this way before she left the classroom; it was no different on her return.

Constructivist reforms developed in the state policy and instantiated in literature-based textbooks call for a much different approach. Irwin, however, does not read them that way. These ideas, she contends, are not new because she has supplemented her basal reading instruction with trade books for a long time. Reforms, then, confirm rather than challenge her teaching practice. "I've always done it this way," she said, "Why is this [supposed to be] so different?"

Because she believes reforms echo her extant ideas and practices, Irwin feels that she has little new to learn and that she has access to all she needs. Irwin belongs to no professional organizations, reads very little professional literature, and attends no professional development opportunities outside textbook inservices. What she learns about reforms comes from local sources and from her own experience. She attended the SBG inservices and she carefully read the textbooks and teacher's guide. Beyond that, Irwin counts on her principal to relay necessary information:

> There are really not too many teachers who are going to sit down and read the guidelines. . . . It's really up to the district or the administrator they work for to relay that information. . . . In this building we have extremely strong leadership and we are aware of what we are supposed to do.

Irwin embraces some parts of the reform agenda, but she interprets reforms as extensions of views she already holds. She sees little new to learn and she is confident that she can learn all that she needs from a few local sources.

A Complex View of Reading.   Marie Irwin's view of reading has two distinct dimensions. One centers on skills instruction and the belief that learning to read means practicing and accumulating reading skills. The other dimension emphasizes reading real literature and appreciating good, well-written stories. Such a compound view does not easily fit into the standard categories of reading which pose these as disparate and incompatible approaches (Harste & Burke, 1977; Richardson et al., 1991); nor does it reflect the viewpoint of most elementary school teachers, who generally adopt skills-based approaches alone (Harris, 1993). Irwin believes, however, that one dimension complements the other. She said, "I wouldn't want to teach the textbook (i.e., reading skills) without the novel option."

Reading skills and reading literature may be complementary, but they are not equal partners. Skills-based textbook study is the heart of Irwin's view of reading. Literature is an important part of reading, but it is only a part. "I think of [classroom novels] as a supplement to the textbook," she said, "but not to replace it. . . . The text is based on skills. Novels add [among other things] reading for fun."

What complicates this is that Irwin's sense of skills differs from that of many in the reading field. Classroom observations show that she teaches both *skills* (i.e., discrete decoding processes such as identifying prefixes and suffixes) and *strategies* (i.e., cognitive processes for making sense of text such as predicting, summarizing, and classifying). Although reformers make much of this difference (Richardson et al., 1991), Irwin has little patience with such distinctions. Instead she uses the term skills to reflect both conceptions.[3]

> I used to see skills isolated, separate from the readings [in the old textbook] and not incorporated in the reading. . . . The way [they're] presented in this book (SBG), I see them as really incorporated. . . . There is still skills instruction, but the skills are tied more directly to the story.

Irwin applauds this change. It "just makes sense" to her that students' skills improve when they can see them used in a real piece of text. The new reading textbook, then, represents both a positive and a comfortable change; the old, familiar skills are there, but they appear in a new and more engaging context.

Skills define the center of Irwin's view of reading, but not its entirety. Agitated by a sense that reading had been reduced solely to a mass of discrete skills and boring basal selections, Irwin decided to act. With her principal's encouragement, she applied for a $600 district grant to purchase and use trade books in place of the old basal. Her rationale was: "I was feeling that reading was getting away from reading, that there wasn't enough reading taking place during reading class." A third-grade colleague agreed to join Irwin, and for a semester, both taught reading from classroom novels.

Students' positive responses confirm Irwin's belief that reading literature is important to their experiences as readers, but nothing in those responses led her to believe, as some reading reformers and teachers do, that the textbook could be dropped. Instead, she remains convinced that textbook instruction, supplemented with literature, reflects the proper direction for reading instruction.

A Look at Current Reading Practice. Marie Irwin's twin interests in reading skills and reading literature play out in her practice. Textbook lessons highlight reading skills and strategies, while lessons with classroom novels emphasize language and storytelling. In both settings, however, a mix of old and new practices can be observed.

Many elements of Marie Irwin's reading practice reflect reforms. One example is her use of trade books:

> Irwin directed students to take out their copies of *The Black Pearl* (O'Dell, 1967), a pencil or pen, and a sheet of paper. She asked students to write the title of the book and the chapters they were examining that day (4 and 5) at the top. Then she said, "Without looking in your books, I want you to write down whatever you can remember from chapters 4 and 5. This is not for a grade, but to trigger your thinking . . . just write down what you remember . . . this is not a test. If you can't remember anything, please write that down as well. . . . Just write, 'I don't remember.'" Students immediately began writing. Most wrote continuously for the approximately 10-minute period. Only one or two students wrote, "I don't remember."

Irwin believes that the unabridged stories in trade books offer students a significantly different experience than basal readers do. Reformers (Goodman, 1986; Goodman et al., 1988) concur. They would also applaud her use of reading strategies such as summarizing as a means of building comprehension.

Later in the same lesson, Irwin emphasized another reading strategy, identifying metaphorical language:

> Irwin read the phrase "wound like a snake." She asked, "What picture do you get in your mind. . . . What do you think of?" Several students offered images. Nodding, Irwin described the phrase as a "special technique that

authors use." She wrote "simile" on the board and explained that similes compare two different things, joining them through the words "like" or "as." By comparing a channel (of water) with a snake, she said, "You can see what the channel looks like because you know what a snake looks like." Later, after describing of one of the main characters, Irwin asked if students could form a picture of him in their minds. Several smiled and nodded.

Sensitizing students to how authors use language to convey ideas is one more strategy for helping them understand text. Irwin often emphasizes the use of literary devices during trade book lessons. The new literature-based textbook provides another site to teach such strategies. A recent lesson began this way:

Irwin distributed a worksheet related to the story the class had been reading. She read from her teacher's guide: "The sea rushed up the shore like a liquid army. Foot by foot it captured the gleaming sand." She said, "In these sentences the sea is being compared to something. What is it being compared to?"

Students:	To an army.
Irwin:	Good. Can you get a picture of it in your mind? Does the sentence create an image?
Students:	Yes.
Irwin:	What do we call that?
Randy:	Figurative language.

Irwin nodded and directed students to the first sentence on the worksheet: "The giant wave hit the shore like a hundred cymbals."

Irwin:	What is the sentence talking about?
Sam:	A wave.
Irwin:	A giant wave. Good. What does the wave sound like?
Sarah:	Cymbals.
Irwin:	Okay, what image does that create?
Sarah:	Like a humungous wave that goes biiing!
Irwin:	Good. That's an interesting way of saying this.

Irwin read the next sentence, "The angry seas rose up and tossed the boat violently."

Irwin:	What is this sentence about?
Tina:	Seas.
Irwin:	Okay, what do seas do?
Larry:	Toss the boat.
Irwin:	What does the sentence tell us about the seas? What image do you get?

Randy:	I get the image that the sea just jumps up and throws the boat.
Sue:	I see a big hand throwing the boat on the land.
Suzanne:	I see Gilligan's Island and the waves are going all over the place.
Irwin:	Okay, okay. But what kind of seas do you see?
Tony:	Stormy.
Irwin:	Good. So now write "The waves were stormy" (in the space after the sentence).[4]

The ostensible purpose of this lesson is to identify and understand the use of figurative language. Yet other reform-minded practices are also evident. For example, Irwin no longer divides her students into ability-based reading groups with differentially leveled texts. Whole-class instruction around a common text is now the norm. Irwin also provides opportunities for students to talk about their ideas. Not long ago she stressed silent, individual work. Today, students more actively participate in their learning.

Gone are the ability-based reading groups, the sole reliance on the textbook, and the endless worksheets. Has Irwin's reading practice changed? Some of the content is different. Reading strategies such as summarizing and identifying literary devices surface frequently and students do their work in new contexts, yet much remains unchanged. Irwin's instruction continues to be teacher centered, textbook based, and didactic. Lessons come primarily from the teacher's guide and textbook and they are delivered in recitation form.[5] And classroom talk usually converges on right answers. Irwin acknowledges that many elements of her instruction remain unchanged:

> The content has changed a lot, but my approach to teaching has not changed. I still follow the basic format in a lesson that fits a recommended format.[6] The way I structure my classroom or the way I manage my classroom has been basically the same for a long time.

In fact, Irwin contends that one of the most attractive features of the new SBG textbook is that "it's set up to follow through just about the way that I do things."

Irwin's reading instruction is sensitive to students' experiences and understandings. Learning skills and extracting the right meaning from text, however, remain the primary goals. She said, "I want [students] to arrive at the suggested meaning that is in the [text]book, so I try to get them as close to that as possible." In a recent lesson, Irwin gave students two SBG worksheets after students had read a mystery story. The first worksheet asked them to interpret a series of clues. After the lesson, Irwin described the task this way:

The students could answer depending upon what they thought the question meant. So the directions weren't really specific. And as they were working on it, they would come up to me and say, "Is it this or is it this?" And my direction was that you could put them both down. I wasn't going to grade it, so it wasn't that important to me.

The second worksheet listed questions designed to extract the main ideas and events of the story. Here, Irwin said:

I want them to be able to determine for themselves how accurate their answer is compared to the given answer . . . they're analyzing the accuracy of their own response. . . . The answers to the story are generally pretty cut and dry. There's not a whole lot of room for interpretation, so the closer they come to the book, the more right they are.

Irwin wants her students to read widely and to appreciate the telling of a good story, but learning to read is largely a function of eliciting the right answers from text. Irwin endorses reading reforms which promote, among other things, comprehension and constructing meaning. In practice, however, students are often encouraged to construct the right answer. She underscores this point: "I'm trying to encourage students to think," she said, "[but] sometimes their thinking is right and sometimes it is not right."

A Static View of Teaching and Learning Reading. Big portions of Marie Irwin's reading practice are different today. She uses new texts and new teaching strategies. She organizes whole-class instruction and provides students more opportunities to discuss their ideas. These efforts come less from outside pressures than from Irwin's own interests: She wrote the proposal to purchase trade books and she volunteered to pilot the new reading series. She took on the additional work in order to promote deeply held beliefs.

Those beliefs have not changed. Despite her reformlike efforts, Irwin maintains she does only what she thinks is important. Reforms confirm her beliefs, but do not engender them. Moreover, those beliefs are centered in conventional textbook skills, didactic instruction, and extracting the right answers. The changes Irwin introduces strengthen her practice, but they do not challenge it. New activities appear, but they do so within a static and conventional framework.

Adding on to a Traditional English Practice

Marie Irwin's additive approach to reforms is particularly evident in her writing instruction. A few reform-minded practices such as journal keeping and creative writing are evident. A sharp separation exists, however, between these practices and Irwin's primary instruction, which focuses on mechanics.

Learning About Writing Reforms. Marie Irwin senses writing reforms in newly adopted district textbook and school-level initiatives. The new SBG English textbook (Gray & Davies-Toth, 1990) features the writing process. "We're expected to do it as part of our English program," Irwin said, "the textbook is geared to it." To learn about this approach, she attended the publisher-sponsored inservices and made a careful study of the textbook. A school-level literacy program also pushed Irwin to consider new ideas about writing. At Principal Tom Nettles' urging, the Sanford Heights faculty agreed to support daily reading and writing requirements for all students. The writing requirement can take either of two forms. *Journals* are spiral-bound notebooks in which students make entries based on their interests. The *publishing center* refers to the school-wide requirement that every student submit at least one piece of writing for publication and display in the school lobby. Teachers are expected to schedule time each day, typically 15 minutes, for work either in journals or on publishing center pieces.

Reforms like the writing process, journal keeping, and creative writing are new for Irwin. If she is uncomfortable or uncertain about them, she neither acknowledges nor takes any steps to address these feelings. Irwin knows that opportunities to learn more exist, but she does not pursue them. Instead, she seems satisfied with her current level of knowledge.

A Compound View of Writing. Marie Irwin recognizes new ideas and approaches to writing as something different from her long-held views. In that view, writing was called English and focused on the formal study of mechanics—grammar, parts of speech, and sentence construction. Irwin still holds this view:

> I think grammar is important and I don't think you can write well if you can't put together a good sentence, and I don't know how students can learn to capitalize and punctuate if it isn't taught. . . . I do the writing, and I put a lot of energy to that, but I would never not teach grammar.

Few reformers would urge Irwin to abandon all grammar instruction, but most would suggest teaching grammar as part of a real writing task rather than as a discrete activity (Graves, 1983). Calkins (1986) states the point bluntly: "The research is conclusive. Teaching formal grammar has no effect on the quality of student writing" (p. 195). Continuing, she explains, "English is a skill to be developed, not content to be taught, and it is best learned through active and purposeful use" (p. 204). The authors of the Michigan writing policy (Michigan State Board of Education, 1985) concur:

Limit instruction in grammar and mechanics in isolation, because application is dependent upon the students' abilities to express themselves in an organized way. Some knowledge of grammar is useful, but too much time spent on the study of grammar steals time from the study of writing. Time is much better spent on writing and conferring with the teacher or other students about each attempt to communicate in writing. (p. 5)

Irwin has read neither Calkins' book nor the Michigan policy. She is aware of suggestions to deemphasize traditional English instruction, however, and she is not persuaded.

Despite her strong belief in teaching English, Irwin does not ignore all new ideas about writing. She recognizes that her students have not done much writing in the past and that the writing they did was short and perfunctory, including writing lists of sentences with appropriate punctuation, and rewriting sentences with the correct parts of speech. Making time for free writing each day is difficult, but Irwin fully supports the school writing initiatives and she willingly schedules time each day during which students can write in their personal journals or work on pieces of writing for the publishing center. Opportunities to write are important. "I see it as an opportunity for [students] . . . to voice things they want to say," Irwin explained. Yet these opportunities are supplemental rather than integral to her English instruction. "I don't see it (the school writing program) as an instructional kind of thing," she said. Writing and English, then, are parallel activities in Irwin's view. Both are important, but they do not intersect.

A Look at Classroom Writing Practice. The segregation of reform-minded and traditional approaches surfaces in Marie Irwin's daily instruction. The mainstay is English mechanics and, ironically, Irwin uses her reform-minded textbook to accomplish this. She can do so because the text is divided into two parts. One part features the writing process and offers abundant suggestions for real writing activities. The other part, however, is a standard English grammar text. Irwin acknowledges that she does not use the text as it was presented in the district inservice:

When we were first introduced to this textbook, we were told that . . . the emphasis should be on the writing and we should not put grammar in the primary role. [But] I do, because I think grammar is important and I don't know how you can write well if you can't put together a good sentence.

Irwin says she teaches chapters from both sections. The following vignette, however, is typical of the classroom lessons I observed, which focus on discrete grammar skills and seem distant from reforms:

Irwin directed students to take out their English books. "What we've been talking about are verbs," she said, "Remember yesterday we began talking about the three forms of verbs. Does anyone remember what they were called?" A few students volunteered partial answers. Irwin summed their responses: "Okay, the forms are the present, past, and past participle. And remember that when you use irregular verbs, they change as you go from past to present."

Irwin directed students' attention to page 130. Present, past, and past participle forms of the verbs "break" (break, broke, broken) and "choose" (choose, chose, chosen) were displayed. She asked, "Can anyone recognize a pattern in that group of verbs?" Tommy said, "You add an ending to the past to get the past participle." "And what is that ending?" asked Irwin? "E-n," he replied.

"Okay," said Irwin, "Now let's look at the next set of verbs (become, became, become). What is the pattern here?" Jill said, "The past participle is the same as the present." Irwin nodded and said, "Good. Now if everyone will look at the third box (say, said, said). What's the pattern there?" Jean offered, "The past and the past participle are the same."

Irwin then wrote examples on the board (e.g., I break a glass, I broke a glass, I have broken many glasses) and asked students to do the same. Later, she distributed a worksheet on which students were to fill in the appropriate verb form:

- Nature _____ forth a number of wonders.   (bring, brought)
- This delicate creature has _____ its cocoon.   (break, broken)
- Finally the caterpillar has _____ a butterfly.   (become, became)

Such lessons typify Irwin's instruction. In fact, grammar is so important that Irwin and some of her Sanford Heights colleagues use an ancillary grammar program to provide extra practice. This program suggests daily grammar exercises using two sentences. Irwin writes the sentences on the board and reviews students' corrections at the beginning of each day. This vignette is typical:

After the Pledge of Allegiance and morning announcements, Irwin turned to the sentences on the board: he had lain the groceries on the counter but had forgot to put the ice cream into the freezer; betty her cousin should have visited the us. She described the corrections while she made them on the board—"Capital S on 'she,' 'laid' instead of 'lain,' a comma after 'counter,' change 'forgot' to 'forgotten,' and a period at the end." Chris asked if "laid" and "forgot" were acceptable. Irwin said, "Oh, you changed the verb tense. They don't want you to do that." The boy nodded and corrected his paper.

Irwin turned to the next sentence—"Okay, capital B on 'betty,' a comma after 'betty' and another one after 'her cousin,' and capitalize and put periods after 'u' and 's'." Clarence raised his hand and explained that he had interpreted the letters "u" "s" to be "us" rather than "U.S." "I just took out the 'the'," he said. Other students concurred. Irwin smiled and said, "I thought you might get fooled by this one." Clarence demanded, "So is it wrong?" Irwin said, "Yes." Clarence looked annoyed, but said nothing. To the class, Irwin said, "I took these right off the paper, so you can see if you can do them correctly."

Whether from the textbook or the ancillary program, Marie Irwin teaches grammar as decontextualized bits, important for its own sake. The instruction is teacher centered and didactic. Students participate, but passively. The purpose of the lessons is to determine the right answer—the correct punctuation symbol, the appropriate verb tense—and there is little room for interpretation as the exchange between Irwin and Clarence attests. Here, Irwin will not entertain the idea that a different construction of the sentence is as viable as the one listed on the paper. That Clarence's answer did not match the given response is sufficient justification for calling it wrong.

These vignettes illustrate Irwin's English instruction. She handles writing much differently. Irwin typically provides the first 10 to 20 minutes of the school day for journal and publishing center activities. Students may work on either journals or publishing center pieces during the scheduled time. The only requirement is that they work quietly and individually. Irwin typically takes a nondirective role; she walks around the room, stopping occasionally to talk quietly with individual students. The conversations are short and often related to mechanics, how to spell a word or to use a punctuation symbol. Occasionally she edits pieces students want to submit to the publishing center.

A Conventional View of Teaching and Learning Writing. Marie Irwin's writing instruction represents a mix of practices. Irwin accepts the reformers' call for more and more engaging writing activities, but this call represents no substantive challenge because the two activities do not interact. Irwin simply makes time both for students to write and for her regular English instruction.

Reforms seemingly have had little effect on Irwin's beliefs about teaching and learning. She sees benefit in students expressing their views through writing and she takes a less didactic teacher role during the writing exercises, but these changes have not pushed deeply into Irwin's practice. Instead, she holds tightly to traditional notions about knowing and teaching grammar.

Ignoring Mathematics Reforms?

Marie Irwin approaches mathematics reforms even more cautiously than writing reforms. She has added a few bits of reform-minded content, but her practice is mostly traditional drill and practice. There is a difference, however. While she is at once comfortable with and hesitant to make changes in her mathematics instruction, Irwin reports a stirring interest in change.

Learning About Mathematics Reforms. What Marie Irwin knows about mathematics reforms is unclear. What is clear is that she has pursued few opportunities to learn.

Through faculty-room talk, Irwin learned that the mathematics portion of the MEAP test had been revised with more emphasis placed on problem solving and the use of calculators. She knows nothing, however, of the new state mathematics policy or of national reform efforts like the NCTM *Standards.* Irwin does remember attending two or three inservices in the late 1980s when the current SBG textbook and ancillary manipulatives kit (Orfan & Vogeli, 1988) were adopted.[7] She knows that district inservice programs are routinely offered and that university courses are available. She chooses not to attend. This seems interesting because Irwin cannot count on school-level resources to help her because the staff interest in literacy does not extend to mathematics:

> I don't think there's been the building-wide emphasis on math as there has been on writing, and certainly on reading. . . . I don't think it was of any concern. I think people were fairly comfortable with how things were, and what was being done.

Irwin adds, "We've been using this series for probably four or five years," she said, "I'm pretty comfortable with the sequence I follow, the approach I use."

A Changing View of Mathematics? Until recently, Marie Irwin ignored mathematics reforms. The sequence she followed and the approach she used supported a traditional view of mathematics. That view emphasizes swift computation and memorization of the algorithms for addition, subtraction, multiplication, and division of whole numbers, fractions, and decimals. Students "have to know how to do the math," she said, but doing mathematics means performing computations quickly and correctly.

Although new ideas and practices have been in the air since her return to the classroom, Irwin has felt no need to respond. One reason is that, contrary to reformers' claims, she believes reforms are not really about the subject matter of mathematics. "The content just isn't that different," she said, "math is math." Irwin sees reforms as new techniques or fads. Estimating is just another step in finding the right answer. Calculators are just another way of doing computation. Manipulatives are just another way to represent a problem. She does not disagree with these practices, she simply views them as superfluous. For example, Irwin feels that while manipulatives are important at lower grade levels, once students reach sixth grade, they are no longer appropriate. "I certainly felt they were appropriate for younger grades," she said, "but I felt that by sixth grade skill mastery was such that a manipulative wasn't necessary to teach something that they probably already had at least a basic understanding of."

If reforms are perceived as "just other ways of doing the same thing," then it makes some sense to ignore them. Moreover, there is little incentive for Irwin to do otherwise. The district instructional monitoring system is geared toward a conventional view of mathematics. Irwin's students seem to respond to her instruction and they perform well on assessments. Why rock the boat?

However, the story does not end here. Recently, Irwin revealed that she is rethinking her views on mathematics and teaching mathematics:

> There has been some change in my personal acceptance of what mathematics is and what's going to happen in the way of mathematics for these students. . . . I'm probably going to make myself accept that and make more of an effort and teach it more effectively.

Change in her "personal acceptance of what mathematics is" is developing on a couple of fronts. Irwin now questions her standard practice of reviewing computation algorithms for 8 weeks at the beginning of each school year. "There's always going to be students who aren't going to have it, and I know they're going to need it," she said, "but that doesn't mean the whole class needs to go over it." Irwin will not abandon practicing algorithms, but she is reconsidering how these elements might be more effectively taught.

Another change she contemplates is more use of mathematical manipulatives. In the past, Irwin saw manipulatives as "play things, toys." "I used to be hesitant to use those things," she said, "but I'm starting to change my mind and see the effect they might have. I do think they have their value."

Deemphasizing computation and using mathematical manipulatives are frequently cited as central to a new view of mathematics (Michigan State Board of Education, 1990; National Council of Teachers of Mathematics, 1989, 1991). Where Irwin's questions will take her is unclear. She may be on the brink of asking some very hard questions of herself and her teaching. She may find, however, that the answers will require more learning and even more change.

A Look at Classroom Practice. While Marie Irwin's talk reflects a nascent interest in mathematics reforms, her practice does not. Virtually all of her lessons come directly from the textbook and focus on rules and procedures. Even when lessons concern topics ostensibly related to reforms, the in-

struction is didactic and the learning is centered on right answers. Consider
a recent lesson about estimation:

> Irwin distributed a worksheet on estimating quotients. She asked, "What is
> a quotient?" and "What is estimating?" Students answered respectively: "The
> answer to a division problem" and "Rounding off to the nearest number."
> Irwin then talked through the example written out at the top of the
> worksheet.

Estimate 516 ÷ 9.7.

$$9.7 \overline{)51}$$

$$10 \overline{)516} \quad \text{Round the divisor to its greatest place.}$$

$$\begin{array}{r} 5 \\ 10 \overline{)516} \end{array} \quad \text{Find the first digit of the quotient.}$$

$$\begin{array}{r} 50 \\ 10 \overline{)516} \end{array} \quad \text{Write zeros for the remaining places.}$$

516 ÷ 9.7 is about 50.

Turning to the first problem (90 ÷ 8.8), Irwin said, "All right, the divisor
is 8.8. Round that to the largest place in your head." "Nine," a student called
out. When Irwin asked how many agreed, hands flew into the air. "All right.
I would like you to re-write the problem as 90 divided by 9. Now divide 9
into 90. That goes . . ." "Once," another student volunteered. "Right," said
Irwin, "Now you just fill out the rest with zeros."

The class worked through the next few problems in similar fashion.
Irwin read the problem and asked how the divisor (and dividend, if appropriate) would be rounded. Students seemed to understand the operation; they readily volunteered answers and asked no questions. The problem 130 divided by 12.7, however, engendered this exchange between
Irwin and a student, Danny:

Irwin: Look at the next divisor. What is the highest place in 12.7?

Linda: Ten.

Irwin: Okay, so you put a one in the tens place. (pause) So 12.7 becomes
10.0.

Danny: Why wouldn't you put 13?

Irwin: That's a good point. But in this lesson, we're putting a zero in after
the first digit.

Danny: Oh.

Irwin: Do you see what we're doing? (Danny nods.) What you suggest is
right, but it doesn't follow the procedure. You'll need to know it
this way for the end of the chapter test.

Asked later about this exchange, Irwin said:

> His answer wasn't wrong in terms of checking his division. But it was not
> right following the procedure. It would've been marked wrong on the [test]
> because you only need a non-zero number in one place. Everything else has
> to be zeros. And then that's confusing too.

I said that it had confused me. Irwin expressed her own confusion:

> I know it, I know it, but if I said that was okay then when I give them the
> test at the end of the chapter, which is a standardized test, these kinds of
> answers aren't going to be there. So I hope that I made it clear to him that
> his thinking wasn't wrong, that it made sense. He just didn't follow the
> process.

Estimation is a key construct in the mathematics reform literature.
Authors of the Michigan mathematics policy (Michigan State Board of
Education, 1990) propose that "mental arithmetic and estimation receive
more attention and are given greater importance" in part because "three
fourths of the everyday use of mathematics is without pencil and paper"
(p. 5).

That a lesson on estimation is included in Marie Irwin's textbook and
that she teaches it implies some attention to reforms. Yet her instruction
takes a pedantic turn. The nominal title of the lesson is estimating, but
there is one right answer to each problem. Instruction focuses on identifying basic terms (e.g., quotient, estimating) and practicing procedures
(e.g., rounding decimals) rather than on helping students develop a rich
understanding of the concept. The sole instructional representation is a
worksheet; no reference is made to everyday applications. Finally, the measure of the lesson is narrowly defined—performance on a standardized test.
When Danny offers an alternative answer, Irwin acknowledges it. The standard she applies to it, however, is neither mathematical nor common sense,
but rather if it reflects an upcoming test.

A Changing View of Teaching and Learning Mathematics? Marie Irwin's
personal discomfort increases whenever she moves into the unfamiliar
territory of estimation, problem solving, and other reform-minded ideas.
Irwin is a thorough professional, however, so if estimation and problem-
solving lessons arise in a regular textbook unit, she will teach them:

> I hate problem solving. I just hate it. I wasn't good at it when I was a kid
> and it's probably that I'm still not. But it's obviously the direction that math
> is going and it's a skill that these kids are going to have to learn.

When unfamiliar lessons seem optional, however, Irwin avoids them. An extensive mathematical manipulatives kit accompanied the textbook Irwin uses. The teacher's guide cross-references textbook lessons and manipulatives, such as beans and cups, base 10 blocks, and fraction bars. The references are frequent, but clearly optional. Irwin usually opts out.

Irwin recognizes that mathematics reforms challenge her practice, however, she has ignored them thus far. She has sought no opportunities to learn about reforms and she has instituted no substantive changes in her teaching. Irwin will do a reform-minded activity like the estimation lesson, but she teaches it as she would any skill: She emphasizes following the procedure and getting the right answers. Not surprisingly then, Irwin shows little interest in examining her beliefs about teaching and learning mathematics.

However, a change may be developing. Irwin reports asking herself: "What could I do, what would make [mathematics] more tangible? What would help [students] understand [it]?" It is not clear what impels these questions, but at least part of her answer lies in her willingness to try new approaches:

> There are references in the teacher's edition [to using manipulatives]. It's not like those aren't there. You know you hit the page on polygons and it says, "Use the geoboards." But in the past I probably would have looked at that and said, "I don't need to do that." This year I said, "Well, maybe that would be effective. I'll try it."

Irwin claims the lesson went well. In her typical taciturn style, she said simply, "It worked. They did okay." Encouraged, she plans to teach her fractions unit using fraction bars.

Responding to Reforms in the Context of Schooling

I have examined Marie Irwin's responses in the context of her classroom practice. The classroom is only one relevant site, however, because school, district, and community contexts also influence her responses.

Managing the Regularities of Schooling

Marie Irwin teaches in a district that defines a number of instructional parameters. The Hamilton instructional guidance system tells her what to teach, how long and in what order to teach it, what materials to use, and how to assess what students know.

In such a comprehensive system, one might guess that typical anxieties about time, content coverage, and testing are eased. Irwin acknowledges that some comfort comes from a scheme which outlines so many of the expectations she faces. Nevertheless, she finds she must still negotiate a number of issues related to the day-to-day exigencies of teaching.

One of those issues is time. The district monitoring system divides the school day into instructional units with specific time allotments for each subject. Sixty minutes are apportioned for reading, 45 minutes for mathematics, 30 minutes for English, and so forth. Irwin wryly notes that the entire scheme adds up to more than the length of a school day. So, like teachers everywhere Irwin must manage the problem of too much to do in too little time:

> You are always taking time away from something else. You have to take 5 minutes here and 5 minutes there and 5 minutes from somewhere else to get [for example] 15 minutes to write in [student] journals. So the amount of time in all the other subject areas is reduced, which reduces either instruction or practice, so there's got to be some loss that way.

The rationality of the system breaks down in the crucible of the classroom because despite this guidance, Irwin finds she must constantly make real and difficult choices about what to do, how long it will take, and what will have to be sacrificed.

Knowing what is expected, having objectives mapped out on a pacing chart, and becoming familiar with a textbook might help Irwin understand what kinds of time and content compromises she can make within the monitoring scheme. After doing so for a period of years, Irwin acknowledges that she has reached a certain level of comfort with the way she manages her instructional time. However, what will happen if, for example, Irwin changes her mathematics instruction? Using more manipulatives and teaching more problem solving may mean more pressures (Heaton, 1994). As it stands, the time and content area requirements established under the central office instructional scheme already demand more than a school day. How will Irwin manage if she reconstructs her practice?

Irwin's fledgling interest in changing aspects of her mathematics practice has implications for a second factor—content coverage. District pacing charts, keyed to textbook units, enumerate the content in reading and science as well as in mathematics. Yet just as the instructional time allotments add up to more than a school day, Irwin feels that the pacing charts require more content than can be reasonably taught in a school year. Consequently she must make adjustments:

> I think we pace our instruction specifically in math to make sure that we are getting that quantity of work done. . . . We are very aware that we have to turn those [monitoring] sheets in. I think we're all aware of what we have to teach, what objectives are tested, and what we can leave out in order to cover the maximum amount of material.

Pacing charts make practices such as using trade books difficult. During the year she received grant money to purchase and use trade books, Irwin continually faced the familiar dilemma of what to teach and what to leave out.

> We are still trying to adjust to using [trade] books in cooperation with our [textbook] series. There was a lot of concern about getting the series done and the skills done and what we could get away with not doing because obviously doing [trade] books took time.

Irwin hopes the new reading series will moderate some of these pressures. "The new series is based on literature, and therefore time for literature is written right into the program," she said, "Our old series had six units, this series only has four. That allows for time to read a book." In addition to this inventive packaging, the publisher's instruction to not worry about completing every lesson in every unit eases the press of covering material. Irwin still finds she must make difficult choices and that "sometimes it's hard to choose because there are so many good things to do." However, she relishes this flexibility and wonders, "Why didn't somebody think of this before?"

One last regularity is assessment. The district instructional guidance system emphasizes testing. In the course of a year, Irwin administers chapter, unit, and cumulative review tests, in addition to the district Essential Skills test, and the California Achievement Test. The foci of each of these tests are reading and mathematics, and the tests are heavily oriented toward assessing basic skills.

Irwin thinks the district does too much testing, but she does not disagree with the focus of these tests. "We all feel that it is still important to test the skills," she said, "You need to know whether the students are growing in that area." Yet Irwin has some concerns. She worries that skills-based tests may not accurately assess what her students learn through reading trade books or through using mathematical manipulatives. District tests, she observes, have been "strictly skill oriented" and "very narrow in their approach." Irwin's students, like their Sanford Heights peers, traditionally perform well on standardized assessments. She wonders what will happen to those scores if she decides to make changes in her practice.

Managing Relationships

Marie Irwin cites the Sanford Heights school community as a rich source of structure and support. The schoolwide reading and writing initiatives are a particular source of pride. Students benefit from the additional opportunities to read and write. The faculty also benefits as teachers feel less isolated and more willing to talk and share ideas. The growing sense of community initiated with the literacy program manifests itself in active staff participation, in staff development activities, and in the eager response to piloting the new reading text. The net result is that Irwin feels a solidarity among the Sanford Heights staff.

Many teachers would envy the professional relationships Irwin enjoys. As she manages changes in her teaching practice, however, some aspects of those relationships may become problematic.

Take the case of mathematics. One reason Irwin ignored mathematics reforms may be the district instructional emphasis on skills and procedures. Another may be her peers. Over the last 8 years, literacy goals have preoccupied the Sanford Heights staff while mathematics has gone unattended. A few teachers at Sanford Heights actively incorporate mathematics reforms into their teaching, but Irwin hints that the building and district ennui fed her own discomfort with mathematics and tacitly sanctioned her inattention to new ideas and practices.

Now that Irwin is questioning her prevailing approach to mathematics one wonders how these changes will be received. Will her peers support a decision to deemphasize computation practice in favor of other topics? Will her principal support a decision to do fewer units as she spends more time in those she does teach? Will district administrators support her if her test scores fall off? The district rhetoric is toward site-based management, but curriculum control has been held at the district level for many years and Irwin does not expect that to change.

Irwin must also manage relationships with parents. Sanford Heights parents are strongly supportive of education in general, and of the school in particular. They like the additional reading and writing opportunities the schoolwide literacy initiatives provide, but they also like the consistently high standardized test scores. Irwin recognizes that Sanford Heights parents are test-wise and anxious that scores remain high. Irwin wonders what implications venturing into new forms of instructional practices could have on her students' test performance. At this point, Irwin is not overly concerned. As she considers changing her mathematics practice, however, concern for parents' reactions could weigh heavily.

Conclusion

While Marie Irwin is not averse to reforms, she does not seek them out. She believes her practice is essentially sound, and profound changes do not interest her. Irwin is willing to try new approaches, especially in reading and writing, but when she perceives a threat, as in mathematics, her instinct is to avoid them.

This observation suggests a second: Irwin's satisfaction with her practice varies. Irwin seems quite comfortable with her current writing and English practices. She is also sanguine about her reading practice, especially now that a literature-based series will be adopted. Mathematics provides the contrast because here, although she ignored reforms for years, she now entertains questions that imply a measure of dissatisfaction or concern.

Irwin's willingness to take risks also varies with the subject matter. Her cautious nature is most evident in her accommodation to writing reforms: She adopts a couple of new activities while preserving her extant practice. The new activities are strong representations of the reforms, but Irwin manages them in ways that do not challenge what she already knows and does well.

Similarly, Irwin has made no profound changes in reading or mathematics. In both cases, however, she has taken some risks. Acting on her belief that students need to read literature, she won a grant to purchase and use trade books. From the safe confines of district textbooks, pacing charts, and assessments, this could be perceived as an enormous risk with few ostensible rewards. Remember that this happened well before the district began piloting literature-based texts. Irwin knew she had her principal's support, but she had no idea how district administrators might react. The other risk Irwin deals with is in mathematics. Her actions have been tentative (e.g., raising some questions, using manipulatives), and it is not clear where Irwin will take this. One should not miss the point that simply raising questions about her mathematics teaching practice is a big personal and professional risk. Irwin does not know much about mathematics and she feels anxious when she teaches this subject. Moreover, she cannot know how those around her will react. Given her colleagues' indifference and the district emphasis on basic skills, she is likely to stand on uncertain ground.

NOTES

1. Unless otherwise indicated, all quotes come from interviews with Marie Irwin conducted between 1991 and 1993.
2. The phenomenon of teachers learning from textbooks is addressed in Cohen and Ball (1990), McDiarmid et al. (1989), and Stake and Easley (1978).
3. There is no reason to conclude that this is an unenlightened view. The Michigan *Essential Goals and Objectives for Reading Education* (Michigan State Board of Education, 1986), for example, states, "Strategies and Skills are used interchangeably throughout this document" (p. 10).
4. I later learned this was the "answer" provided in the teacher's guide.
5. Irwin generally follows the recommended lesson plans from her teacher's guide. She does not follow them blindly, however. She sometimes replaces and sometimes skips textbook exercises altogether. Irwin also occasionally changes the order in which units are presented. When she does this in subject matters like reading, which are monitored by the district,

she feels obligated to inform the principal even though he has never questioned her decisions.

6. This reference is to a Madeline Hunter (1983) inservice Irwin took. The Hunter Instructional Theory Into Practice (ITIP) program emphasizes a standard approach to planning and delivering lessons.

7. The SBG textbook is an interesting mix of old and new. Attention to reforms is evident in reform-minded topics such as estimation, mental math, and problem-solving and in references to guide teachers' use of manipulatives. The bulk of the text, however, has a traditional cast with discrete lessons focused on rules and procedures and pages of practice exercises.

Chapter 6

Seeking a Balance:
The Case of Paula Goddard

Paula Goddard hears the call to reform. Until a couple of years ago, she taught reading, writing, and mathematics in conventional ways and she saw no reason to change. Since then, she has up-ended her reading and mathematics practices and is attempting the same in writing. Goddard does not manage these reforms in uniform ways or in ways that mirror any one of the teachers discussed in previous chapters. Instead, she represents yet another case of varied responses across teachers and reforms.

In reforms, Goddard sees an opportunity to question her practice, to learn about new instructional approaches, to take risks, and to make changes. Like Bonnie Jones, she has become an eager reformer, but unlike Jones, Goddard feels tugged between reforms and the status quo. Because both are insistent, Goddard continually strives to find a balance.

A European-American woman in her early forties, Paula Goddard has taught second graders at Sheldon Court Academic Center (SCAC) for 5 years. Before that, she did long- and short-term substituting until her children reached school age. Goddard is of quiet manner and voice. She has warm eyes and a generous smile.

Goddard runs a tight ship. Lessons move quickly and little time is wasted during or between assignments. Goddard also acts swiftly to halt any student indiscretion. SCAC has an extensive student disciplinary code and Goddard strongly supports it. Infractions of any kind are assessed checks which, as they accumulate, result in increasingly strong punishments. Goddard believes that this system, combined with parent cooperation, effectively eliminates discipline problems. The net result: "We actually get to teach in this program."[1]

The structured disciplinary system is a central tenet of the Sheldon Court program. Another is a basic skills curriculum. Traditional courses in reading, mathematics, and grammar define the school day; skills-based textbooks and worksheets define the content; seatwork and recitation define the instruction.

Goddard believes the disciplinary and curriculum mandates contribute equally to the school's success. That success is measured by consistently high rankings on local, state, and national assessments, strong support by the school's parents, and a long waiting list of applicants. Recently, however, concerns about the basic skills program have emerged. Neither parents nor staff question the school's disciplinary structure, but Goddard reports that she and some of her peers worry about the exclusive emphasis on discrete reading, writing, and mathematics skills. While students' performance on standardized tests may be high, Goddard worries that "students may not be able to think for themselves."

That concern emerged in recent textbook adoptions. The Sheldon Court academic program is textbook centered. Teachers draw on ancillary materials, but the textbook determines their planning and instruction, and at SCAC revising the curriculum means reviewing, piloting, and adopting new textbook series. Each adoption introduced a range of reforms and one now sees a mix of old and new, form and reform in SCAC classrooms.

Consider the mix of old and new in Goddard's classroom. Near the hall door are two sets of posters. One set, reflecting reading reforms, outlines the elements of a *story grammar*—characters, problem, events, and ending. The other set details standard punctuation symbols—quotation marks, question marks, periods, and exclamation points. In the back of the room, dust-covered boxes of mathematics manipulatives line the shelves. Open and well-used boxes of mathematics flash cards lie on a nearby table. A class-composed poem, displayed on one wall, epitomizes the balance between old and new:

One, two
Use your glue.

Three, four
Touch the floor

Five, six
Fix the bricks

Seven, eight
Don't be late

Nine, ten
Get the pen.

This piece represents the students' first effort as a class to produce a common text. "The kids really liked doing it," Goddard said, "I never thought they would be able to do such a good job." When she created the poster version to put on the wall, however, Goddard felt compelled to add a traditional twist: underlining the phonetic sounds. "I just couldn't resist," she said. Farther along this same wall, posters illustrate the sequence of events from the story, "The Tortoise and the Hare." Students created these accounts in small groups, a form of classroom organization Goddard had not used before. "I didn't know how they were going to do together," she said, "And they worked it out by themselves. I was really surprised." Underneath these posters, however, are bins for homework, seatwork, and boardwork, all overflowing with worksheets of subtraction problems, alphabetizing exercises, and punctuation drills.

That old and new coexist along the walls of Goddard's classroom makes sense. Goddard taught only traditional skills for several years. She honors the successes of SCAC's basic skills orientation and the commitment of the staff who made those successes possible, and she will not abandon it easily. At the same time, Goddard is excited by the call to reform. She is asking difficult questions of her teaching; she is seeking new answers, a new balance. Her responses look uneven and awkward at times, but given the context in which she teaches, the distance she must travel, and the uncertain support she faces, Goddard is taking big steps toward reforms.

Responding to Reforms

Elements of Paula Goddard's varied responses to reading, writing, and mathematics reforms recall those of the preceding cases. Like Bonnie Jones, Goddard believes reforms challenge her extant practices and she understands that change involves reeducating oneself. Like Marie Irwin and Frank Jensen, the mix of practices in Goddard's classroom often favors the old.

The cross-teacher variation is instructive because it demonstrates something of the range of response reformers may see as reforms are enacted across classrooms. Equally as instructive, however, is the cross-reform variation, because we see again that how an individual teacher makes sense of reform can vary dramatically. Goddard embraces reforms in reading and writing. Her reading practice shows changes in purpose, instruction, and text. Similar changes may be occurring in writing, but to date, Goddard's response has been additive; new practices supplement rather than supplant traditional grammar instruction. Her response to mathematics reforms illustrates yet another variation, for here Goddard has reversed course. Drawn to manipulatives-based reforms a couple of years ago, she revamped much of her conventional skills-based approach only to return to it a year later.

Looking at teachers' responses in the context of their classrooms is instructive. The classroom is not the only relevant frame, however, because Goddard teaches in a school context far different from Jones, Jensen, or Irwin. Sheldon Court Academic Center is part of the Hamilton district and follows most of its guidelines. The factors that make it unique, such as a prescribed mission and student population, a staff united by and supportive of the mission and students, deep parent support and involvement, and a long history of emphasis on textbooks and tests, shape SCAC and its success. These factors exert considerable influence on teachers like Goddard, who appreciate both the direction and certainty the SCAC mission provides, and the potential power reform-minded changes offer. In this sense, Goddard faces a double challenge. Embracing reforms means she must be willing and able to challenge not only her own practice, but the explicit and commonly held practices of the school. "We have it a little tougher," Goddard explained, "Because we not only have to change what's in our classrooms, but we have to convince everybody else in the building that this is the way to go." It is an enormous challenge, and not surprisingly Goddard often speaks of trying to find a balance.

Taking Up Reading Reforms

Paula Goddard once described herself as a very traditional reading teacher. Then, she grouped students into homogeneous reading groups, read from vocabulary-controlled basals, assigned mountains of seatwork exercises, stressed discrete word recognition and word attack skills, and gave little attention to what students brought to, or understood from, their reading. Learning to read meant practicing endless skills and subskills.

Reforms challenge this approach and Goddard believes she has made big changes in response. There is evidence for this claim because whole-class instruction, reading strategies, literature-based text, trade books, and connecting reading with other subject matters are now functional parts of Goddard's reading practice.

Learning About Reading Reforms. Paula Goddard learns about reading reforms from several sources. One is the new state policy which she first heard about in the mid-1980s when Ann Laurel, the school reading teacher, talked about a new definition of reading. A second encounter with the policy proved more influential. After volunteering to pilot the Houghton Mifflin (Pikulski & Cooper, 1991) reading series,[2] Goddard enrolled in a reading education course at a local state university. This course fit her MA program in elementary education and offered a quick route to new ideas about reading. It proved to be more than that. The instructor covered a range of reforms, including whole language, reading strategies, and the writing process, using the new state policy as the principal text. The experience was eye opening:

> It just kind of opened up a whole new idea of what reading is. . . . I hadn't put that much thought into [the new policy]. Then I took the class and thought, "Whoa." That professor tore it apart and said, "This is what it really means."

The reading course had a powerful effect. Not only did the instructor offer a different vision of reading instruction, but she pushed students to reflect on their own reading practices. Among other things, Goddard learned that research no longer supported her skills-based instruction. She remembers feeling surprised and angry that she had been trained to teach in ways that now seemed unproductive.

While the reading course and literature-based textbook raised questions about Goddard's past practice, they also encouraged her to see that she could do things differently. The new textbook was particularly valuable in this sense:

> The literature-based [reading text] has allowed us to be a little more free. And what's nice about it is the textbook said we could do it. I mean it's there in the textbook. I mean it's not like you're working on a project that you feel is important, but that's not in the basal. . . . Now you've got permission to do it because it's in the textbook.

The reading course and new textbook proved to be important learning opportunities. It was a personal experience, however, that cemented Goddard's commitment to teaching reading differently. Virtually a nonreader before, Goddard's daughter blossomed in the fourth-grade classroom of a committed whole language teacher. "I've seen the benefit [of literacy reforms]," Goddard explained. Seeing the impact on her child persuaded her that she might have a similar effect on her students.

Reforms call for Goddard to know and do new and different things, and she understands that she has much more to learn. She would like to join the state reading association and attend conferences and workshops, but a growing family and an excess of after-school meetings drastically reduce her time. Goddard relies on district workshops and reading "a lot of stuff on my own."

A New View of Reading. Paula Goddard describes her skills-based view as "the old way of teaching reading." Then, she explained, "The kids learned how to read skill sheets. Reading was not fun. Kids dreaded it." Her instruction was defined by three sources—the basal reader, the teacher's guide, and an ancillary phonics program. These sources promote what Richardson and her colleagues (1991) call a skills/word approach. Word recognition and decoding skills form the heart of this view; comprehension matters, but it is clearly secondary:

> You go through skills everyday with kids if you're doing the basal program. I mean, we may go over ten skills in reading a day if I were teaching from the basal. Then we choose a day to read the story for fun and maybe ask a few comprehension questions like, "What was this guy's name" and "What did this guy do" and "What color was his room?" Just real basic comprehension questions. And then we'd be back to skills.

Goddard did not question this approach. "[It was] the way I was taught," she said, "That's the kinds of reading we had. . . . That's the kind of reading I thought was valuable." This view also fit well with the SCAC emphasis on basic reading skills.

Goddard's view began to change about a year ago, when a confluence of factors including the new reading program, a university reading course, and her own child's experiences in a whole language classroom pushed a reconsideration of that view. Her developing view is multifaceted, revolving around reading strategies, comprehending text, and integrating reading across the curriculum.

Goddard makes a distinction between reading skills and reading strategies. Among other things, *skills* refer to the discrete word recognition and decoding tactics prominent in reading basal and phonics programs. Goddard still believes these skills are important and she will not abandon them. In fact, she praises the new Houghton Mifflin textbook's presentation of skills within the stories students read rather than in decontextualized worksheets. "Now the skills that we are teaching make more sense," Goddard said, "because the children see them right in the story." As an example, she cites the text's treatment of quotation marks:

> The story ["The Tortoise and the Hare"] had a lot of dialogue. And so there's a lot of quotation marks. So they took that particular skill and put it with the story so the kids could pull that out and say, "Yeah, the tortoise is saying something. Those are quotation marks." It's [the skill] related to the story.

Reading *strategies* are something different. In Goddard's view, strategies are less about understanding individual words than about understanding text. As she and her students work through stories, Goddard teaches comprehension strategies like previewing and surveying the text, distinguishing between text structures, and accessing prior knowledge.

Goddard's changing view of reading also includes a concern for the kind of text students read. Once satisfied with the basal reader alone,

Goddard now supplements the new textbook with trade books. A trial run at the end of the school year produced good results. "I got really excited," she said, "and so did the kids. . . . There's less emphasis on skills . . . but it's just as valuable. The kids learned just as much." Goddard explains that trade books are more versatile than the textbook in that they support cross-disciplinary activities that integrate reading, writing, and art. Goddard will not abandon the textbook in favor of trade books, but she feels she has a valuable new addition to her reading practice.

As she redefines reading, Goddard has an ally in Ann Laurel, the school reading teacher. They share a common view that embraces the possibilities reforms promise, but reserves judgment in the event that reformers are wrong:

> [Laurel] likes the idea that there's a balance. . . . She doesn't want to say let's go all whole language. She's more like what I'm saying, let's be sure the kids also know the skills . . . because we don't know. Five years from now, [researchers] might say, "Whoops. [Whole language] wasn't that valuable." And you've got 5 years of kids that don't know the skills.

Like veteran teachers everywhere, Goddard and Laurel know that the glitter of reform can quickly fade. Goddard is making some big changes in the way she approaches reading, but she retains a slice of the past for balance.

A Look at Classroom Reading Practice. If Paula Goddard's view of reading is changing, so too is her instruction. A recent lesson about reading expository text illustrates several reform-minded changes.

Goddard directed students to the story "Air Is All Around You" in their literature-based reading textbooks (Pikulski & Cooper, 1991) and the accompanying journal.[3]

Goddard:	We're going to do a little reviewing of this story. Then we'll learn some more about it when we read it. What is the topic?
Quinn:	Air
Goddard:	What is it about? Why is this story different?
Jamar:	It's important.
Goddard:	Okay, but so are the other stories. How is this one different?
Nicole:	They were fiction and fantasy. (The previous unit featured fantasy characters.)
Shanequa:	This is information text.
Goddard:	Okay, what have we talked about? What topics?
Jamar:	Dinosaurs
Ebony:	Stars.

> Goddard: The topic today is air. And we're looking today for main
>   ideas. So get ready to do some strategies. I want you to look
>   at the title, then look at the pictures, and then write some-
>   thing down you'd like to know about the story. (pause) All
>   right. What is the title?
>
> Ebony: "Air Is All Around You."

This vignette highlights three reforms. First, it reflects the notion that all
students can learn and that all students should have access to the same
curriculum (Anderson et al., 1985). Goddard organizes her students for
whole-class instruction around a common text. Four of her students receive
extra reading assistance from the school reading teacher, but in this lesson,
they read and respond to the same story as their peers. Second, Goddard
sets a context for the reading by asking students to compare the topic and
genre of this reading with those of earlier readings (Michigan State Board
of Education, 1986). Third, strategic reading is emphasized when Goddard
surveys the text. Gaining information about text through reviewing features
like titles, pictures, and headings is a common reading strategy (Paris et
al., 1984; Paris et al., 1991).

Strategy instruction is central to Goddard's new instructional approach
and to her new purposes for reading which emphasize comprehension.
An example is the reading strategy known as KWL. KWL is an acronym
for what students *Know*, what they *Want* to know, and what they *Learn*
(Ogle, 1986). This strategy helps increase students' comprehension by
teaching them to question both the text and themselves. Goddard uses a
version of this technique in this vignette:

> After surveying the text, Goddard turned students' attention to their journals.
> She told them to record any questions they had in the first section and what
> they found out, after reading the story, in the second. Goddard asked for
> "sample questions." Students volunteered—"When you go in outer space,
> can you see with a telescope?" and "How do you go into outer space?" After
> each, Goddard urged the student to "think about air." She offered these
> examples—"Does air weigh anything?" "What is the experiment in the picture
> about?" She then asked for more examples from students. They responded—
> Is there any air in space? Is there any air in water? If there wasn't any air,
> what would we do? Is there air in a balloon? Goddard praised all of these
> questions but the last. To that question she said, "I think most of us know
> the answer to that."

Later, after reading the story, Goddard returned to the questions students
wrote, asking them if they would "share some of the questions and answers
you wrote." Before beginning, however, she advised, "Now proofread what
you have written to see if it makes sense. And ask yourself, 'Is this something

I want to share?'" In the ensuing discussion, Goddard praised all student efforts, but said little about the substance of the questions or answers:

Tiffany:	(reading her question and answer) "What was the experiment about?" It was about air is all around us.
Kendrick:	"How can people breathe when they is [*sic*] in outer space?" They breathe with air in tanks.
Ebony:	"Is there air in water?" There is air in water.
Doris:	"If there wasn't air in the world, what would people do?" The story did not answer my question.
Goddard:	Is that right? (A boy raised his hand and said, "We'd die!") Right.
Janay:	"I wonder if air is in space?" The story did not answer my question.
Goddard:	I think it did, Janay. (The girl looked up and said, "No?" Goddard nodded.)

One other reading strategy evident in the lesson is accessing prior knowledge. Before reading the story aloud, Goddard brought out several pieces of chart paper. The previous day, she and the class talked about two questions in preparation for this story: How do we know air is there everyday? How do we use air? Student responses to the first question included: flags flapping, blowing bubbles, wave hand, the air we breathe, and clouds moving. The second question featured these responses: breathing, blowing balloons, blowing out candles, paper airplanes, drying clothes, and sailing a boat. Goddard displayed the charts and quickly read through them. She later told me the class had spent 20 minutes developing these ideas as a warm-up for the story. She said, "You need to get out their ideas, their prior knowledge, for the story to make sense to them."

Other reform-minded changes are also evident. One is the public or social nature of reading. Reformers (Cazden, 1992; Goodman et al., 1988; Kulleseid & Strickland, 1989) encourage teachers to consider reading as a social as well as individual activity. Goddard's students have many opportunities to express their ideas. She often solicits multiple responses and airs students' questions and their answers. She also encourages students to form relationships around text. At the end of this lesson, for example, she encouraged students to "share read" with a partner. One last reform involves writing. Connecting reading and writing is a common theme in the reform literature (Anderson et al., 1985). The KWL strategy is one vehicle. After surveying the text, students list the questions that occur to them; after reading, they write their answers. Goddard emphasizes the connection between reading and writing by modeling the KWL strategy in front of the class.

Whole-class instruction, setting a context for reading, teaching reading strategies, making reading more public, and encouraging writing are significant moves away from skills-based practice. Still, vestiges of "the old way of teaching reading" remain. Many of Goddard's questions are low level and call for a single right answer. Students' talk is primarily in response to these questions with little lateral talk, student-to-student. Writing opportunities are sometimes limited to developing questions and recording answers. Consider this vignette:

> As students entered the classroom and stood in line to hang up their coats, Goddard directed their attention to the boardwork assignment:
>
> Boardwork—Underline the soft <u>c</u> or g
> 1. We like to read big books about giants.
> 2. Are you going to play games in the gym?
> 3. He came to school with a new red pencil.
> 4. Cindy likes to cook rice on the stove.
>
> Goddard distributed the seatwork assignments: two pages from a phonics workbook, two pages from a spelling workbook, and a math skill sheet on addition and subtraction. After the opening exercises, Goddard directed students to the boardwork assignment. She reviewed the "soft c and g rule": These letters are pronounced softly if they are followed by a vowel. She called on individual students to identify the soft c or g in each sentence and to explain their choices.
>
> Kendrick: (reads) "We like to read big books about giants." Giants.
> Goddard: How did you know?
> Kendrick: The "g" is followed by an "i."
> Goddard: Good. Jamar, read the next sentence.
> Jamar: (reads) "Are you going to play games in the gym?" Gym.
> Goddard: Okay. How did you know?
> Jamar: The "g" is followed by a "y."
> Goddard: Good. And is this an asking or a telling sentence?
> Jamar: Telling?
> Goddard: Telling? What?
> Jamar: Asking.
> Goddard: Okay.

This pattern continued through the rest of the sentences. Students were attentive and responsive; hands waved continuously in the air. After completing the boardwork review, Goddard dismissed students by rows to deposit their work in the boardwork basket in the back of the room. As they took their seats, she turned their attention to the seatwork assignments.

Here are all the elements of skills instruction: discrete word attack skills taught in decontextualized fashion, an emphasis on getting the right answer, and teacher-centered and didactic instruction. Learning to read in this context means learning letter sounds in order to correctly identify and pronounce words. Consideration of text and ideas lies some distance away.

However, these points are insignificant when one considers the distance Goddard has traveled. Today, her students work in instructional settings, they read texts, and they talk and write about ideas that their peers, only a few years ago, would never have experienced.

A New View of Teaching and Learning Reading.   Paula Goddard's reading instruction reflects a mix of practices. However, all this evidence suggests that an important shift is occurring.

Goddard's response to reforms has taken her far from her familiar skills-based practice. She teaches toward new purposes, making meaning from text rather than accumulating skills. She treats students more as active learners than as passive recipients. She still emphasizes right answers, but Goddard more often accepts the possibility that multiple answers exist.

Elements of Goddard's practice still look quite traditional. In fact, she consciously and intentionally reserves part of each school day for skills instruction. As she redefines her reading practice, however, skills play a new and diminished role. Skills instruction gives Goddard's practice a necessary balance, but it is a balance which takes up key elements of the reforms.

Tilting Toward Writing Reforms

Paula Goddard's approach to writing is also changing. Here too, Goddard hears the call to reform and she asks hard questions of her past practice. In this area, however, she seems less sure of herself: The uncertainty is stronger, the changes are more fragile, and the mix of old and new is more evident.

Learning About Writing Reforms.   Paula Goddard has neither seen nor heard about the state writing policy. Instead, her introduction to writing reforms began when SCAC adopted a new Houghton-Mifflin English textbook (Stewig & Haley-Janes, 1990), which combined mechanics with reform-minded ideas like the writing process, peer editing, and creative writing.

Goddard claims to embrace the reforms, but only in the last year. Reminiscent of her initial response to the state reading reforms, she first ignored the reform-minded sections and continued her conventional grammar instruction. As her interest in reading developed, Goddard began thinking more about writing. She has some concerns, though. About teaching the writing process, for example, she said, "It's a hard process to get into because it's so different from the basal. . . . I would really like to see how other people do it [the writing process]."

Opportunities to see how other people do it are available. Goddard has attended inservice sessions about the textbook and about using student writing portfolios. She would like to do more, but as with reading, Goddard's interest in opportunities to learn outstrips her time and energy.

A Changing View of Writing? Several parallels between Paula Goddard's response to writing and reading reforms emerge. First, her past practice focused on discrete skills. Writing meant practice and mastery of mechanics such as grammar, punctuation, and sentence construction. Second, she interpreted reforms as a direct challenge to that practice. A third parallel is Goddard's use of new textbooks as a vehicle for change. The new reading text stresses reading strategies, using literature, and integrating reading and writing. The new English textbook features the writing process and real writing tasks.

Interestingly enough, Goddard may have anticipated writing reforms. Based, as she said, on "something I read," Goddard began using writing journals a year before adoption of the new English textbook. Journals are spiral-bound notebooks in which students record their ideas, stories, pictures. "There's a real value in having kids write and read in their own language," Goddard explained, "It's fun to see how that emphasis on writing has really turned them into writers."

Although it is not clear that the students consider themselves writers, now they have more opportunities to write. As in reading, Goddard seems to be changing her purpose for teaching writing. Learning mechanics is no longer sufficient as Goddard wants students to become clear and purposeful writers. Where grammar rules and usage once dominated her instruction, she now supplements those topics with concern for content and expression: "Now I ask them, 'What did you want to say here? What did you really mean?' Last year, I would have never done that. It would have been all skill sheets, bonus sheets, doing this little ditty or that."

Goddard's talk reflects less emphasis on skills and more emphasis on meaning, yet she worries about holding students accountable for doing their best work and about grading students' work for content or effort. She also wonders about a wholesale shift from a skills-based approach to a writing-process approach:

> It's real hard to know when to expect them to write in complete sentences and to have the right content. . . . [The writing process] is a real hard process to get into because it's so different than the [old textbook]. You need to find out what's valuable there.

While Goddard values her students' efforts and enthusiasm, she fears the writing process may produce little more than "cute writing." Her compromise is to provide more writing opportunities while holding students to strict standards of grammar: "I tell my kids I'm looking for sentences. 'Did you answer in complete sentences? Did it make sense? You get so many points. Did you capitalize and period?' Putting periods in, I even bring that into it."

As with reading, Goddard asks questions and considers alternatives to her extant views. At the same time, she finds that questions and alternatives come without easy answers and that balancing competing interests is no mean feat.

A Look at Classroom Writing Instruction.   Paula Goddard's writing instruction mirrors her talk because both conventional and reform-minded practices are evident. At the same time that students have more, and more realistic, writing opportunities they study conventional grammar quite apart from their writing. Unlike Goddard's reading instruction wherein new practices are displacing old, in writing, old and new practices are equally evident.

Attention to reforms is most obvious in Goddard's use of writing journals. First, journals reflect the call to provide students an opportunity to write each day (Calkins, 1986). Though there is no set time, Goddard usually creates a 10-to-15-minute journal period each day. Second, journals offer students an occasion to exercise their voice (Calkins, 1986; Graves, 1983). Goddard occasionally assigns topics, but more often the choice is open ended. Students' stories, poems, and letters, all colorfully illustrated, fill the pages. Goddard does not grade these entries. Instead she reads them and writes a response once a week. Third, journals are a vehicle for making writing public. Sharing one's writing with others is a common theme in the reform literature (Atwell, 1987; Calkins, 1986; Michigan State Board of Education, 1985). Her students can keep their work private, but Goddard encourages them to share their journals with one another as well as with her. Finally, as a real writing task, journals provide an informal assessment of students' writing progress. As she reads entries, Goddard notes students' ability to express their ideas clearly and to use mechanics properly. In fact, she wonders if journals do not provide a better context for assessment of mechanics than do worksheets:

> The problem [is] . . . they can do it on the worksheet. I can give them a worksheet on capitals . . . [and] they can zip right through that. Good, they know the skill. But, no, they don't know the skill because they're not using it . . . [but] I didn't know they couldn't use it because I didn't have enough writing to show me that they weren't using it. . . . Now I can see it everyday.

Journals provide fertile ground for reform-minded practices. New practices also occur at other points during the school day. The journal accompanying the new reading textbook also offers students a place to write. It has a workbook-like feel as the tasks are largely pedantic and students are rarely asked to write more than a few sentences. In Goddard's eyes, however, it is a significant improvement over the old workbook which offered only fill-in-the-blank and multiple-choice questions. More ambitious opportunities to write are also present. For example, after a recent unit about adventure stories, Goddard asked students to write their own adventure stories. This activity reflects her sense that bigger pieces of writing help students develop ideas about characters, setting, and plot.

These efforts stand in some contrast to Goddard's recent writing instruction. As little as 2 years ago, students wrote virtually nothing. Worksheet tasks occasionally demanded that students copy a sentence using the correct part of speech or punctuation symbol. More often, however, they presented multiple-choice questions and students simply circled the correct response. Goddard notes, "We taught all these skills, but we never used them. The kids never wrote."

Discrete skill instruction remains a significant piece of Goddard's writing practice. Worksheets about parts of speech, grammar, and punctuation from the English textbook are a regular part of each school day. In fact, she feels grammar skills are so important that she and some of her peers adopted the same grammar program Irwin and the Sanford Heights staff use. Goddard contends these activities "strengthen [students'] skills," but, she also acknowledges that similar items appear on the district Essential Skills test and the California Achievement Test. Such exercises, then, serve as "good practice for the tests."

A Changing View of Teaching and Learning Writing? These vignettes suggest the mixed flavor of Paula Goddard's writing instruction. Mixed practice was also evident in her reading instruction. Here, however, the mix of old and new seems more equal. Goddard may be beginning to see ways to connect grammar and writing. At this point, however, they remain largely distinct pieces.

Recognizing a gap between her current practice and the reforms, Goddard pursues some opportunities to learn about reforms. Changes in her daily practice suggest that she is willing and able to pursue new ideas. Of the four teachers in this study, she alone seems to see the potential for teaching mechanics through writing. Where the others have added-on pieces, only Goddard senses that students' journals magnify their use of mechanics as well as their creativity.

Goddard recognizes that she has much to learn. She does not view herself as a writer and she has had virtually no training as a teacher of writing. She hopes to learn about conferencing with students about pieces they are writing and by collecting their work in portfolios. However, she wonders where she will find the time to learn about these practices and to plan and make the necessary changes.

Reversing Course in Mathematics

Before reading and writing reforms captured Paula Goddard's attention she focused on mathematics. Although she reports knowing nothing about the new state mathematics policy or changes in the state test, Goddard abruptly recast her mathematics program, setting aside a procedural approach based on computation skills in favor of a more conceptual approach based on mathematical manipulatives. Flash cards, drill sheets, and math facts suddenly gave way to beans, fraction bars, and tangrams. Individual seatwork gave way to partners and small group work, and textbook lessons and worksheets gave way to mathematics stations. A year later, and just as abruptly, Goddard reversed course. The flash cards and worksheets reappeared and the manipulatives began gathering dust. Students went back to their individual seats and textbooks units became *de rigueur*.

Two events triggered Goddard's rush to reform. One was a university course in mathematics education. The instructor highlighted ideas and practices current in the reform literature: taking a conceptual view of mathematics, de-emphasizing computation, encouraging student conjecture about mathematics, using alternative representations to illustrate mathematical concepts, and organizing math stations[4] around the classroom. Some of these ideas were familiar, for Goddard's Houghton-Mifflin mathematics textbook (Duncan, Quast, Haubner, & Cole, 1985) emphasized algorithmic knowledge and skills, and also encouraged use of mathematical manipulatives. Up to that point, however, Goddard rarely used them. Like many elementary school teachers, she had little coursework in mathematics and little confidence in her understanding of mathematics. The manipulatives were attractive, but Goddard was not sure how to use them or what benefit they represented.

In the university course, Goddard heard a convincing rationale for rethinking her mathematics practice. "When our kids graduate . . . [employers] aren't going to look necessarily at how well [they] can do a multiplication problem or an addition problem," she said, "They're going to look at . . . how much are you thinking about this?" Goddard also learned that there are "a lot of different ways to teach math" including problem-solving strategies such as estimation and mental math, and alternative representations like manipulatives. More important, however, she saw lessons she thought she could replicate. She said, "There were some really good ideas on how to teach the different concepts . . . and I thought [at the time], 'Gee, I can really use this.'"

Goddard notes these "good ideas" became more viable when her own children came home excited about the mathematics they were learning in their classrooms. "[Their teachers] are pushing more estimating and measuring and those kinds of skills rather than memorizing facts," she explained, "They want [students] to be able to use what [they] know rather than to just know it." Again, the experiences of her own children provided Goddard insights into reforms and incentives to pursue them.

At about the same time, Goddard's emerging interest got a boost from a different source. After attending a *Mathematics Their Way* conference, an SCAC teacher urged Goddard, the other primary grade teachers, and the school principal, Natalie Simon, to adopt the program as a supplement to the textbook. *Mathematics Their Way* (Baratta-Lorton, 1976) is a manipulatives-based program reflecting the idea that students understand mathematics concepts and procedures better when they can use concrete objects (e.g., beans, fraction bars). Principal Simon gave her blessing as an experiment. Goddard received the *Mathematics Their Way* materials, but she did not attend any workshops about their use. This point seems critical because Goddard has a weak background in mathematics instruction and an even weaker knowledge base in mathematics itself. She may have assumed that she only needed to follow the *Mathematics Their Way* teacher's guide, but reform-minded materials often presume teachers have more knowledge than they really do (Heaton, 1994; Remillard, 1991).

By some accounts, the experiment was a success. Students' scores on the district Essential Skills test rose over those of the previous year and Goddard said that both she and the students liked the change. "The [math] stations worked well last year," she said, "The stations are fun and they do teach a lot of things."

So why change back to a skills-based approach? Goddard cites testing as one reason. Her students performed better than the previous class on the district test, but Sheldon Court scores on the whole went down slightly. Test scores mean a lot to the SCAC staff and parents, consequently falling scores are of immediate concern. Principal Simon did not demand the pilot teachers abandon *Mathematics Their Way*, but she did direct all teachers to develop what Goddard described as "a list of the basics . . . objectives for mastery in mathematics" to address the problem of low test scores. For whatever reason, Goddard and her colleagues responded by pulling out their old mathematics textbooks. Citing the need to list "everything [students] need to pass in order to get on to the next grade," the teachers scoured the text and determined that computation skills and algorithmic knowledge were the most important objectives. Goddard defined the outcome this way: "These are things that [students] absolutely have to know to get out of second grade. Like counting to 100. Counting by two or . . . [being] able to add and subtract up through fifteen, a total of fifteen."

Whether this activity alone was enough to cause Goddard to reverse course is impossible to know because it coincided with a second factor—

Goddard's realization that a manipulatives-based program demands considerabie time and energy. Setting up math stations, allowing students time to work through the activities at their own pace, and discussing students' ideas about mathematics all took more than Goddard felt she could give. In a tired voice, she said:

> This year I'm following the math book and I'm not doing as much with the manipulatives and stuff as I did last year because there is just so much. . . . It's not that I don't want to do it, but setting up the stations just takes a lot of time.

All things being equal, Goddard might have coped. The reading textbook pilot, however, proved too much. "The reading is taking over," she said, "I guess because reading is so emphasized this year, I'm not really that up on the math."

Will Goddard return to the reform-minded mathematics practices when the reading pilot is over? The answer isn't clear. Goddard declares manipulatives-based instruction beneficial, but she is not sure it is worth the effort:

> I think the manipulatives are good for the kids and they really teach them a lot. But I think I'm going to get the same results [on standardized tests] doing it this way this year. I think the kids last year had a little more fun with math than they are having this year, but I'm finding the kids are really, they're learning the same, the results are the same.

Goddard values her students' classroom experiences. She senses, however, that students are learning as much mathematics through textbook instruction as they did through manipulatives. She has not put aside her interest in reforms; she hopes to "find a balance" in the future:

> Next year, once we settle down with the reading and it becomes more familiar, maybe I can find a balance. . . . It's not like you're either teaching a structured math or you're teaching with the manipulatives. A lot of teachers out there are doing both, you know? They've got the pages [of math skills] and they've got the manipulatives and that's what I'll probably go with.

In one sense, Goddard's intuition about her students learning the same and getting the same results was borne out. Students' test scores rose after a year of conventional textbook instruction. "They did very well," Goddard said, "They scored better than the kids (under the *Mathematics Their Way* program) did the last year." How Goddard understands this result or what it will mean as she tries to "find a balance" remains to be seen.

A Mix of Old and New Views of Mathematics. Paula Goddard's view of mathematics presents an interpretive challenge.[5] Goddard talks positively of her experience with *Mathematics Their Way* and the activities and materials reflecting new ideas about mathematics. Those activities and materials, however, seem not to have translated into a new view of mathematics because today Goddard's talk reflects a jumble of old and new.

On the one hand, Goddard seems comfortable with a conventional view of mathematics, stressing math facts and procedures. She talks about students mastering the basics. She sees nothing problematic in her principal's request to define "things that [students] absolutely have to know to get out of second grade." She does not question the decision to emphasize traditional objectives.

At the same time, her talk is sprinkled with references to reforms. That talk centers on the use of mathematical manipulatives to illustrate procedures such as re-grouping for subtraction. Other reform ideas (e.g., encouraging students to develop and discuss multiple conjectures, teaching computation in a problem-solving context), however, are notably absent.

A Look at Classroom Mathematics Instruction. Classroom observations suggest little remains of Paula Goddard's excursion into mathematics reforms. Lessons are typically textbook centered, didactic, and focused on math facts and procedures. Even when she uses manipulatives, Goddard's instruction has a conventional cast. A recent observation is illustrative. The lesson began with a brief review and a mathematics test:

Before the test, Goddard wrote "How many more?" on the board and said, "I've written this sentence on the board. You will often see it in your story problems. What does it say?"

Janesa:	(reads) "How many more?"
Goddard:	So if I have 10 baseballs and 5 bats, *how many more* baseballs do I have?
Janesa:	Five
Goddard:	So what does "how many more" mean?
Jimmy:	Subtract.

Goddard then moved to another point. She wrote on the board:

$$4 \text{ tens} = \underline{\qquad} \text{ tens} \underline{\qquad} \text{ ones}$$

She asked, "How we can say 4 tens differently?" A student responded, "You could put 10 in the ones and put a 3 in the tens." Goddard, nodding, asked if there were any questions. Seeing none, she handed out the test.

The exam was a unit test from the Houghton-Mifflin math workbook. Half the test questions resembled those Goddard reviewed: subtraction problems written with the phrase "how many more?" and place value questions where values were redistributed. Problems in addition and subtraction of two-digit numbers, measurement, and telling time filled out the two-page test. While students worked, Goddard circulated, reminding students, "It's the same thing we did on the board."

After the test, Goddard directed students to this problem on the board:

The discussion went this way:

> Goddard said, "I'm going to give you a clue, and you've had this before, the arrow always points at the lower number." She then asked Kesha which way the arrow should point in the example. Kesha said, "Toward the 5." Goddard nodded, drew in the arrow, and wrote the next example on the board (36____63). "All right, Stesha," Goddard said, "Which way should the arrow point?" Stesha replied, "Toward the window." Goddard nodded, drew an arrow pointing toward the "36," and wrote another example (27____36) on the board. After Stesha used the expression "toward the window," Goddard asked students whether the arrow should point toward the "window" (on the left side of the classroom) or the "calendar" (on the right side) on the next examples.

The conceptual understanding and real-world connections mathematics reforms call for are absent here. Instead, Goddard emphasizes procedural knowledge and math facts. That conclusion is demonstrated when Goddard coaches students to do "the same thing we did on the board" during the math test and when the recitation about the relative size of numbers degenerates to the mathematically irrelevant properties of "toward the window" and "toward the calendar." Rather than develop deep understandings of powerful concepts, Goddard's students learn school math—discrete, decontextualized bits of mathematics practiced and mastered outside of any meaningful context. Several mathematical concepts are evident: addition, subtraction, place value, number relationships, measurement, and time, but each idea is adrift, unanchored to any larger idea or practice other than an upcoming test.

The mathematics is no more clearly anchored when Goddard uses manipulatives. A lesson about money, for example, centers on procedural knowledge about the absolute and relative value of coins, and makes little connection to real-world situations. The lesson involved naming and identifying coins individually and in combinations. An example of the discussion follows:

Goddard: Today we are looking at the quarter and the half dollar. If I wanted to use different coins for 25 cents, what could I use?

Loreen: Two nickels and two more nickels and a nickel. (As the student spoke, Goddard drew five circles on the board and labeled each "5 cents.")

Goddard: Okay, let's count by fives. (She and the class counted aloud to 25. Goddard clapped her hands in time.) Good. Is this money if I just write 25?

Students: No. Cents sign.

Goddard: What other coins equal 50 cents?

Tara: A dime, another dime, another dime, another dime, and another dime. (Goddard drew 5 circles and labeled each "10 cents.")

Goddard: How about another way to say 50 cents?

Nicole: One penny and another penny . . . (students and Goddard laugh).

Goddard took the class through several combinations. She then turned on the overhead, displayed transparent versions of each coin, and asked volunteers to identify them.

In the next part of the lesson, students tore a page from their math workbooks. The first side featured photographs of a quarter and a half-dollar at the top and several coin combinations below. Students were to add the coins and record the totals. On the back, students were to draw lines from a quarter to the various coin combinations that equaled 25 cents (a similar exercise using a half-dollar was on the bottom of the page).

Aside from the presence of manipulatives, this lesson resembles the first. Real-world connections are ignored and identifying the right answer is emphasized. Goddard's didactic instruction puts students in largely passive roles, their contributions largely confined to brief responses to her questions. Finally, although Goddard uses manipulatives in the second lesson, she does so toward entirely traditional ends. If this lesson is representative of the balance she seeks, one suspects it is a balance tipped decidedly toward conventional instruction.

A Conventional View of Teaching and Learning Mathematics.   Paula Goddard reports overhauling her mathematics practice a couple of years ago. Today, little seems different and one wonders about the fragility of real classroom change.

Goddard embraced reforms, at least initially. She acknowledged a gulf between her extant practice and that promoted in her university course, and the *Mathematics Their Way* materials. She substituted a manipulatives-based view of mathematics for the skills-based approach of her mathematics textbook and skillsheets, and she added the use of math stations to her whole-class mathematics instruction.

These changes in daily instruction seem profound, yet one suspects they were built on an unsteady foundation because Goddard constructed these practices without much knowledge of mathematics or of the new pedagogy. The university course and *Mathematics Their Way* program opened the possibility for profound change. When her fledgling innovation was challenged, however, Goddard had insufficient resources to continue. Returning to a conventional practice makes sense given the external pressures, but it also makes sense given Goddard's weak knowledge and instructional background.

Responding to Reforms in the Context of Schooling

Paula Goddard manages reforms in her classroom every day. The classroom is not the only relevant context, because the norms and expectations unique to Sheldon Court Academic Center are also important. How Goddard manages those regularities and relationships reflects on her responses to reforms.

Sheldon Court Academic Center arose from a concern that African American students were not succeeding in public schools. Success was defined as high scores on standardized tests, and the means to that success were a strong parental presence, a strict disciplinary code, and a basic skills curriculum. By most accounts, SCAC has succeeded. Students whose circumstances might push them in undesirable directions have a place to feel safe, to work hard, and to see the benefit of their efforts. Parents and staff are fiercely proud of their work.

The Sheldon Court community is active. As an alternative school within the public system, the faculty and principal constantly feel pressed to explain, justify, and promote their work. Parents are active as well. They serve on the school's governing board and expect to receive and give regular feedback on their children's progress. There is no complacency here, but neither is there much incentive to reconsider or recast the SCAC mission. Reforms are not necessarily discouraged or ignored, but the SCAC community holds tightly to vehicles like the basic skills curriculum, which they assume got them where they are.

It is against this background that Goddard's questions about the basic skills curriculum must be judged. She raises no objections to the strict disciplinary code or to the active parental involvement, but in Goddard's classroom and a few others, challenges to the basic skills curriculum are developing. As they do, Goddard feels tugged between reforms and the status quo.

Managing the Regularities of Schooling

Sheldon Court Academic Center's designation as an alternative school in the Hamilton system means that it lies outside the district instructional guidance system. The SCAC program, however, mirrors the district system in most ways. The district instructional time allotments were adopted. SCAC students take the same battery of standardized tests—the district Essential Skills test, the California Achievement Test, and the MEAP—that other Hamilton students do. Teachers must maintain pacing charts in reading, mathematics, and science, which record the units taught and students' chapter and unit test scores. The SCAC staff may, and often does, choose textbooks different from district adoptions, but the SCAC instructional program is as textbook-bound as the district's. That fact, combined with the widely supported basic skills mission, means that Goddard faces significant difficulty and uncertainty in moving toward a more ambitious pedagogy.

One difficulty concerns what to teach. Until recently Goddard took her cues from the assorted textbooks on her shelf and she took seriously the task of completing each text during each school year. Although she inevitably faced time constraints, she felt confident that she was teaching the right content.

Reforms undermine her comfort. Her university courses, district inservices, and new textbooks send a similar message: Skills-based instructional approaches are passé. Goddard hears that message and embraces it. Doing so offers little consolation, however, for rather than proscribing what she should do, reforms open up more possibilities. Moreover, reforms have not stilled the voices of convention. Her frustration shows: "There are so many skills and there's so much curriculum that you really don't know what the most important things are." Goddard hopes to find a balance between the disparate voices of old and new. Perhaps she envisions some point where reform-minded and skills-based practices will fit harmoniously together. For now, however, Goddard straddles a difficult and tenuous gap. "I want the freedom [to follow reforms]," she said, "But yet I want to know that what I'm doing is what . . . the rest of the teachers will be doing in the second grade."

The persistent lack of time compounds the difficulty of deciding what to teach. Goddard always has more to do than the time allotted; attending to reforms only exacerbates that problem. New reading textbooks, new math programs, and new ways of organizing students for work simply take much more time: more workshop and inservice time, more preparation time, and more class time. These demands are, in turn, complicated by the family demands of two small children. The strain is palpable. In a weary tone, she said, "There are days when you just want to give them the book and throw paper at them and say, 'I'm sick of this!' " Goddard hopes to attend conferences and inservices about reading and writing because she sees the value of this knowledge, but she wonders where she will find time to attend, much less understand what she learns and make it part of her practice.

A third difficulty is assessment. In Goddard's case, this issue has two dimensions: classroom assessment and standardized assessment.

By second grade, SCAC students expect highly routinized instruction with clear, simple assessments of what they know. Introducing changes, Goddard finds, can be problematic:

> Sometimes [students] don't take it seriously if they aren't graded on their answers. Now the kids have to think differently. Some of the kids didn't want to put in the effort. They were used to filling in the blanks; the skills took very little effort. Now they have to pay more attention.

Pushing students to do more is not easy, and students have resisted. Goddard can understand this, but it feeds her uncertainties because what she learned about reforms was directed at changing her views and actions. She recalls no mention of the possibility that students might not readily comply.

SCAC parents and staff place great stock in standardized test scores, especially the district Essential Skills and California Achievement tests. As tests of basic skills, these assessments have been a good match for the SCAC curriculum and the SCAC community takes pride in its students' success. Goddard understands, however, that the stronger content and instruction called for in reforms demands a corresponding change in student assessment. Highly visible basic skills tests undercut reform efforts in two ways. First, there is little incentive for teachers, comfortable with the basic skills curriculum, to pay much attention. Second, if test scores decline, pressure to change instruction may not be in the direction of reforms, but instead toward more basic skills. A case in point is the reaction of SCAC principal, Simon, and her staff to lower math scores. Simon's directive, to develop objectives for mastery, and the teachers' decision (including Goddard) to focus on computation had a decidedly skills-based flavor. Goddard explains the point bluntly, "Unfortunately teachers know what they are going to test on the [Essential Skills] test. And that's what we're going to push."

Managing Relationships

In addition to managing the regularities of content, time, and assessment, Paula Goddard finds she must manage relationships with her peers, principal, and the Sheldon Court parents.

Most of Goddard's peers have taught at SCAC since it opened, and their devotion to the students, to the program, and to one another runs deep. They sense that their status as an alternative school with a select student population, full-time aides, strong parent support, and freedom from district mandates creates jealousies. "[Other teachers] think this is a cush job," Goddard explained. "Cush" job or not, the SCAC staff is protective of their students, of each other, and of the program.

Goddard has thrived here. Although the school and students differ from those she experienced as a student, the clear discipline and curricular guidelines and her colleagues' ready support eased her adjustment. She has been comfortable with her practice and is a solid proponent of the SCAC program.

Goddard's reform efforts have not been openly challenged or criticized, but they are not always shared or encouraged. For example, an effort to convince her second-grade colleague that the new reading series was a good idea fell flat. This confirmed basic-skills teacher's response was direct and unequivocal: "I already know how to teach reading. I taught reading all of these years. I know what it is." Goddard encounters similar resistance when she brings up new ideas about teaching writing. Diplomatically, she said, "Some teachers take writing more seriously than others."

The other in-school relationship Goddard must manage is with her principal, Natalie Simon. Simon, an African American woman in a district dominated by white male administrators, has fought many battles on SCAC's behalf. Goddard recognizes and honors Simon's work, but she perceives the principal as unnecessarily heavy handed and insensitive to staff needs. Moreover, Simon is an inconsistent supporter of reforms. For example, while she initially supported the *Mathematics Their Way* effort, the first time test scores fell, improving the scores took precedence over supporting reform-minded change. Although Simon has not directly challenged any of her efforts, Goddard still worries: "Is this [changing her practice] going to really work? I mean is this something that I can make work? Or is this something that my principal is going to come in and say, 'Well, why aren't you doing this [other thing]?'"

Given the origins of SCAC, Goddard must also consider parents' reactions. She believes parents will support the new reading text and her efforts to encourage more writing. She also believes parents have certain expectations about the kind of work their children will do. One of those expectations is phonics. "Parents," she said, "want phonics because they like the extra work." It is not clear that Goddard would abandon phonics if she could, but what is clear is that she will maintain at least a semblance of a phonics program until she becomes convinced that parents will understand and support a change. A similar situation exists with spelling. Goddard is considering an integrated approach to spelling—teaching spelling as part of reading and writing lessons. She worries, however, that parents will balk. "The parents have to see that the spelling books come home every year," she explained.

Goddard's perceptions may be wrong. To date, no parent has complained about any of the changes she has made, and those parents who ask, for example, about the new reading textbook, seem satisfied with her response. However, Goddard believes parents can be fickle. If their expectations about the kind and amount of work their children do are upset or if test scores dip, then she expects to be called to account.

The need to manage regularities and relationships adds yet another layer of complexity and uncertainty to Goddard's response to reforms. "It kinda feels like you are out there by yourself, forging ahead," she mused. At the same time, Goddard appears sufficiently autonomous to pursue a range of classroom changes without sanction or rebuke. Difficult to assess, however, is what she might do given a more supportive and reform-minded environment.

Conclusion

While she uses no phrase like "cycle of change," in many ways Paula Goddard is as attentive to reforms as Bonnie Jones is. In fact, given the tradition of basic skills at SCAC, one could argue that she is even more ambitious than Jones. It is not always clear how Goddard will forge the balance she seeks, it is hard to ignore the range of changes she has undertaken.

Goddard remains dissatisfied with her practice. Although she is especially interested in new ideas about writing, she continues to read and think about her reading practice. Goddard also expresses some dissatisfaction with her mathematics instruction. In this case, however, her students' newly improved test scores, her principal's uncertain support, and the limits of time and energy would seem to undercut any significant efforts toward reforms.

However, Goddard is clearly willing to take risks. From her initial foray into mathematics reforms through her offer to pilot the reading textbook, and now in her attention to writing reforms, Goddard has shown a determination to raise questions and to make changes. This is unusual behavior in any teaching context (Lortie, 1975), but it is particularly so at SCAC where adventurous instruction has been so clearly outside the limits of the school mission.

NOTES

1. Unless otherwise indicated, all quotations come from interviews with Paula Goddard recorded between 1992 and 1993.
2. Some SCAC teachers, like Goddard, are piloting the Houghton-Mifflin text. Others are piloting a Silver Burdett & Ginn (Pearson & Johnson, 1991) textbook. Goddard favors

the Houghton-Mifflin textbook contending that the stories are "more interesting" and the reading strategies are "more clear."

3. The Student Resource Journal accompanies the textbook. In some ways it looks like a conventional workbook as a variety of exercises coincide with each story. Goddard defines a workbook as a collection of skills exercises unrelated to the stories. In her eyes, the Journal is much different.

4. A math station is a designated area in a classroom where the teacher has placed a variety of materials for students to explore a particular mathematical idea. For example, Goddard reports placing beans and cups in one station to illustrate place value. In another, she placed several items that all represented the number five. Two days a week, she said, students rotated through these stations in small groups.

5. I began interviewing Goddard and observing her practice after her switch back to more conventional approaches. Consequently, I know her views of reforms because she tried them and has since reversed course. The timing of this study undoubtedly figures into my interpretations of what I see and how I interpret what Goddard says about her practice.

Epilogue

Variation in Teachers' Responses to Reforms: Marie Irwin and Paula Goddard

In the first set of cases, Bonnie Jones and Frank Jensen teach under similar circumstances, yet respond to reforms in dramatically different ways. The reverse is true here: Marie Irwin and Paula Goddard teach in widely different contexts, yet their reform responses share some strong similarities. I attempt to explain this phenomenon in chapter 7. Now, however, I want to highlight the cross-teacher and cross-reform variation that emerges in this second set of cases.

Variation in Responses Across Reforms

Marie Irwin's and Paula Goddard's reform responses can be generalized: Irwin is a teacher who keeps reform-minded ideas at arm's length; Goddard is a teacher who hopes to balance reform and traditional approaches. Looking underneath these generalizations is important, however, because the variation in how Irwin and Goddard manage reforms within their respective practices is as great as the variation between their practices.

The Variation Within Marie Irwin's Responses

The similarities across Marie Irwin's reform responses are significant. She rarely pursues opportunities to learn about new practices and she has not questioned her basic assumptions about teaching and learning. Nevertheless, numerous differences arise in the way Irwin views reforms vis-à-vis her past practice, and in the way she incorporates reforms into her daily instruction.

Irwin segregates writing reforms. She accepts that students do not do enough writing, and she is willing to provide time, opportunities, and encouragement. Yet writing reforms provoke no uncertainty because they challenge neither Irwin's current approach nor her underlying assumptions about teaching and learning writing. She adds journal writing and publishing center activities to a busy schedule, but she does so such that these activities are unrelated to the formal study of English grammar. Irwin accommodates new writing activities as long as they do not impose on her established practice.

Irwin manages mathematics reforms quite differently. First, while her response to writing reforms has been modest, Irwin has not hesitated to act. By contrast, she ignored mathematics reforms for several years. She knew ideas about problem solving and mathematical manipulatives were circulating, but whenever possible she avoided them. Second, while Irwin does not view writing reforms as a challenge to her knowledge and practice, she now views mathematics reforms this way. Although she largely ignores them in practice, Irwin understands that reforms push in directions much different from her traditional approach.

Her response to reading reforms offers yet another variation on Irwin's cautious approach to new ideas. Here, instructional changes are more obvious and run throughout her practice. Trade books, reading strategies, and the like are not separate activities, but instead are part of an overall view of reading. Irwin makes distinctions between teaching textbook skills and teaching literature, but these distinctions lie within a practice which echoes big chunks of the reforms.

Changes are less obvious below the surface. Irwin does not interpret reforms as a challenge to her knowledge and practice, she sees little need to learn more, and her basic beliefs about teaching and learning reading remain firm. Irwin is changing the broad surface of her reading practice, but the core remains solid.

The Variation Within Paula Goddard's Responses

Some similarities emerge across Paula Goddard's responses to reforms. New ideas interest and excite her. She is willing to consider how reforms differ from her practice and she is interested in learning more. These generalizations describe a teacher engaged in the difficult work of reconstructing her teaching. They tell only a partial story, however, because in the details of how Goddard manages each reform are substantive differences.

Although she initially ignored reading reforms, Goddard does so no longer. She sees clear distinctions between her traditional approaches and those of reforms. She understands, for example, that constructivist views of students as constructors of meaning differ sharply from traditional views which emphasize practicing skills and extracting meaning from text. Accepting that difference means reshaping her instructional practice, and Goddard has not hesitated. She is making numerous changes in her daily instruction including new texts, new instructional strategies, new groupings, and new forms of discourse. She is also reexamining her long-held assumptions about teaching and learning reading. If some traditional practices remain, Goddard's response indicates a profound shift is building.

Goddard seems to want similarly impressive changes in writing. Writing reforms are most evident in the journals and writing assignments she makes. Goddard senses, however, that reforms must be balanced with instruction in discrete grammar knowledge and skills. Even so, Goddard understands that she needs to learn more about writing before making profound changes.

Goddard's reading and writing practices are changing as she pushes herself to try new approaches and to hold old approaches up to scrutiny. By contrast, her mathematics practice is moving away from reforms. The momentum of a year ago has stopped and the reform-minded changes have ebbed. So too have the big questions Goddard was asking of her practice. Her current practice reflects little substantive change, and Goddard's energies now seem directed elsewhere.

The Variation Across Teachers

Given her unique context, one might expect Paula Goddard's individual responses to be radically different from the other teachers, but they share some commonality with each of the earlier cases. Because they mirror no particular teacher, however, Goddard's responses illustrate yet another variation on how teachers manage reforms.

On the surface, Goddard's classroom response to reading reforms most directly resembles Irwin's. Both teachers center their instruction in new literature-based textbooks, use trade books as supplements, set aside ability-based reading groups in favor of whole class instruction, and teach both reading strategies and skills.

Changes in daily instruction are one piece of a response. In most other ways, however, Goddard's response is radically different from Irwin's (and by extension, Jensen's). First, Goddard recognizes the distinction between traditional and constructivist approaches and understands that the distinction has important classroom implications. Jensen blurs this distinction.

Irwin may understand it, but she seeks an accommodation, incorporating trade books and the like into her conventional approach. Second, Goddard realizes she needs to learn more. Teaching toward different purposes demands knowledge and abilities she does not have. Irwin and Jensen, by contrast, believe they already possess the requisite knowledge. Finally, Goddard is willing to entertain questions about her pedagogical beliefs. Embracing reforms involves more than changing textbooks and incorporating a few new strategies. Unlike the other two teachers, Goddard understands that reconstructing her practice means reconstructing who she is and how she understands her role as a reading teacher.

Whereas Goddard's efforts in reading clearly differ from those of Irwin and Jensen, they also differ from those of Jones. Jones no longer relies on textbooks, she has virtually eliminated discrete skills instruction, and she teaches reading throughout the school day. Goddard's efforts seem pale by comparison. However, two conditions must be considered: Jones has been working with these ideas considerably longer than Goddard has, and she has done so in a context wherein teachers have considerably more autonomy. Jones' colleagues may not understand or support her efforts, but the laissez-faire context provides great freedom of movement. These conditions suggest the possibility that Goddard's responses may be just as ambitious as Jones'.

In writing, Goddard's reform responses reflect two commonalities with the teachers in this study: All view reforms as different from their extant practices and each (except for Jensen) adds new ideas and approaches to a skills-based practice. Beyond that, Goddard's response is more similar to Jones' than to the others' because these two teachers are dissatisfied with their current knowledge and want to learn and do more. Jensen and Irwin, by contrast, seem satisfied with their current knowledge and practice.

Finally, there is Goddard's complex response to mathematics reforms. We have seen numerous examples of teachers' responses changing over time, but in each instance the direction of change is toward reform-minded practice. Goddard's response represents a retrenchment, an ambitious response followed by retreat to more familiar terrain.[1]

This response is distinctly different from those of the other teachers. Jones appears to be headed toward continuing change. Jensen appears satisfied with his current efforts. Irwin is entertaining questions that could mean substantive changes, but have yet to take hold. Goddard, by contrast, seems caught between competing impulses. Her informal assessment and students' improved test performance convince her that students learned mathematics during the *Mathematics Their Way* year, but test scores improved again when she returned to a more conventional approach. Goddard argues that she could not justify her students' enthusiasm for the manipulatives-based program with the time and energy necessary to effect it. Her talk about finding a balance suggests that she is not done with reforms, but at the same time, she has no immediate plans to learn more or to try anything different.

NOTE

1. Richardson and her colleagues (1991) suggest this is a common phenomenon and that one reason "weak and ineffectual" attempts at change occur is because teachers try to use new materials and activities without understanding the content and pedagogical thinking behind them.

Part III

UNDERSTANDING REFORM
AND CHANGE

The Interaction of Personal, Organizational, and Policy Factors: Explaining the Variation in Teachers' Responses

The variation in teachers' reform responses raises many questions. Two of those questions, what explains the variation in teachers' responses and what implications arise for systemic reform, frame this chapter and the next. In chapter 8, I look at the relationship between the rhetoric of systemic reform and the realities of policy and schooling in Michigan, and I conclude that the systemic solution goes against the grain of the Michigan experience in a number of important ways. Here, however, I focus on explanations by exploring the question of why teachers' responses varied across teachers and across reforms. I argue that, while discrete explanations may seem obvious, a more powerful explanation develops when one considers several factors in interaction.

Some of the variation in the Derry and Hamilton teachers' reform responses might have been anticipated. Research and common sense suggest that teachers and teaching vary across classrooms. It is a pretty small leap to imagine that different teachers might interpret reading reforms differently. This is not to say that we understand this phenomenon well because analysts have traditionally viewed variation as an aberration (McLaughlin, 1990). As researchers increasingly see variation as the norm, more useful studies of teacher behavior have resulted (Cohen et al., in press; Porter, Floden, Freeman, Schmidt, & Schwille, 1988; Schwille et al., 1983).

Even less visible and understood, however, is the cross-reform variation. How are we to understand a teacher like Bonnie Jones who embraces reforms in reading and mathematics at the same time that she ignores them in writing? Or Frank Jensen who gives reading and mathematics

171

reforms only the slightest attention, while he constructs a reform-minded writing practice? Or Marie Irwin who asks tentative, but potentially powerful questions about mathematics while she manages reading and writing reforms toward more conventional ends? Or Paula Goddard whose ambitious moves toward reading and writing reforms developed after she abandoned similar moves in mathematics?

How then can we account for responses that vary across teachers and across reforms? In chapter 1, I offered several discrete possibilities. Some involved the nature of policy and the special problems of subject-matter reforms. Others entailed features of the organizations teachers work in, and the autonomous nature of teachers' labor. Still others highlighted issues of learning and teachers' individual knowledge, beliefs, and experiences. While evidence of each permeates the cases, these factors explain responses neither discretely nor generically. Instead, more complex and more satisfactory explanations develop when one looks at personal, organizational, and policy factors in interaction and in context. In short, the variation in teachers' responses reflects policy and organizational influences, but only as those influences interact with individual teachers' knowledge, beliefs, and experiences.

For clarity's sake, I separate the explanations for each type of variation into two distinct sections. In the first, I offer explanations for the variation across teachers' responses. In the second, I focus on each teacher individually, and explain the variation in his or her responses across reforms.

EXPLAINING THE CROSS-TEACHER VARIATION IN TEACHERS' RESPONSES

The classroom lives of teachers are messy research sites because each teacher's instructional decisions reflect a complex of factors. All is not chaos, however, currents and cross-currents of influence are discernible. In earlier work (Grant, 1996), I describe the interaction of personal, organizational, and policy influences on teachers' content and pedagogical decisions. I return to those constructs as a means of explaining the cross-teacher and cross-reform variation in teachers' reform responses.

Policy Factors

Policies at the national, state, and local levels can influence teachers' instructional decisions (Cuban, 1990; Firestone, 1989; McLaughlin, 1987, 1990). These policies can take many forms. Curriculum initiatives might come from a national organization (e.g., the National Council of Teachers of Mathematics), a state education department (e.g., the Michigan *Essential*

Goals and Objectives for Reading Education), or the central office of a school district (e.g., the Hamilton instructional guidance system). Assessment policy takes shape in the many standardized state- and district-level tests teachers administer. Finally, issues like school-level governance may be covered by state and local policies.

Policy affects these four teachers' classroom practices, but it does so in no single fashion. Consider reading as a case in point. All four teachers report reading the new Michigan policy and yet they made very different sense of it. Jones embraces the state policy as a challenge to her long-held, skills-based practice. She is making substantive changes in her daily classroom instruction and in her basic assumptions about teaching and learning reading. Jensen's talk echoes the policy, but his practice is a hodgepodge of old and new. He sees no important differences between reforms and his extant practice, and the few changes in his daily practice seemed tacked on. Likewise, Irwin sees no profound challenges in reforms. Although she has made notable changes in her reading instruction, she entertains no questions about her basic pedagogical assumptions. Finally, after initially ignoring the policy, Goddard now embraces it as the basis for some profound changes both in her instruction and in her assumptions about teaching and learning reading.

One way of explaining this cross-teacher variation is by considering the nature of educational policy. One issue is that policy is, by nature, vague and subject to multiple interpretations (Firestone, 1989; Kirst & Walker, 1971). Policy can serve as a vehicle for conceptualizing and broadcasting new ideas (Fuhrman, 1993b; Weiss, 1990). The various Michigan curriculum policies, for example, promote new, constructivist views of teaching and learning. However, these reforms, like most others that deal with "core technologies" (Hawley et al., 1984), offer no simple prescriptions or blueprints for enactment. As a result, it should surprise no one that teachers interpret these policies differently.

A second issue is that policies tend to arrive in bunches and compete for teachers' time and attention. One way that policies bunch up is that new initiatives often come from multiple sources. In reading, for example, the state reading policy, the reading portion of the MEAP test, national proposals like *Becoming a Nation of Readers* (Anderson et al., 1985), and district textbook adoptions all competed for teachers' attention. Another way policies bunch up is over time. Recall that in addition to initiatives in reading, writing, and mathematics, these four teachers also face reforms in health and school-level governance. Although these policies did not all land on teachers' desks at the exactly same time, the proximity of their arrival suggests that teachers had to choose what they would attend to and how much energy they could devote to any one issue. The most poignant example of this phenomenon is Goddard's decision to abandon reforms in mathematics, in part, because she felt the press to attend to reading reforms.

These two conditions—the vague, non-prescriptive nature of policy and the blizzard-like form in which policies surface—help explain the cross-teacher variation in responses to reforms.

Organizational Factors

It is tempting to look no farther than policy to explain the cross-teacher variation. Doing so would ignore an important interaction, however, because policies do not come to teachers unencumbered. Policy does matter, but so too does the organizational context in which teachers learn about and respond to reforms.

Organizational or structural influences on teacher behavior are widely accepted and the relevant literature is expansive. Some observers posit the influence of organizational cultures (Cusick, 1983; Hargreaves, 1994; Little, 1982; Sarason, 1982), organizational structures (Chubb & Moe, 1990; McNeil, 1988; Meyer & Rowan, 1978), and the nature of bureaucratic work (Lipsky, 1980). Still others cite the influence of organizational players such as teaching peers (Lortie, 1975) and school and district administrators (Spillane, 1996, 1998).

Just as there is little question that policy can influence teachers' practices, so too is there little argument about the influence of organizational factors. The point to remember, however, is that policy and organization are not discrete influences. Instead, they interact in myriad and complex ways. Using reading as the case in point, consider how organizational factors in both Derry and Hamilton interact with state and local policy to help explain the cross-teacher variation.

The Organizational Context in Derry. Three factors—opportunities to learn new ideas, norms and expectations of teachers, and the relationships between teachers and others—define the organizational context of reading reforms.

Derry teachers had a variety of opportunities to learn about reading reforms beginning with a week-long district inservice. There, Jones and Jensen learned about the state policy and a range of related ideas, including using trade books, teaching reading strategies, motivating student as readers, and integrating reading and writing. Another district learning opportunity was the adoption of a literature-based textbook series and the publisher-led workshops. School-level reading resources were also available. For example, classroom sets of trade books were purchased with special school funds.

Also important in defining the organizational context in Derry are the norms and expectations of teachers and the relationships they have with school and district administrators, parents, and students. A major feature of classroom life in Derry is the autonomy teachers hold. Teachers are encouraged to cover material, but there are no pacing charts or monitoring sheets. Standardized tests are required, but chapter and unit testing is done at teachers' discretion. Textbooks are adopted, but their use is not mandated. The importance of teachers' autonomy figures into their relationships with others. Consider the example of Teresa Jensen, the district reading coordinator, who was primarily responsible for bringing the state reading policy and other reading reforms to Derry teachers. She is available to assist teachers who want to try new approaches, but her power lies in persuasion rather than in force, because she can only assist those teachers who request her help. Similarly, neither the Donnelly-King principal nor the school parents exert much influence on teachers. They may try, as in the case of the parent who complained that Jones had not distributed the class mathematics book, but this action had no important consequence.

These organizational factors help explain the variation across Jones' and Jensen's reform responses. Jones believes her embrace of reading reforms developed in spite of the district. She admits that the district inservice was valuable. She believes that other district actions, such as adopting textbooks instead of tradebooks and administering standardized basic skills tests, however, undermine rather than support her efforts. Of course, Jones would feel much more constrained if she actually had to use the reading textbook and if she had to teach directly to the tests. She does not. The district norm of teacher autonomy means that she uses texts, develops lessons, organizes classes, and assesses students as she deems most appropriate. Jones pushes very ambitious changes in her reading practice and she does so because she believes this is what students need. She also does so because she knows she can. Jones may not feel well supported, but she has the organizational latitude to act on her convictions.

So does Jensen. The "special dispensation" and "bubble of privacy" he believes adhere to the Challenger program allow him maximum discretion in his reading practice. Jensen knows about the push for a more constructivist-based approach to reading, but he senses no external pressure to change his practice in fundamental ways. He uses the new textbook as part of a shotgun approach, but if he decided not to, he would expect no reprimand from his principal, from his students or from their parents. Jensen's sense of autonomy also extends to testing. All of his third and fourth graders take the district basic skills test, and the fourth graders also take the MEAP reading test, yet Jensen seems unconcerned about either set of scores or what consequences might develop from a poor showing. External factors, then, have relatively little influence on Jensen's reading practice. His individual knowledge, beliefs, and experience guide the majority of his instructional decisions.

Understanding each teacher's interpretation of the organization helps explain his or her different responses to reading reforms. The latitude that enables Jones to interpret reforms as a challenge to her extant practice, to seek resources outside the district, and to pursue big changes in her instruction also enables Jensen to interpret reforms as supporting and justifying what he already knows and does. That which makes it possible for Jones to push her teaching allows Jensen to preserve his.

The Organizational Context in Hamilton. Compared to the Derry teachers, Irwin and Goddard have fewer and different opportunities to learn about the state policy and related reading reforms. They first encountered the state policy in 1986 during afternoon workshops led by their respective school reading teachers. In 1993, when the district began its literature-based textbook pilot, Irwin and Goddard attended publisher-sponsored inservices. During the intervening years, neither teacher remembers any district reading initiatives. At the school level, however, Irwin and her Sanford Heights colleagues constructed a rich reading and writing program outside of the district curriculum. Goddard and her Sheldon Court colleagues took no similar actions.

Classroom autonomy and the relationships teachers have with others also differ from Derry to Hamilton. The Hamilton instructional guidance system reaches far into teachers' classrooms. That system defines *content* as skills-based instruction in reading and mathematics. It defines the *instructional means* as textbooks, tests, and paced lessons. Each week, teachers complete monitoring sheets, recording the lessons taught and the students' progress. The impetus is to cover as much material as possible while maintaining high test scores.

School principals play a pivotal role in this system. They collect and review the monitoring sheets before sending them to the district office. Principals also deal with any problems that develop such as teachers failing to maintain pace or low student test scores. Principals enforce district priorities, yet those priorities are not all-encompassing. Hamilton principals have the latitude to construct enhancement programs like the Sanford Heights literacy project and the Sheldon Court *Mathematics Their Way* experiment, though not all do.

School and district influences are stronger in Hamilton than in Derry, but so too are parental influences. This is especially true at Sheldon Court where parents are intimately involved both in their children's classroom lives and in the way that the school operates. Parents are less directly involved at Sanford Heights, but the principal and Irwin both noted an intense parental interest in standardized test scores.

Again, cataloguing organizational factors helps explain the variation in teachers' reform responses. Irwin faithfully followed the district skills-based reading program. She quietly supplemented that program with trade books, however, because she felt that students needed richer literature experiences than the basal readers provided. She interpreted the new state policy and the school literacy program as support for her approach. Taking advantage of a district mini-grant program, Irwin received money to purchase additional trade books. Two years later, when the district began piloting a literature-based textbook/trade book series, she saw her long-held beliefs confirmed. The system, which she once viewed as confining, now seems enabling.

Unlike Irwin, Goddard held no deep or hidden ambitions for reading before encountering the state policy. Instead, she held tightly to the skills-based approaches in which she had been trained and which defined the Sheldon Court mission. Rather than a constraint, the textbook-based instructional program made Goddard's work possible as it defined what to teach, when to teach it, and how to know if one was successful. Against this background, Goddard's initial rejection of reading reforms makes sense: She felt comfortable with and supported by the extant instructional program. She interpreted the light attention given reforms by school and district administrators to mean she should stay the course. It is impossible to know how she would have responded to the literature-based textbook pilot had she not been reintroduced to reforms through a university course, and had her own children not had positive experiences in a reform-minded classroom. What is apparent, however, is that Goddard perceives the new textbook as a vehicle for enacting changes in her classroom, and it is of no small importance that her principal supports these changes. Goddard worries that parents may have trouble with newer approaches and so she maintains elements (e.g., phonics worksheets) that reflect the old program, but today Goddard imagines herself on the road to becoming a very different reading teacher.

In some sense, Irwin and Goddard are worlds apart. While Irwin interprets the school organization as confirming beliefs she already had, Goddard interprets it as liberating her from her past practice.

Personal Factors

Policy and organizational factors tend to get more attention (especially from policymakers), but personal factors such as teachers' knowledge, beliefs, and experiences are widely acknowledged as powerful influences on their behavior.

Personal factors represent the lived background character of individual teachers. We can talk about a broad array of factors: personal knowledge and beliefs, personal and professional experiences, personal history or narratives, and capacity and will. What makes these factors personal is the notion that no two people have lived the same lives nor are they influenced by their experiences in the same ways. What teachers know and do is affected by their unique pasts. We should not be surprised to learn, then, that the variation in teachers' responses to reforms reflects the influence of personal factors.

The death of her child shook Jones both personally and professionally. As she put her life and career back together, she did not like what she saw in her classroom. She had become a "ditto queen" and she felt burned out. Moreover, she sensed that students were bored with her skills-based instruction and their worksheet lives. She resolved to do something, and the new state reading policy provided a focus, something she could try. She now considers her response the beginning of a "cycle of change."

Reading reforms call for Jones to know and do very different things, and she knows she has much to learn about text, interpretation, and pedagogy if she is to effect reform-minded changes. This is no mean assignment, for she believes local learning resources are thin and inconsistent. Jones is determined to change, however, even if this means expending considerable time, energy, and money to attend richer learning opportunities outside the district, and running the risk of administrator and parental questions about her practice.

Individual factors also help explain Jensen's response to reading reforms. As a "Challenger type kid," Jensen now believes his affective and cognitive needs were misunderstood. Jensen knows his students need what he didn't get—sensitivity to affect, as well as intellectual flexibility. New language and ideas clearly excite him, but they have no bite, because Jensen perceives no important differences between his instruction and reforms. Reading reforms "fit" and "justif[y]" his approach. His slight response is not due to a problem of capacity or of will. Jensen knows what he needs, and he is doing all that he intends to. With virtually no external pressures, he picks and chooses pieces which support his current practice and advance his affective goals.

The difference between Irwin's and Goddard's responses also reflects different personal knowledge and experience. Irwin is a confident, skilled, and thoughtful reading teacher. She attributes little direct influence to reforms, although she interprets them as consistent with her views. Consequently, she believes she has little new to learn. She attends obligatory district inservices and scrutinizes her textbook, although she finds nothing startlingly new. Irwin believes reading skills and strategies are important and that a textbook approach is appropriate if not sufficient. Irwin also believes students need literature and she acted on that belief in two ways: She wrote a grant proposal to purchase trade books, and she volunteered to pilot a literature-based textbook series. Irwin could easily have done otherwise. The Hamilton instructional guidance system prizes traditional instruction. Irwin willingly pushed against this system.

In Goddard's case, neither school nor district influences push consistently toward reforms. With the status quo privileged, Goddard could easily ignore reforms, and until recently she did. Local resources play a role in Goddard's ambitious response because the literature-based textbook she pilots made ideas she had heard about but could not envision seem real. It was the knowledge she gained in the university course and her child's positive experience in a whole language classroom that sealed her interest in reading reforms.

Cognitive psychologists tell us that we interpret new information through old, that our cumulative knowledge, beliefs, and personal histories influence our interpretations of new ideas and contexts (Fiske & Taylor, 1984; Nisbett & Ross, 1980; Resnick, 1987). That teachers could read the same policy document, and in the case of Jones and Jensen, be part of the same organizational context, but interpret it in very different ways is not surprising.

In this account of the cross-teacher variation, we see a web of interactions. Teachers read policy, but their readings reflect no single perspective. Individual factors such as knowledge, beliefs, and experiences interact with the opportunities organizations offer and the norms and relationships teachers encounter. Teachers interpret policy as individuals, but they do so through social and organizational contexts. As individual and organizational factors interact, then, variation across a set of teachers' responses becomes more likely, and explaining that variation involves looking at the ways multiple factors intersect.

EXPLAINING THE CROSS-REFORM VARIATION
IN RESPONSES

The variation across teachers' responses to reforms will not surprise many school observers. Explaining this variation is complicated, but recent studies (Cohen et al., in press; Jennings, 1996; Porter et al., 1988; Schwille et al., 1983) increasingly document the phenomenon. Less apparent or understood, however, is the variation within an individual teacher's responses across reforms.

We do know some things. We know that most elementary teachers are competent readers and confident reading teachers; we also know that few hold these qualities in mathematics or writing (Ball & Cohen, 1995). Moreover, we know that teachers respond to multiple reforms simultaneously and that it makes intuitive sense that they might manage reforms in one subject matter differently from another, but what explains this variation?

To explain the cross-teacher variation, I explored the interaction of policy, organizational, and personal factors. The interaction of those factors also helps explain the cross-reform variation within each teacher's practice.

Organizational Opportunities and Setting:
The Hamilton Response Across Reforms

Before developing explanations for Irwin's and Goddard's varied responses across reforms, let me reintroduce features of the Hamilton district context relevant to the three subject-matter reforms.

The Hamilton instructional guidance system manages mathematics teaching and learning much as it does reading: The curriculum is textbook based and emphasizes discrete knowledge and skills, lessons are paced, and testing is frequent. Teachers' progress and students' scores are monitored each week. Teachers use district-adopted English textbooks, but instruction is not monitored.

As noted, the Hamilton response to reading reforms is considerably less enthusiastic than Derry's. The response to mathematics and writing reforms is also muted. In both cases, the principal approach is to adopt a new textbook series. These texts offer some evidence of reforms. For example, the mathematics textbook comes with a manipulatives kit, and the English textbook has a section about the writing process. Beyond the publisher-sponsored workshops, however, teachers have few other district resources because there are no district mathematics or writing coordinators.

Hamilton schools reflect the district lead. First, Hamilton principals give considerable attention to the district instructional guidance system. Principals collect and review monitoring sheets in mathematics, but writing instruction is left to teachers' discretion. Schoolwide enhancement efforts like the writing project at Sanford Heights and the *Mathematics Their Way* experiment at Sheldon Court are not supported by the district, but neither are they actively discouraged.

Second, school-based resources are scant. For example, there are no head teachers in writing and mathematics. Irwin and her Sanford Heights colleagues promote writing through the schoolwide literacy project, but there is no comparable effort in mathematics. Goddard and her primary-grade colleagues at Sheldon Court received the *Mathematics Their Way* materials, but they had no professional development opportunities to support them and there was no school-level attention to writing.

Marie Irwin

In chapter 5, I argue that Irwin manages reading, mathematics, and writing reforms in similar ways, by assimilating them into her extant practice. There are important differences, however. A knowledgeable and confident reader and reading teacher, Irwin is a passive teacher of mathematics. She focuses on the conventional approaches in her textbook and avoids anything unfamiliar or optional. In fact, Irwin's nascent interest in mathematics reforms is all the more noteworthy given the district emphasis on basic skills, her colleagues' disinterest, and her avoidance of any mathematics-related learning opportunities.

Irwin's response to writing reforms is a different matter. The principal influences there seem to be external—the schoolwide literacy initiative and her new textbook. Irwin willingly schedules writing time and gives some attention to the writing process, yet her belief that grammar is critical has not changed. She adopts some reform-minded activities, but maintains a rigid separation between them and her traditional English instruction.

Individual factors like knowledge, beliefs, and experiences help explain Irwin's varied responses. Not exclusively, however, for how Irwin interprets reforms interacts with her interpretation of the local setting and the available resources.

In reading, Irwin's strong beliefs about what students need guided her embrace of the literature-based textbook and trade books, reading strategies, and whole group instruction. Given the Hamilton instructional guidance system, she could not have instituted these changes on her own. The system's emphasis on basal textbook instruction and its initial reluctance to move away from discrete skills made such changes unlikely. Even systems seemingly as tight as Hamilton's have cracks, however, which determined teachers can exploit. With her strong interest in literature and her principal's backing, Irwin exploited one of those cracks by taking advantage of the district mini-grant program to purchase classroom sets of trade books. Combined with her literature-based textbook, Irwin can now teach reading in the way she believes most appropriate for students.

With a set of strong personal beliefs, Irwin interprets the local organizational context in ways that support her ambitions in reading. In writing and mathematics, however, equally strong sets of beliefs encourage her to read the nuances in the school and district context so that she can preserve much of her traditional instruction.

Irwin attends to reformers' calls that students need more, and more engaging, opportunities to write. To that end, she supports her school's writing program and she uses those portions of the district English textbook which promote reform-minded instruction. At the same time, however, Irwin believes that grammar instruction is critical. She allows students time to write and she teaches some elements of the writing process, but her sense that students need intensive work with mechanics, combined with the lack of organizational pressures to change, means that Irwin can maintain her traditional grammar instruction.

A similar scenario emerges in mathematics, although Irwin's avoidance of reforms is stronger than in writing and stems from a different source.

Rather than guiding her response with a considered set of beliefs, Irwin responds to mathematics reforms based on a weak knowledge base and personal discomfort with the subject matter. She knows about new approaches to mathematics, but she reads the mixed messages evident in her textbook as justification for ignoring reforms. Without school or district support, encouragement, or pressure to do otherwise, this response makes sense. It also, however, makes her fledgling questions about mathematics more intriguing and more problematic. Irwin has a sense of what she wants to do and she may be able to make some changes through her determination alone. Substantive changes will be difficult, however, given her thin subject-matter knowledge and the weak organizational resources available.

Paula Goddard

Goddard's determination to initiate big changes in her reading practice is echoed in writing. She offers students more and more authentic writing opportunities, and she hopes to incorporate writing conferences and portfolios. Goddard intends to pursue the appropriate learning opportunities, but she wonders where she will find the time and energy.

Goddard's response to mathematics reforms, however, seems to be moving in the opposite direction. Once, she understood that a gap existed between reforms and her extant practice, and she eagerly adopted several reform-minded changes. The venture produced some success—her students' enthusiasm and test scores rose. Those successes did not continue, however. A year later, few of the reforms remain and an emphasis on basic mathematics knowledge and skills is in place.

As with Irwin, Goddard's varied responses across reforms are best explained as an interaction among policy, organizational, and personal factors.

Goddard's complex response to mathematics reforms is a good example. Today her practice looks quite conventional and her reading of organizational influences seems a large part of the explanation. One piece is her principal's mandate that teachers list basic knowledge and skills objectives in order to stem declining standardized test scores. Another is the time-draining, literature-based textbook pilot. These factors might have been enough in and of themselves to turn Goddard back toward textbook instruction in mathematics. They take on added importance, however, when one understands Goddard's weak knowledge of mathematics and the stress created while trying to teach mathematics in new and ambitious ways.

Goddard's determined response to reading and writing reforms seems to be taking up where her interest in mathematics reforms left off. There are two important differences, however. First, Goddard seeks opportunities to build her subject-matter knowledge and pedagogy as she makes changes in these areas. Rather than simply plunge in, Goddard seems to understand that reforms call for her not only to do different things but to know different things as well. Given the various demands on her personal and professional time and energy, she may not pursue all the opportunities she hopes to. In contrast with her naive efforts in mathematics, Goddard's response to literacy reforms seems more considered.

The second difference is that Goddard reads the organizational context as more supportive of reading reforms (the case is less clear in writing) than of mathematics reforms. Recall that her initiation to mathematics reforms came largely through the *Mathematics Their Way* program. Her principal supported the venture, but it was clearly billed as an experiment. By contrast, the literature-based textbook pilot was sanctioned by both school and district administrators. Some of Goddard's colleagues read their more traditional aims into the textbook and their practices are little changed. Based in part on the university course she took and on her children's positive experiences, Goddard interprets the new textbook as a genuine move toward reform and as a warrant to make extensive changes in her practice. This is not to say that all traces of skills-based instruction are gone, for Goddard reads some aspects of the SCAC context as continuing to promote the status quo. She maintains a separate phonics program, for example, partially because she is not comfortable giving it up. She also does it because she believes parents like the extra work.

Organizational Opportunities and Setting:
The Derry Response Across Reforms

The Derry district response toward reading reforms is considerably stronger than that toward writing or mathematics. The new state mathematics policy received little, if any, attention. There is no district-level mathematics coordinator and there has been no district-sponsored inservice. The adoption of a new mathematics textbook series and a few publisher workshops define the district response. The response has been even weaker in writing. There, only Teresa Jensen's efforts in individual teachers' classrooms (like her husband's) are visible. No inservices have been arranged and no textbook has been adopted. Also, in contrast with reading, there are no school-level resources available in mathematics or writing.

Although the organizational climate differs across reforms, the laissez-faire stance taken toward teaching and learning continues. Ambitious teachers have the latitude to develop reform-minded practices, but they find little support.

Bonnie Jones

Jones' "cycle of change" began with reading reforms. It extended into mathematics, where despite her weak content and pedagogical background, she pushed herself to learn about reforms and to initiate a series of profound changes in her practice. The personal courage to accept this challenge is notable in and of itself, but it is also distinctive in comparison with her response to writing reforms because the confidence with which Jones tackled reading and mathematics reforms did not carry over into writing. Recall her pained comments about writing being "a weak area of mine" and something "I avoid . . . because I'm not very good at it." Jones knew that writing reforms existed and that they challenged her traditional approaches. Until recently, however, she ignored them. As she becomes increasingly comfortable with her new reading and mathematics practices, Jones appears more willing to take on writing reforms. She seeks new opportunities to learn, and she said, "I'm trying to push myself to do more writing this year."

Jones faced tremendous personal and professional challenges. The person who emerged, however, carries the courage to look hard at her teaching and the determination to make deep changes. She does not do this in a vacuum, however, for the variation across Jones' reform responses reflects differences in her interpretation of reforms and of the local context.

One example is her different responses to reading and mathematics textbooks. Jones knew a lot about reading and text when she abandoned the district textbook in favor of trade books. The university courses, conferences, and workshops she attended outside the district convinced her that trade books were a viable option and that she could use them instead of a textbook. Given this response, one might expect Jones would also reject new mathematics textbooks. She embraces mathematics reforms as strongly as she does reading, she knows that math textbooks have problems, and she has ancillary materials to use as a substitute. However, Jones also recognizes that she knows considerably less about mathematics and teaching mathematics than she does about reading. As her knowledge and confidence grows, she supplements the text with ancillary materials. Until she feels more capable, however, she will continue to center her mathematics instruction in the textbook.

The interaction of personal, organizational, and policy factors also helps explain Jones' response to writing reforms. Although Jones has attended conference sessions about writing for several years, she dismissed much of what she heard because her response to writing reforms is shaped less by what she needs to learn than by how she feels about writing. She chose to maintain her conventional grammar instruction largely because she felt uncomfortable with herself as a writer and as a teacher of writing. That there has been no concerted school or district support for writing undoubtedly played into Jones' response. This point only underscores, however, the significance of her recent determination to deal with this difficult subject. Given the local ennui, Jones has carte blanche to make radical changes in her writing instruction, but she could just as easily not.

Frank Jensen

Jensen's eclectic response to reading reforms resurfaces in mathematics. He is drawn to the language of problem solving, mental math, and patterns, but little else. The few changes he has made are superficial and reflect little knowledge of mathematics. As in reading, Jensen senses no external pressure to do more nor does he express any particular interest in making additional changes. In sharp contrast is Jensen's recent embrace of writing reforms. Whereas once he ignored writing, last year he constructed an energetic writing project. Although this represented a profound change in his daily practice, Jensen perceives no need to learn more about writing reforms.

One might be tempted to explain the variation across Jensen's responses by citing the extensive organizational autonomy given his "special dispensation" and "bubble of privacy." After all, he seems immune from virtually all external factors. The concerns about curriculum coverage, time, and tests, which preoccupy most teachers, are absent. Instead, Jensen charts his own instructional course. This last point, however, could also figure into a much different explanation. One might explain Jensen's responses primarily in terms of personal predilections. Jensen's shotgun approach to instruction, his penchant for student affect, and his glib familiarity with reforms seem part and parcel of his personal knowledge, beliefs, and experience.

As persuasive as either of these arguments might be, it seems likely that they interact because the "special dispensation" and "bubble of privacy" that Jensen claims adhere to his work in the Challenger program are simply that: claims. The school and district postures toward teachers and their work offer considerable classroom autonomy, but autonomy is not a commodity to be picked up by teachers along with their classroom keys. Instead, as teachers interpret their organizational contexts, one piece of that interpretation is their sense of the control they can exert over their instructional day. Thus the "special dispensation" and "bubble of privacy" exist only in Jensen's mind. Because he believes and acts as if they exist, they do.

As Jensen's idiosyncratic approach to teaching and learning interacts with his sense of instructional freedom, one should not be surprised by any turn his attention takes. In reading and mathematics, his principal response has been to grab any and all ideas, grafting them onto practices which seem to have little focus or direction. Why Jensen reacted so differently to writing reforms is puzzling. There are no clear school or district pressures to do so. Jensen admits his wife's interest in writing influenced him, but remember that her equally strong interest in reading produced no similar result.

IMPLICATIONS

The notion that policy, organizational, and individual factors would figure into explanations of the cross-teacher and cross-reform variation in teachers' reform responses is not news. After all, substantial literatures exist which posit each of these factors as influential. My analysis departs from conventional wisdom, however, in the sense that these factors interact. Strains of policy, organizational, and individual influences can be detected. No comprehensive account of the varied ways these four teachers manage reforms, however, can emerge without acknowledging the ways each set of factors shapes and is shaped by the others. Teachers construct individual responses to reforms, but they do so in both organizational and policy contexts.

Two implications seem clear. One is that as influences, policy, organizational, and individual factors are potential rather than fixed. Influence is a social construct; how a teacher responds to new ideas reflects his or her reading of the nature of the reform, the relevant classroom, school, and district contexts, and the knowledge, beliefs, and experiences he or she brings to bear. Thus, the importance of district testing is differently perceived by Jones and Jensen based on their different readings of policy, organizational, and individual factors. Similarly, the different ways that Goddard and Irwin interpret new ideas about writing reflect their own idiosyncratic interpretations of the relevant factors. Consequently, it becomes difficult to see policy, organizational, and personal factors as individual influences. The relevance of these factors seems more potential than real.

The second implication is that what counts as an influence may change over time and circumstance. That is, factors which seem of particular importance at one point and in one context may be supplanted by other factors as time and situations change. Examples of this phenomenon can be seen in Jensen's recent embrace of writing and in Goddard's retreat from mathematics. Though different, each response demonstrates the teacher's sensitivity to conditions changing over time and context.

If these two points ring true, then we can begin to evaluate the promise and problem of substantively changing teaching through efforts like systemic reform. I now turn to that issue.

Chapter 8

If the Problem Is Systemic, Is the Solution? Considering the Prospects for Systemic Reform

In this chapter, I return to the issue of systemic reform. More specifically, I explore how the recent experience of Michigan policymakers, administrators, and teachers helps us to understand the prospects for the systemic agenda.

Systemic reformers offer an insightful analysis into the problem of education. They see a range of issues including curriculum, assessment, professional development, and educational governance that push in multiple, and often conflicting directions. Particularly problematic is the sense that past reform efforts have done little for those students who traditionally have been poorly served. By identifying the educational system itself as the problem, reformers develop a powerful analysis of the complexity of educating all children to ambitious levels.

From that analysis, systemic reformers propose a solution based on an activist state-level agenda. They assign to the state the role of critical actor and the responsibility for constructing a vision for educational change through the development of new curriculum frameworks, coordination of key policies, and changes in school-level governance. Underlying these actions is the belief that better schooling for all children depends on a more coherent educational system, made so through the alignment of various system components.

Systemic reformers' assumptions about the problem of education fit Michigan. Before systemic initiatives began, educational structures in Michigan were fragmented, complex, and multileveled. Past curriculum and assessment efforts worked at various purposes; state actions were weakened by a traditionally strong belief in local control, and by strong and competing policymaking at local levels. Moreover, prevailing patterns of privilege existed: Students across the state received very different resources and educations, with the least advantaged receiving the short end of both. All in all, the problems of education in Michigan fit the systemic analysis.

But if the problem is systemic, is the solution? Not necessarily. In the bulk of this chapter, I look at four instances wherein the experience of Michigan policymakers, administrators, and teachers rubs against the systemic reform grain. I conclude by raising two issues that further problematize the systemic solution.

SYSTEMIC REFORM: SOLUTIONS AND SLIPPAGES

The rhetoric of systemic reform has a genuine appeal in no small measure because it is clear and rational. Reality, however, is rarely as clear or as rational as theory. It is reasonable, then, to suspect that there might be some tension or slippage as the rhetoric of the systemic solution interacts with the realities of life in state education departments, local district offices, and school classrooms. It is also reasonable to suspect that some slippages are more important than others. From this study of Michigan policy and practice, the four most important slippages occur around:

1. the definition of the state as the critical actor;
2. the proliferation of policy;
3. the division between policymaking and enactment; and,
4. the role of teacher interpretation.

Slippage One: The State as Critical Actor

One instance where rhetoric and reality rub in this study involves the assignation of critical actor status to the state. Systemic reformers believe that a key part of their solution is positioning state-level actors to provide leadership and coherence to an unruly educational context. They may be right. In the case of Michigan, however, defining the state is no simple matter.

True to form, state-level actors have pushed an assertive and activist state agenda in Michigan. With the exception of textbook adoption, virtually all areas of schooling—curriculum, assessment, certification, professional development, graduation requirements, even the length of the school year—have been reviewed and modified by state policymakers. Changes of this scope would have been unimaginable no more than 10 years ago, for in addition to challenging prevailing school practices, these policies also challenge the traditional norms of local control.

The rise of state influence and the pervasiveness of state policy in Michigan is undeniable, but that reality only exacerbates the problematic nature of defining the state. State-level policymaking increased in Michigan, yet as time passed, it became increasingly clear that the state was no single entity.

Systemic reformers suggest that there may be some warring as the state position becomes clear (Fuhrman, 1993b), yet they take no stance on whether the state will be represented by the state department of education, the state legislature, the governor, or some coalition of all of these. In Michigan, the road to systemic reform began in the state education department (MDE) with revisions to the state curriculum frameworks and the MEAP in the mid-1980s. With no response from the legislature and the governor's office, the state was the state department of education. While MDE actions continued during the 1990s, increasingly state lawmakers and the governor became involved. Following PA 25 a series of legislative acts addressed more elements of the state education scene. Many of these initiatives dealt with areas, previously unaddressed by MDE actions, such as professional development, accreditation, diploma standards, and the length of the school year. Others, however, seemed to conflict with MDE efforts. For example, while PA 25 required schools to submit school improvement plans to MDE, legislation enacted in 1995 eliminated that requirement. The impact of these actions had not yet trickled down to teachers when this study ended, and it is easy to imagine questions emerging about who was in charge of state education policy.

Competition for the mantle of state spokesperson was not limited to the upper levels of state government. Tensions around whose messages would dominate also developed within the state department of education. There, one form of competition swelled between specialists in curriculum and in assessment.[1] Although arguments between curriculum and assessment specialists are nothing new, a long-standing distrust simmered between the two departments in the MDE (Cohen et al., in press). The principal result of this distrust was parallel but independent work. Curriculum specialists led the revisions of the various subject matter policies while assessment specialists led the revision of the MEAP. Each effort represented a substantive change from past practice, but as noted earlier, the MEAP revisions had less influence than those developed in the frameworks. The revised reading section of the MEAP, for example, represented something of a shift toward constructivist thinking through the inclusion of real text, longer passages, and higher-level questions. Test makers also made changes, but balked at abandoning such staples as a multiple-choice format. On one level, this might be read as a matter of mixed messages about the nature of reading. On another level, however, this seems like a conflict about which department, curriculum or assessment, would prevail as the official state view.

Confusion over defining the state yields two implications. One is that the state's message, assertive though it was, weakened over time. In addition to the MDE actions, no less than four major pieces of state legislation were passed. As more and more actors entered the stage and as the reform agenda grew, tensions emerged between new and old initiatives.

A second implication follows. If the state's messages were muddied, then it stands to reason that the state's role as critical actor was undercut. Basic to the systemic reform argument is the state's role in creating a strong vision for educational change. The scramble for leadership and control of the state message undermined the potential for a coherent vision. As I show in the next section, that scramble also undercut the power of the state position. The state presence was undoubtedly stronger, but it was far from preeminent.

Given the state's constitutional authority over education, the systemic reformers' impulse to assign leadership to the state makes sense. As the case of Michigan suggests, however, the state is no uniform entity and speaks with no single voice.

Slippage Two: The Proliferation of Policy

A second instance of slippage between the systemic solution and the case of Michigan involves policy proliferation. The systemic reform argument presumes that as state-level activity increases, a corresponding decrease in policymaking at other levels will occur. In Michigan, the reverse is true: Despite their expansive actions, Michigan policymakers failed to stem the profusion of policymaking at levels above and below the state.

State-level policymaking in Michigan expanded tremendously beginning in the mid-1980s. National policymaking, beginning with *A Nation at Risk*, did too. Recall, for example, that the new Michigan mathematics policy emerged about the same time that the National Council of Teachers of Mathematics offered a massive set of new curriculum, evaluation, and professional standards. The Michigan reading and writing policies also emerged concurrently with national reforms.

Even more surprising, however, was the steady pace of local policymaking. Local Michigan administrators were used to directing their own change efforts. The state introduced a range of new initiatives, but this action in no way curbed local undertakings. For example, Derry administrators brought in a huge professional development program (ODDM), adopted new reading and mathematics textbook series, and developed a trade book program at Donnelly-King Elementary school. Hamilton administrators also developed new policies. The multifaceted instructional guidance system with textbook adoption, instructional pacing, and assessment monitoring components reflected just one set of local policies. Other district initiatives included piloting new reading textbooks and purchasing mathematics manipulatives kits for all elementary school classrooms. School-level policies, such as the reading and writing program at Sanford Heights Elementary, also developed and grew during this period.

One implication of this policy proliferation is that not only did local policymaking expand, but local efforts did not closely follow the state lead. Two points are important here. One is that local policymakers generally addressed perceived local needs rather than state policy. The Derry ODDM project and the Hamilton instructional guidance system, for example, were massive undertakings. Each, however, was initiated independently from state influence. The second point is related, because local policy reflected local needs, and local policymakers apparently felt free to ignore state initiatives. True, some local efforts paralleled the state agenda. The Derry reading textbook adoption, for example, was promoted as a response to the new state reading policy. In other cases, however, local actors clearly disregarded state directives. Neither Derry nor Hamilton administrators, for example, gave the state writing policy any explicit attention.

A second implication of the policy explosion is that, with diverse sources of policy, it is reasonable to expect that teachers realize diverse messages. Consider first Jones' experience in reading. Jones supports the direction established by the state policy. She believes the school policy about tradebooks is sympathetic. She disagrees strongly, however, with the district textbook choice and the decision to devote district resources to other areas such as ODDM. In the first case, Jones believes the new textbook conflicts with the state's curriculum message. In the second case, she contends that the district is moving too fast: Many teachers, including herself, need more time to understand and adopt new reading practices before moving onto another set of changes. Irwin presents a different example. She is only vaguely aware of the push to reform writing; recall that she did not know there was a new state writing policy. She is, however, very aware of the importance of writing in her school through the literacy program, and she devotes a lot more time to writing now than she used to. At the same time, the district textbook sends conflicting messages, alternatively promoting traditional and reformist perspectives. Goddard also sees conflict among policy messages. Goddard began changing her mathematics practice by taking advantage of the district manipulatives kit and her principal's encouragement to use *Mathematics Their Way*. Before those ideas and practices could gel, however, she found herself in the midst of a reading textbook pilot. Overwhelmed, Goddard felt forced to choose between reading and mathematics. Of the four teachers, only Jensen saw no mixed or conflicting messages among the various policies he encountered. This is not surprising, however, given his expansive views and his shotgun approach to teaching. With the exception of Jensen, then, each teacher saw real conflicts between and among the messages broadcast by state and local policymakers. In Jones' case, this provoked considerable frustration and anxiety. In Irwin's case, it resulted in a mix of parallel practices that never seemed to intersect, and in Goddard's case, we see a reformer's worst nightmare: a reform-minded practice dying on the vine.

Systemic reformers rightly grumble about the proliferation of policy, and their solution—assuming that expanding the state policymaking role will reduce the volume of policy made—makes some sense. The Michigan experience, however, suggests otherwise. Not only does state policy not stem policymaking at other levels, it does not appear to hold any privileged position. Ironically, then, increasing state policymaking means more policy and more confusion at other levels, rather than less.

Slippage Three: The Division Between Policymaking and Enactment

The notion that local policymaking is only distantly related to state policymaking spells trouble for another systemic reform solution—separating policymaking from enactment, in general, and separating curriculum from instruction, in particular.

Systemic reformers argue for centering policymaking at the state level, and correspondingly, for centering implementation at the local level. As we have seen, this is problematic: Local administrators continue to make policy largely independently of state efforts. Implementation of the state agenda, if it is going to happen, must happen at the local level. However, local educators, in Michigan at least, enact many agendas, only some of which are the state's.

This point takes on special importance when one considers that systemic reformers assign responsibility for establishing curriculum goals to state actors, and responsibility for implementation of those goals to local educators. They do so based on the premise that, while common statewide goals are crucial, instructional conditions vary across localities. Teaching decisions, presumably then, are best made at the local level. Make no mistake, systemic reformers want instruction to change. They assume, however, that local actors are best positioned to enact those changes.

Here, the Michigan experience closely follows the systemic model. State-level policymakers generated ambitious new curriculum frameworks, revised state tests, and provided money for district-level professional development. MDE curriculum specialists conducted some statewide meetings and inservices relating to these initiatives. Most of the professional development that teachers report attending, however, came through school and district-level workshops and the occasional university course. In this sense, then, Michigan educators followed the systemic reformers' script—policymaking at the state level; implementation at the local level.

As this approach unfolds, however, three implications develop. We have already seen the first: Local actors apparently do not limit their attention to state initiatives. The state may assume that it is setting curriculum policy, but local educators appear to feel free to consider or to ignore the state agenda.

A second implication is that policymaking and policy implementation are not so easily separated because districts play an important role in mediating state curriculum policy. In short, the various actions taken by local administrators can be described easily as both policymaking and implementation. To emphasize this point, consider how each district handled reading, writing, and mathematics reforms.

Derry administrators sent clear messages that reading was primary. This is the only subject matter in which, in addition to adopting a new textbook series, a district consultant was available, a week-long inservice was scheduled, and a school trade book program was developed. By contrast, administrators gave considerably less attention to mathematics and writing: A new mathematics textbook series was adopted and a publisher-sponsored workshop was held; writing received no district-sponsored attention apart from Teresa Jensen's modest individual efforts. Hamilton administrators sent more complex messages. Reading and math were clearly the district's highest concerns, as evidenced by their prominence in the instructional guidance system, but district administrators gave little, if any, attention to state policies in these areas. Hamilton teachers learned about the state reading policy from their school reading teachers, but learned nothing more from the district about reading reforms of any kind until the textbook pilot several years later. District administrators also ignored the state mathematics policy, but in an independent action purchased manipulatives kits for each elementary school classroom. Finally, the district seemed to address writing reforms by purchasing (in advance of the state policy) a new English textbook series that featured the writing process. The importance of these actions was undercut, however, by a lack of district follow-through for teachers who wanted to learn more.

All this suggests that local administrators attended as much to the ends of these reforms as to the means. In other words, in making decisions about what they would and would not attend to and what resources would be devoted to each area, local administrators were establishing curriculum goals as well as enacting them. In this sense, then, district administrators mediated the state policy agenda. Doing so did not preclude teachers from pursuing their own interests. In fact, each of the teachers in this study demonstrated some interest in areas beyond their districts' explicit priorities, Jones and Irwin in mathematics, Jensen and Goddard in writing. Those interests meant, however, that Jensen and Goddard had relatively few local resources from which to draw.

This last point about the nature of district resources suggests one other implication of the systemic solution which separates policymaking from implementation. Simply put, systemic reformers assume that district leaders will know how to teach teachers to transform their practices, and that they will have the appropriate resources to do so. In practice, however, this assumption is highly suspect. One problem is that districts try to do too much too fast. Like teachers who aim for content coverage rather than for student understanding, district leaders push a constant stream of reforms past teachers. This study reports about teachers' responses to reforms in three major curriculum areas. Remember, however, that each teacher also deals with reforms in science and health; and, for the Derry teachers, with outcome-based education. At the very least, this blizzard of change blows teachers' time, energy, and attention in multiple directions. At its worst, it promotes a sense of moving on before real instructional changes can gel. Covering reforms is covering the curriculum: It is unlikely to produce substantive and sustained learning and change.

A second problem is the promotion of incompatible goals, especially relating to teaching and testing. With the exception of Jensen, each of the teachers in this study expressed some version of the concern that making fundamental changes in their practices could disadvantage their students on standardized tests, particularly those administered locally. The Goddard case is instructive here. Recall that her students' scores increased the year she began using the *Mathematics Their Way* program. Recall also, however, that students' scores went up even more the next year when she returned to a skills-based practice. Goddard's experience suggests it is no foregone conclusion that scores will fall if teachers change their practices, but her case also underscores the notion that matching teaching to tests can pay off. Districts want teachers to improve their pedagogy, but they also want high test scores. To the extent that teaching and testing push in different directions, then, instructional changes may continue to be modest as both teachers and their administrators hope to avoid falling test scores.

There is one other problem with the systemic assumption that districts will be able to help teachers make the kinds of changes reformers envision. Current reforms challenge much of what teachers know and do. Reformers agree that in order to teach reading, writing, and mathematics differently, teachers must learn to read, write, and do mathematics in deep ways. This sounds right, for how can one expect students to think and act in new and rigorous ways unless their teachers can?

Yet this premise is problematic given the present professional development system. Among other things, there is a fundamental difference between professional development that focuses on training and that which emphasizes education. The majority of professional development efforts take a training approach which assumes that teachers already possess much of the requisite knowledge and experience. Professional development, in that context, consists of demonstrating new instructional strategies which teachers can incorporate into their extant practices. By contrast, professional development as education implies that teachers will reexamine and revise their practices in light of new conceptualizations of teaching and learning. Behaviorism and constructivism are different ways of conceptualizing teaching, learning, and subject matter. Most teachers were schooled in the former; reforms are rooted in the later. To teach in reform-minded ways, then, requires education rather than training.

Other considerations emerge because of the way district-level professional development is typically presented. First, professional development facilitators often rely on short-term workshop approaches rather than on extended learning opportunities. Education is a long-term process. Changes of the types reformers envision simply will not come during one-shot, 30-minute workshops held after school (Grant, Peterson, & Shojgreen-Downer, 1996). Second, professional development facilitators often fail to understand that teachers bring very different resources to their learning. Elementary teachers generally have much more knowledge and experience as readers than they do as writers or mathematicians (Ball & Cohen, 1995; Graves, 1983). Consequently, opportunities to learn about reading may need to vary considerably from those about writing and mathematics. These two considerations suggest a third: Professional development facilitators need to know and do much that is new to them. Just as students may not learn to think and act in ambitious ways if their teachers do not, it stands to reason that teachers may not learn to teach in ambitious ways if their teachers, the professional development facilitators, use conventional approaches. Ironically, however, professional development facilitators often teach reform-minded ideas in entirely pedantic ways (Grant, 1997a). One last consideration involves time and resources. While these issues are always important, they are particularly so given the type of professional development sketched above. Training implies a certain efficiency. Education, especially when it challenges much of what one knows, is messy, complex, and slow. Some teachers, like Jones and Goddard may be motivated and resourceful enough to find the means necessary to learn about reform-minded practices. The experiences of Irwin and Jensen, however, suggest that standard professional development practices do not suffice.

Systemic reformers assume that ends can be constant and means can vary, yet these are not unrelated phenomena; ends often define means and vice versa. Viewing local actors as only implementors, then, misses an important feature of local context: School and district administrators not only mediate the messages the state sends, but also the means by which teachers come to understand those messages. In doing so, however, local administrators face problems of trying to do too much too fast, of promoting incompatible goals, and of transforming their professional development efforts.

Slippage Four: The Role of Teacher Interpretation

Systemic reformers slip one more time when they assume that the messages the state broadcasts are the ones that teachers hear, and that what they hear is what they will do. As we have seen, one problem is that state messages can be drowned out by messages from other sources, both national and local. Another problem is that there is no direct pipeline from state-level policymakers to teachers. School and district administrators play an important mediating role. Even if these problems did not exist, the systemic solution would still be problematic for the simple fact remains that systemic reformers underestimate the role of teacher interpretation in responses to reform.

In fact, systemic reformers rarely mention teachers and classrooms in anything other than a general sense. This seems odd, given the small but powerful literature (Firestone, 1989; Schwille et al., 1983; Weatherly & Lipsky, 1977) which casts teachers in an activist role in the policymaking process. It is difficult to imagine that systemic reformers are unfamiliar with this literature. For whatever reason, however, they do ignore the activist role of teachers, banking instead on the power of state efforts to drive coherence and change down through the system and into classrooms.

The Michigan experience suggests this expectation is problematic for several reasons. First, teachers were unaware of some state reforms. All had read the state reading policy, but only one had read the new state mathematics policy, and none had seen the writing policy. All four teachers knew that prevailing views were changing in these areas, but what they knew came largely from local, national, or university sources rather than from the state. Second, even when teachers perceived reforms, from whatever source, they sometimes ignored them. Irwin knew about new approaches to mathematics for several years; she had even been given a mathematical manipulatives kit. Until recently, however, she continued her skills-based practice without a second thought. Similarly, Jones knew that her writing instruction was out-of-step with current thinking, yet she too maintained a traditional instructional approach. Finally, when teachers perceived reforms and made changes in their practices, these changes were remarkably varied. Knowing about the state reading policy, for example, did not lead to a common interpretation. Similarly, each teacher reacted differently to the textbooks their districts piloted or adopted. From these experiences, we understand that teachers may or may not see reforms as a challenge to their past practices, they may or may not see a need to learn anything new, and they may or may not make changes in their extant thinking and practices. Teachers recognize reforms as potential influences, but they interpret those influences in many ways.

From a systemic view, this variation might be explained as a predictable result of the mixed messages sent by state and local policymakers. Reformers might be dismayed by this result, but could hold out hope that this is a flaw in the particular actors rather than in the theory. Perhaps it is. As I suggest in chapter 7, however, it is difficult to sustain an argument that posits only policy and organizational influences on teachers' actions. State and local actions do matter, but they do so in interaction with individual factors. This effect is most clearly seen in Derry where Jones and Jensen were exposed to virtually the same range of state and local messages. These messages clearly had some effect on their respective practices. The variation in their responses, however, only makes sense when one considers their individual knowledge, beliefs, and experiences. For example, Jones interpreted state policy as a basic and direct challenge to her whole approach to reading, and she made large-scale changes in her practice. Jensen interpreted the same policy as part and parcel of his extant approach, and his practice remains largely unchanged. A similar situation developed around the district-adopted mathematics textbook: Jones uses it as part of an expansive, reform-minded practice; Jensen uses it as the basis of his traditional skills-based practice. This pattern breaks down in writing, however, for neither teacher reports a serious state or local influence, yet Jensen's writing instruction looks significantly more like reforms than Jones' does.

Three implications develop from these problems with the systemic solution. The first concerns the relationship among policy, organizational, and individual influences. The systemic solution gives clear priority to the first. State-level policy should alternatively encourage or drive change downward or both. Michigan policymakers brought potentially powerful influences to bear in the form of new curriculum frameworks, revised assessments, and the like. These efforts did influence some teachers' actions, but they influenced teachers in varied ways, and they did not influence teachers more than local administrative actions or more than the teachers' own knowledge, beliefs, and experiences. Influences exist, but they come from multiple sources, they interact, and they vary over time.

The second implication concerns the nature of the changes teachers make. Reforms call for new instructional approaches in reading, writing, and mathematics. Each of the teachers in this study made changes. Only rarely, however, were those changes as sweeping and profound as reformers envisioned. In a gross sense, most changes are small and tacked on; they are different from what the teacher did in the past, but they do not signal a profound shift in the teacher's thinking or practice. Irwin's response to writing reforms is a good example. She now assigns more and more am-bitious writing projects. The bulk of her writing instruction, however, re-mains rooted in grammar and mechanics. Jones is perhaps the best case of a teacher trying to enact profound changes in her practice. Given where she started, one could argue that she is transforming her teaching, at least in reading and mathematics. However, elements of traditional practice remain. Pages of worksheet math problems and literal comprehension reading questions regularly appear. I mention this not to denigrate Jones' efforts because her case tells a stirring story of a teacher powerfully com-mitted to more rigorous teaching. Jones' practice simply reminds us that no change is wholesale and that teachers' best new efforts still reflect past practice in some fashion.

One last implication is a special case of the nature of the changes teachers made. Systemic reformers make no distinctions among the changes they expect from teachers: Transforming one's teaching is pre-sumably no different in mathematics than it is in reading. It is easy to see where this assumption comes from, because the various subject matter reforms have a common root in constructivist thinking. The observation, then, that a teacher like Jones could make profound changes in reading and virtually none in writing does not make sense. However, teachers clearly bring different resources to bear when they encounter different reforms, so change in one area has no particular implication for change in another. The four teachers in this study, like elementary teachers across the country, tend to know more about, and feel more skilled, as readers than as writers or mathematicians. This fact did not disable them because some of the most profound changes occurred in these teachers' mathe-matics and writing practices. Nevertheless, the sense remains that the changes teachers made in their reading instruction were deeper and more sustainable than those in other subjects.

By definition, the systemic solution focuses on actions some distance from teachers and classrooms. Doing so makes some sense because teacher autonomy is a generally accepted dimension of classroom life, but it is not complete. The influences on teachers' practices are multiple, complex, and tenuous. State initiatives are part of the policy, organizational, and individual mix, but they hold no special sway. Thus, despite efforts toward alignment and coherence, teachers' responses to reforms vary considerably.

PROSPECTS AND PROBLEMS

These slippages signal a range of problems for the systemic agenda. To conclude this discussion, I raise two problems that seriously undercut the prospects for systemic reform. One is the problem of coherence. Another is the question of whether the systemic agenda is truly system-changing.

The Problem of Coherence

Reformers place great faith in coherence as a means of educational improvement, and in policy alignment as a means of gaining coherence, yet coherence as a policy end is questionable. Coherence is not a fixed quantity or state, but instead is a perception, and is a contextual and dynamic one at that. What appears coherent to one person in one place and at one time may seem quite different to another.

Consider the different ways state policymakers and local classroom teachers view coherence. An MDE policymaker, for example, would be most concerned with coherence in two ways. One is that the policies emanating from his or her department cohere with those of another, as in the case of curriculum frameworks and state assessment tests. The other is that MDE policies cohere with those enacted by the state legislature and signed by the governor. The state policymaker may have concerns about how local actors interpret these policies, but following the dictates of systemic theory, coherence at the state level should drive the proper changes in schools and classrooms. Coherence for systemic reformers in general, and for this policymaker in particular, is set within a state context.

Coherence at the classroom level looks much different. Complicating the issue is the fact that a classroom teacher like Bonnie Jones works within the multiple contexts of district, school, and state. Given that situation, the emergence of inconsistencies or incoherence is easy to imagine. In reading, for example, Jones saw the district message about textbooks as inconsistent with the state reading policy and with her school policy about trade books. She embraces the state policy. Doing so, however, is no simple matter because she must negotiate the different state, district, and school-level terrains. While Jones might prefer to hear a coherent set of messages from these various actors, she is not going to wait.

The idea that Jones would not wait for various policies to cohere raises another issue, the dynamic quality of U.S. education in general, and of educational policymaking in particular. We saw instances of incoherence developing over time at the state level. For example, incoherence seemed to increase rather than decrease in the movement from ambitious new curriculum frameworks to the less ambitious MEAP. Coherence also became a problem over time at the district and school levels. In Hamilton, we saw district administrators initially maintaining a skills-based reading program in spite of the state movement toward constructivist approaches. Years later, the district introduced a textbook pilot. It seemed to support the direction the state was taking, but recall Irwin's comment that, while the heavy district instructional guidance system was suspended during the pilot, she fully expected it to return. If so, teachers would receive textbooks which supported a new conception of reading, but they would be expected to use them within a context which supports the old conception of reading.

In this case, coherence is compromised by mixed messages, and the potential for mixed messages grows over time.

To be sure, one might argue that this study simply represents a case of poorly done systemic reform, and that coherence remains a reasonable goal when set in more congenial contexts and managed with more adept hands. While not denying the possibility that Michigan reformers might have done better, two points undercut this argument. One point is that if the problem of education and its solution is truly systemic, then it seems unfair to argue that it will only work in the right kinds of situations. As reformers cast the problem in terms of the education system in the United States, the argument that Michigan simply is not a good site does not hold. The second point is that studies in other states, especially those with presumably more hospitable conditions, suggest that the issues raised in this study are not unique (Grant et al., 1996; Lusi, 1997; Spillane, Peterson, Prawat, Jennings, & Borman, 1996).

These examples demonstrate that, as a policy objective, coherence is problematic on several fronts. Perceptions of coherence are affected by contexts and time, both past and present. The assumptions that one can build a coherent system, which will be perceived as such by all stakeholders and will hold over time, seem naive at best.

Leaving the System Intact

If one problem is the notion of coherence, a second is the degree to which systemic reform really is about changing the educational system. Systemic reform looks like grand theory—a comprehensive, novel approach to understanding an important social institution. However, the systemic agenda seems limited: tweaking, rather than conceptualizing and promoting, a dramatic change in the current system. Systemic reform still may be grand theory, but it is grand theory cast within familiar bounds.

Two observations support this view. First, the systemic reformers do not change the locus of control. Locating power to create and disseminate policy at the state level is really no change because constitutionally, education has always been a state affair. That some states, notably northern states like Michigan, have let that power devolve to local levels does not change the basic premise that education is a state phenomenon. Reformers might have proposed a truly systemic change by advocating a shift to national control. They do not, arguing instead that the constitutional authority over schooling and the practical control over funding bespeaks state rather than national rule (Smith & O'Day, 1991). They may be right. Certainly the long tradition of state or local control or both in the United States presents a daunting target, but by maintaining the locus of control at the state level, systemic reformers limit the possibility of truly changing the education system.

This point becomes obvious when one examines the slippage between rhetoric and reality around policymaking and implementation. Systemic reformers bemoan the decentralized nature of U.S. educational decision making. Part of their solution is to locate more power, particularly policymaking power, in state hands, and to limit local policymaking by assigning implementation of the state plan to local educators. The Michigan experience suggests, however, that the policy making and implementation relationship is much more complex in practice. In short, increasing state-level policymaking and efforts to control the direction of educational change have a varied effect. Local actors may acknowledge the state message (assuming, simplistically as it turns out, that there is only one), but there is no surety that the message will supplant district or individual teacher agendas or both. Rather than transforming the system, reformers' efforts tend to be swallowed up by the current system (Tyack & Cuban, 1995).

The view that systemic reform is less than system changing is also supported by the fact that reformers do not abandon traditional levers of change (e.g., curriculum frameworks, assessments, and professional development) or measures of accountability (e.g., test scores and accreditation). Reformers bank on the salutary effects of coherence developed through the alignment of new and existing policies. As we have seen, coherence, as a policy goal, is a poor bet. Even if it were not, it is at least mildly surprising to see that reformers hope to change the current system by using conventional approaches. Educators have had long experience with frameworks and tests and accreditation reports. As a means to promote and sustain change, these approaches have the advantage of familiarity. With that familiarity, however, comes the baggage of past experience, much of it negative. Every educator of any experience at all knows two things. One is that the latest new thing eventually will be replaced by the next latest new thing. The other is that responses to the new thing can vary considerably, from disregard to embrace. This study demonstrates that real changes can come from traditional policy approaches, especially when they are rooted in new and provocative ideas, but if the systemic dream of real change for all children is to be realized, it is difficult to imagine that outcome if only traditional approaches are used.

Systemic reform has the trappings of grand theory—a comprehensive analysis of the problems of the current situation and a set of rational solutions. Grand theories are notoriously problematic in reality, however, so in one sense it is not surprising to see some of the slippages noted in this chapter. In another sense, however, systemic reform seems less than grand, because while changes are promoted, those changes are located within the current system rather than in the parameters of the system itself.

Conclusion

I have argued, that while systemic reformers define well the problem of education, the solution they offer is problematic in a number of ways. This seems an odd claim at first: If a problem is systemic, how can the solution not be? Well, the simple fact is that the solution reformers offer, making the system more coherent through the alignment of relevant policies, is just one possible answer. The focus on coherence through alignment makes sense, but only if many assumptions, which were not true under the extant system, suddenly become so. The data from this study suggest this is a naive hope.

There is another point as well. If the goal is to improve teaching and learning, focusing on creating and aligning new and old policies seems to be an indirect means at best. Policy is a blunt instrument, and little evidence exists showing that policy can directly affect the basic teaching–learning relationship.

In chapter 9, I argue that those interested in reforming schools should shift goals from a focus on coherence to a focus on ideas. I then review two strategies which may prove more viable than the systemic solution.

NOTE

1. Thompson, Spillane, and Cohen (1994) suggest that another competitor for state spokesperson was the School Development Unit, which was given primary responsibility for big chunks of PA 25—accreditation, the annual education reports, and school improvement process.

Chapter 9

Looking Ahead:
The Prospects for Systemic Reform
and Change in U.S. Schools

On one reading, this study represents a success story. A state that relied for a long time on local change efforts saw state-level actors offer a range of new ideas and policies designed to give all children access to powerful learning. Those initiatives, combined with national and local factors, influenced changes in teachers' practices. Before encountering reforms, these four teachers' reading, writing, and mathematics practices reflected conventional skills-based approaches. Knowledge consisted of discrete, hierarchical skills; teaching was textbook-based and didactic; and learning was passive. Today, constructivist approaches are evident in some form in each teacher's classroom. Curriculum materials are more complex and more engaging. Teaching is less about telling and more about understanding. Learning opportunities are more varied and learners are more active. The cases can be interpreted to suggest that ideas matter and that teachers can and will change their instructional practices.

A second reading proves to be more puzzling. Reformers hope that their efforts change teachers' practices in coherent and consistent ways. The result seems just the reverse: Teachers' practices were more similar before the current reform movement than now. Today, one sees instances of manifestly ambitious instruction, wherein teachers and students engage new ideas, new texts, and new purposes. One also sees teaching that looks manifestly familiar, with worksheet knowledge, drill and practice instruction, and the emphasis on right answers. One also sees a lot of teaching that reflects a mix of old and new; a new text or a new instructional strategy is used to advance conventional ends. This range of instruction suggests that reformers have received more than they bargained for. Teachers' practices have changed, but not all of them, and not necessarily in the same powerful ways.

In chapter 8, I argue that, while systemic reformers offer a helpful analysis of the problem of education, the solution they advance is suspect. I illustrate that assertion by describing four instances where slippages emerged between the systemic solution and the experience of Michigan policymakers, administrators, and teachers. Based on those slippages, I argue that significant questions surface around the notion of coherence and the nature of systemic reform as a system-changing approach.

If that argument holds, then the prospects for the systemic reform agenda seem dim. In this chapter, I sketch an alternative. First, rather than focus on coherence, I suggest focusing on ideas as a means of leveraging educational change. Second, rather than taking a top-down, state-based approach (or, alternatively, a bottom-up, school-based strategy) I suggest adopting a middle-ground approach.

IDEAS AS LEVERS OF CHANGE

The systemic agenda focuses on policy coherence and alignment as a means of educational change. This study suggests, however, that coherence is less important than are ideas. Whether or not these four teachers perceived coherence among state, district, and school policies is unrelated to whether or not they made any changes in their pedagogy. More important is whether a teacher perceived ideas (from whatever source) as new, provocative, and a challenge to his or her extant thinking and practice. Promoting new ideas, then, may be a more powerful change strategy than promoting coherence and alignment (Ball & Cohen, 1995; Grant, 1997b; Weiss, 1990). As Meier (1995) points out, "A good idea has a natural habit of growing" (p. 40).

Ideas can take many shapes (e.g., a new way to think about numbers, a new approach to teaching writing, or a new sense about how students engage text) and can come from many sources (e.g., subject-matter frameworks, textbooks, workshop presentations, or university courses). Regardless of the form or source, we see the importance of ideas in every case of substantive change in the Michigan teacher cases. Paula Goddard's reading practice reflects her interest in the idea that children could benefit from reading literature and that skills should be taught in a real context. Frank Jensen's writing practice reflects his interest in the idea that students need more opportunities to write and that one of those opportunities could take the form of a big book for younger learners. Bonnie Jones' mathematics practice reflects her interest in the ideas that students must think about mathematics conceptually, that they must know and use a range of mathematical strategies, and that they must do mathematics in real-world contexts.

Conversely, when ideas were perceived as nothing particularly new or as unduly threatening, little or no change is effected. Jensen's modest changes in his reading practice reflect his sense that there was little in either the new state reading policy or the newly adopted district reading textbook that challenged his extant views. Marie Irwin knew that new ideas about teaching mathematics were in the air. She ignored them and maintained her traditional mathematics practice largely because of her personal discomfort with mathematics in general, and with new teaching approaches (e.g., mathematical manipulatives) in particular.

The variation in these responses reminds us that ideas guarantee no particular result. How a teacher responds to a new idea or reform reflects an interaction of several factors. First, teachers may not interpret the instantiation of ideas, in policies, textbooks, and the like, as representing new and challenging ideas. Jones and Jensen had access to the same ideas about reading, writing, and mathematics, but they made very different sense of them. Second, teachers may not have the personal and professional resources necessary to act. Jones knew that new ideas about writing were in the air as Irwin sensed in mathematics. Jones ignored them, however, for reasons similar to Irwin: Jones was uncomfortable with her own knowledge about and ability to write. She seemed interested in changing her writing practice, but acknowledged that it would call for even greater personal and professional resources than the changes she made in reading and mathematics. Finally, teachers may not have adequate organizational support. Here the case of Goddard's response to new ideas in mathematics is instructive. Given some initial school-level support, Goddard embraced new approaches to mathematics and made numerous changes in her instructional practice. When that support was withdrawn and a new set of ideas (i.e., the reading textbook pilot) was introduced, Goddard reversed course in mathematics. Ideas, then, represent the potential for change rather than a sure thing. Without them, however, little substantive change occurs.

If ideas act as levers of change, then three points are important. One is that teachers need access to more sources of ideas (Darling-Hammond, 1990; Hertert, 1996; Meier, 1995). State policies were one source of ideas from which teachers drew, though they were not necessarily the most important and clearly they were not the only one. State actors can probably do more to promote new ideas, but if teachers, like their students, need multiple opportunities to engage ideas in order to understand them, then it makes sense to broaden the marketplace for ideas.

The second point is that the ideas offered need to be substantive. Teachers routinely complain about the pap presented at most workshops and inservices (Grant, 1997a). Typically they perceive the topics to be irrelevant to their current needs or to be weakly developed and of little use. Teachers want new, demonstrably sound ideas about teaching and learning their subject matters. Their experience tells them, however, that they will rarely get what they want.

Finally, ideas need support to grow. The simple fact is that the current professional development system is hard ground for ideas. Not only are the ideas presented often of weak quality, but even when substantive ideas are offered, they are generally offered in pedantic fashion (Grant, 1997a; Little, 1989). Workshops are ubiquitous despite the fact that they often represent the worst of educational practice—bite-sized information delivered by "talking head" presenters in one and one-half hours after school. Teachers scoff at such sessions, and for good reason. As one teacher put it, "If we taught like that, we'd be fired!" (Grant, 1997a, p. 277). For teachers to change their instructional practices, they need to see and experience good pedagogy themselves.

There probably will never be enough time and money to meet all the needs teachers have. Nevertheless, without efforts to make professional development more about educating, or teaching and learning, than training, it is hard to imagine real and sustainable changes happening in more than a few classrooms. This matters, because as Fullan (1996) notes, "We cannot improve student learning for all or most students without improving teacher learning for most or all teachers" (p. 423).

Changing teachers' practice is an enormously complex matter (Fullan, 1993) because a range of policy, organizational, and individual factors figure into the development of teachers' practices. Influencing these factors, however, are ideas about new ways to think about and approach instruction. The power of ideas to spark instructional change is evidenced by the fact that, even given few sources, many weak ideas, and poor pedagogical practices, teachers still seek out ideas and work with them in their classrooms. With a bit more help, they may do even more.

TWO STRATEGIES FOR LEVERAGING CHANGE

This study suggests that top-down, grand theories like systemic reform are problematic. Others (Clune, 1993; Cohen, 1995; Fullan, 1996) agree, though the particulars of their critiques vary. The alternative solutions vary as well, but they can be loosely grouped into two camps. One camp promotes a bottom-up strategy where the impetus for changing teachers' practices comes from local sources. The other camp does not dismiss local efforts. Advocates of a middle-ground strategy, however, argue that state and national actors can positively influence instructional change.

Working From the Bottom Up

The bottom-up strategy is rooted in assumptions that real change is a local phenomenon and that governmental action is, at best, inconsequential (Chubb & Moe, 1990; Cuban, 1984; Sizer, 1996). Meier (1995), founder of the widely known Central Park East schools and perhaps the most articulate spokesperson for bottom-up change, directly rebuts the systemic argument. "Top-down mandates have pretty much reached their limits," Meier asserts (p. 101). Sympathetic with the reformers' concern about widespread school failure, she nevertheless argues that what schools need are "fewer rules, not more of them" (p. 37).

The argument for bottom-up approaches is strong. First, while portraits of failing schools are numerous (Fine, 1991; Kozol, 1991), portraits of strong, school-based programs (Lieberman, 1995b; Lightfoot, 1983; Wood, 1992) continue to surface. These examples give credence to the observation that "reform actually happens in a single school, even a single classroom, at a time" (Kirp & Driver, 1995, p. 608). Second, good schools owe their success to a wide range of factors. Largely absent from the list of important factors, however, is state or national policy. Although ideas are central to the Central Park East schools, Meier discounts the influence of policy. "We will not achieve the reforms we need by fiat," she argues (Meier, 1995, p. 36). Third, a bottom-up approach centers reform where it needs to be, in classrooms and in the teaching and learning of school subjects (Cohen, 1995; Tyack & Cuban, 1995). In this view, policy is a blunt instrument at best, ill suited to influence the "core technologies" of teaching and learning (Hawley et al., 1984; Rowan, 1990). Finally, as many observers note, the bottom-up approach may be the only game in town, given the ability of classroom teachers to make and remake policy. Kirst and Walker (1971) make the point succinctly: The fate of any reform lies in the "pocket veto" of the nation's teachers (p. 505). Real change, then, comes from the extraordinary efforts of school-based teachers and administrators (McLaughlin, 1990). In fact, local actors are so central to instructional change, that Fullan (1996), argues that the only important coherence is that which exists in the minds of classroom teachers. To pursue coherence at other levels may help, but "only when greater clarity and coherence are achieved in the minds of the majority of teachers will we have any chance of success" (p. 421).

A bottom-up strategy has much to recommend it, but it is problematic. One concern emerges around the notion of coherence as a state of teachers' minds. If one definition of coherence is seeing no conflicts among ideas, then Jensen is the only teacher in this sample who fits. Each of the others, to one or another degree and in one or another subject matter, were confused, and uncertain and unsure about their practices. Given the choice, it is hard to believe the self-professed but coherent efforts of a teacher like Jensen are more powerful than the fledgling efforts of teachers like Jones and Goddard, and, to a lesser extent, Irwin. A second concern is the nagging sense that bottom-up approaches have failed to make a difference for all kids. The work at Central Park East and a few other schools notwithstanding, it is hard to believe the necessary financial, professional, and personal resources are already available locally. Serving the nation's neediest students is clearly no mean task. To expect the existing teachers and schools to transform themselves with only their own meager resources at hand seems naive.

A Middle-Ground Strategy

Another solution comes from those observers who advocate a middle-ground strategy (Clune, 1993; Cohen, 1995; Donmoyer, 1995; Hertert, 1996; Scheurich & Fuller, 1995). These observers do not dismiss systemic reform, but neither do they believe it will meet its ambitious ends. As Clune (1993) notes, "Systemic policy tries to cure the problem of incremental change at the bottom through systemic changes at the top, but this merely relocates the problem without solving it" (p. 245). Middle-ground advocates understand and support the power of local change efforts. At the same time, however, they do not discount the potential for positive action by national and state actors. Common across this strategy is the belief that ideas matter and that good ideas can have many sources.

Many of those sources are located at the national level. Middle-ground advocates generally praise the efforts of groups like the National Council of Teachers of Mathematics, the National Academy of Education, the National Science Foundation, and the National Resource Council. Each responded to the call to reform by producing works that are both thoughtful and useable by teachers. These documents are a rich source of ideas about teaching and learning and are a potentially powerful influence on teachers' instructional practices.

They have no power, however, if teachers never see them. This study and others (Grant, 1996, 1997a) indicate that teachers generally have little direct awareness of national reform efforts. One possible role for state-level actors could be to act as a clearinghouse for new practices and materials. Final decisions would be in hands of local actors, but the state would provide a valuable service by more directly connecting teachers and new ideas. This action would also reduce the strain on the typically thin state resources available for curriculum work.

Other possible state-level actions might focus on professional development. New York Commissioner for Education, Richard Mills, for example, talks about creating a "great league" of professional development experts who can rethink the way professional development is offered (Grant, 1997a). This will be no easy task because professional development is currently highly decentralized, and assembling all the providers is probably impossible. State-level actors could, however, push for quality professional development through a variety of actions. States might, for example, reward forward-acting districts with more professional development funds, while demanding that recalcitrant districts meet with state-approved consultants to develop appropriate professional development plans. States might also encourage the development of demonstration sites where a range of approaches to professional development can be explored, researched, and promoted. Finally, states might take a more active role in promoting conversations among teachers. Some of those conversations could be local, but the technical capacity to link teachers across states and countries is increasingly available. State-level actors could play a key role in helping teachers see the potential for professional growth through collegial involvement.

As these examples suggest, a middle-ground approach neither leaves local actors on their own nor underestimates the potential for national and state influence over educational change. It does, however, recast the state role in a key sense. State-level actors may not control the educational change agenda as in the systemic approach, but they would play a vital role in mediating and encouraging change in local schools and classrooms. A middle-ground strategy does not absolve states of their responsibility to pursue equality of opportunity for all kids, but it does allow for and support teachers and schools who are attempting ambitious work.

In advocating ideas as a lever of change, I believe that states can serve teachers better by expanding beyond their traditional policymaking role to include actions that strike more directly at teachers' work—encouraging the development and spread of new ideas and pushing for changes in the professional development system. Such actions may seem like a dilution of state authority. In the long run, however, they may make more sense and have a greater effect than the more narrow policy-based approach advocated by systemic reformers.

Conclusion

In the end I am persuaded that a middle-ground strategy—one that brings a variety of resources together to support the efforts of local actors—is the best approach. I also believe that the American public in general, and educators in particular, owe systemic reformers a debt. While their great hopes are likely to go unrealized, systemic advocates have pushed us to think hard about the nature of American education and about what it might take to make real changes in classrooms.

A middle-ground strategy lacks the grandeur and sweep of the systemic solution. It lacks the democratic and egalitarian vision of a bottom-up approach. My hope, however, is that it marries the best of those visions in a way that honors the good work of those closest to students, while never believing that we cannot do more.

Appendix:
Research Design

Data alone cannot tell a story.

—Buchmann (1984)

This book grew out of my dissertation research (Grant, 1994). That study developed from a larger research project concerned with the relationships between state instructional policy and teachers' classroom practices. The Educational Policy and Practice Study (EPPS) explores issues of mathematics and reading policy and practice in Michigan, California, and South Carolina. As an EPPS field worker, I was interested in teachers' responses to these new initiatives. The more time I spent with teachers, however, the more curious I became about the range of reforms they faced. I turned this interest into my principal research question: How do teachers respond to multiple reforms?

I investigated that question with four Michigan elementary school teachers. Each had originally been contacted for the EPPS study; each subsequently agreed to allow my explorations into other reforms. I chose to study these teachers primarily because they represented an array of contexts: rural, suburban, and urban areas; strong and weak instructional guidance systems; and regular and alternative schools. Using a field-study approach, I used interviews, observations, and document analysis to construct case studies of each teacher. I looked specifically at reading, writing, and mathematics reforms across the cases. The cases illustrate how these teachers responded to an array of reforms, how their responses were similar or different, and what their responses suggested about the role of teacher as policymaker.

After finishing the dissertation, I became interested in how cases of teachers and reforms might help us to understand the growing movement toward systemic reform. Using some of the EPPS data we collected in California, Penelope Peterson, Angela Shojgreen-Downer, and I explored how three elementary school teachers understood mathematics reforms in the context of a state systemic effort (Grant et al., 1996). That work helped me see how I might reframe my dissertation to discuss more broadly the prospects for the systemic reform agenda.

SITE SELECTION

The more than 20 schools and 6 districts selected for the EPPS study in Michigan represent a range of socioeconomic and demographic characteristics. Districts vary by socioeconomic status, size, ethnic population, and geography. They include large urban, medium-urban, suburban, and rural settings. Schools are similarly distributed. Also varied is the response to reforms and the form of instructional guidance system at hand (e.g., strong–weak central office control).

These characteristics are represented well in my study. Although two districts and three schools cannot possibly mirror the field, the strong contrasts between the districts and among the schools proved helpful. The approach toward instructional guidance in Derry and Hamilton varies significantly. District administrators in Derry take a laissez-faire approach. For example, textbooks are adopted district-wide, but the central office does not monitor their use. In contrast, Hamilton central office administrators have a strong and coordinated instructional system. District-developed tests are aligned with textbook units, the teaching of which is closely monitored. District responses to reforms also vary. Hamilton administrators react cautiously to new initiatives (Spillane, 1993, 1998). Derry administrators generally tend to be open to innovations (Jennings, 1996).

The schools also contrast in many ways. Although roughly the same size (approximately 300 students), Donnelly-King Elementary, Sanford Heights Elementary, and Sheldon Court Academic Center vary by the type of school, student population, socioeconomic status, the principal's role, and the school mission. All are public schools, but Sheldon Court Academic Center is a public-supported alternative school which operates outside most district regulations. SCAC also differs from the other schools in having a substantial number of poor and minority students. Donnelly-King and Sanford Heights students are predominately White, but Donnelly-King students come from working-class families while Sanford Heights students are from middle- and upper-middle-class homes. SCAC students are almost exclusively African-American and from poor or working-class families. The principals played a different role in each school. Michael Adams, the Donnelly-King principal, played a largely passive role. He rarely visited classrooms; allowed teachers autonomy in choosing instructional methods, materials, and content; and provided little schoolwide leadership. By contrast, Tim Nettles and Natalie Simon, the respective Sanford Heights and SCAC principals, provided much more instructional direction to their teachers and played a more active role in crafting the schools' missions. Those missions were another point of variance. Simon and the SCAC staff saw their charge as providing a strict, supportive environment for teaching and learning basic academic skills. Nettles and the Sanford Heights staff had a different mission—supporting students' language development by building a literate environment. Adams and the Donnelly-King staff had no explicit school mission.

I chose to work in these diverse settings because I was interested in seeing how reforms play out in different contexts. Gaining access to the schools and classrooms through the EPPS project enabled me to capitalize on the differences already apparent in these sites.

TEACHER SELECTION

The EPPS study focuses on grades 2 and 5 because teachers' knowledge and beliefs about subject matter and their instructional practices seem to vary from lower- to upper-elementary grades. One dimension of the project explores exemplary teachers' practices. The bulk of the sample, however, are cases of what Shulman (1983) calls the "probable"—studies of teachers in a range of ordinary situations. The four teachers in this study fit that description. They were recruited based on recommendations by principals, district administrators, or both, as experienced, regular teachers who were responding to reading and mathematics reforms, and were willing to allow a researcher's interviews and observations during an extended period of time. One might argue that Bonnie Jones is an exemplary teacher; she seems an outlier both among her local peers and within this study. This was not apparent when she was recruited, however, because the big changes in her approaches to teaching and learning appeared after this study began. My early field notes and interviews suggested a teacher who was quite traditional.

The teachers in this study vary along several dimensions such as gender, grade level, years of experience, school and district context, kinds of students, interest and involvement with reforms, and life experiences. Not all of these factors were relevant to understanding how and why teachers responded to reforms as they did. For example, I could attach no significance to the teachers' gender or relative years of teaching experience. Other factors, however, such as the school context and the teacher's life experiences emerged as highly relevant. Being able to look at the similarities and differences in such factors across the cases proved invaluable to my analysis.

DATA COLLECTION

While data collection centered on observations of and interviews with the four teachers profiled, other data sources also proved important. Those sources included interviews with school principals, district administrators, and state officials. Also, classroom documents (e.g., textbooks, tests, and assignments) and district, state, and national documents (e.g., policy statements and tests) were used.

Teacher Observations and Interviews

I observed and interviewed each teacher for several years. I visited Bonnie Jones, Frank Jensen, and Marie Irwin each for 3 years from 1991 to 1993. I visited Paula Goddard for 2 years from 1992 to 1993. I observed each teacher at least twice each year, usually for the whole school day. Formal interviews followed each observation. I also completed several short telephone interviews with each teacher throughout the school year.

Observations. The night before each observation, I conducted a short telephone interview with the teacher about her or his plans for the day. I inquired about the array of lessons, kinds of activities, types of materials, and whether she or he had done similar things in the past. These preobservation interviews helped me (re)orient myself to the teacher and classroom and prepared me for the day.

During the observation, I sat at the back or side of the room so that I could hear both teacher and students and observe facial and body gestures. I also walked around and talked quietly with students as they worked on assignments. Staying the whole day allowed me multiple opportunities to talk informally with the teacher during class breaks.

I noted these informal conversations along with the handwritten notes I took throughout each observation.[1] On the right-hand side of each page, I recorded as much of the explicit classroom instruction as possible (e.g., teacher and student talk, assignments, boardwork). On the left-hand side, I noted questions, conjectures, and extra information (e.g., textbook titles and publishers). I also made careful sketches of the classroom interior including the location, the arrangement of desks, the types and numbers of ancillary equipment and materials (e.g., reference books, globes, computers), and the kinds of informational posters and student work displayed on classroom walls. I also noted the gender and race or ethnicity of each student.

I made these notes using the observation protocol constructed by the EPPS team and based on the observation guides developed for the Teacher Education and Learning to Teach study conducted by the National Center for Research on Teacher Education (NCRTE) (Ball & McDiarmid, 1990a).

The protocol helped me organize my observations by emphasizing textbook use, instructional representations, discourse patterns, and student grouping arrangements. I did not modify the protocol for my research other than to add similar questions about writing, science, health, and cooperative learning to those written for reading and mathematics.

The observation protocol also served to structure my expanded field notes. After each observation, I organized my field notes in line with the protocol structure. Typically this meant an introduction, a narrative description of the observation, and responses to a series of analytic questions. The introduction established a context for the visit. After the first observation, I used the introduction to note relevant changes in the teacher's attention to reforms, classroom practices, and personal experiences. The narrative described the range of lessons, activities, interactions, and materials that emerged during the visit. I inserted illustrative examples of discourse between teacher and students as well as observer notes recording perceptions of what I saw. Writing the narrative this way helped me capture the details of the day. It also helped me form and reform a "big picture" view of the teacher and her or his response to reforms. The last section of the expanded field notes called for brief responses to a series of analytic questions. These questions probed the kinds of texts available and how they were used, the sources of instructional representations and the forms they took, the variety of discourse and interaction patterns between teachers and students, the way students were organized and grouped for instruction, and if and how they changed during the day. Answering these questions was helpful in two ways. First, they forced me to reflect on the observations and my description in the narrative. As a result, I frequently found myself rethinking and revising parts of the narrative as I worked through the questions. Second, the questions provided a measure of consistency across the observations. Keeping track of each teacher's responses to multiple reforms was made easier by using a common set of analytic questions.

These expanded field notes were valuable throughout the study. During the data collection stage, they became an ongoing record of classroom events and interactions. They also provoked initial conjectures and themes which became fodder for future observations. In that sense, these notes formed an important bridge between data collection and analysis.

Interviews. Writing up field notes occasionally sparked questions which I pursued in follow-up telephone interviews. These unstructured conversations were one of the two types of informal interviews I conducted. I also used three structured interview protocols. One was a postobservation guide used immediately after an observation. The second was a longer interview which focused on teachers' responses to reforms. The last was a separate interview protocol I designed to explore teachers' responses to multiple reforms.

Telephone interviews were of two types: preobservation and follow-up. The follow-up interview was usually organized around one or more specific questions that arose in thinking, writing, or both, about an observation. The preobservation interviews, as described previously, focused on the next day's visit. Teachers were always responsive to these calls and often answered at length. During these calls, I made handwritten notes which I either typed individually or added to the relevant expanded field notes.

The postobservation and reforms interviews followed structured protocols modified by the EPPS team from the guides developed in the NCRTE project (Ball & McDiarmid, 1990a). The postobservation interview was approximately 30 minutes in duration. The reforms interview was considerably longer; some lasted as long as 2 hours. I audiotaped each of these interviews, which were then transcribed by EPPS secretaries.

The postobservation interview highlighted several dimensions of each lesson. Questions focused on what teachers were trying to teach, what means they used, what they thought students might have learned, how the lesson differed (if at all) from previous years, and how (if at all) teachers planned to follow up the lesson. Teachers were also asked how the lesson fit into their curricula and whether the lesson might be considered typical.

The reforms interview had four parts. One section dealt with reading and mathematics reforms and inquired about what changes (if any) the teacher had made in her or his practice and what changes (if any) she or he understood were occurring at the school, district, and state level. A second section dealt with teachers' learning and focused on the opportunities available to learn about reforms. A third piece looked at assessment. Here, I explored what standardized assessments were given in the school, and how teachers interpreted their import. The last part, labeled "pedagogical biography," asked teachers to talk about their experiences in school as both students and teachers.

Like the EPPS observation guides, I found the structured interview protocols helpful in my study. Again, I made no major modifications other than adding questions relevant to other reforms. I did, however, create an additional interview guide which I administered either separately or along with the reforms interview. The "multiple reforms" interview probed issues around responding to various reforms simultaneously. The interview began when I asked the teacher to respond to a list of reforms I compiled from previous interviews. Establishing this list helped me to understand the range of reforms to which each teacher was currently attending. Then, I asked a series of questions about how teachers interpreted the reforms individually and in concert, how reforms had influenced their thinking and practice, how others around them interpreted and responded to these reforms, and whether responding to reforms had implications for their personal lives. I also probed how teachers managed the array of ideas, methods, and materials, occasioned by new initiatives. These questions proved invaluable because teachers seemed to reflect on both the daily and larger ramifications of reforms for their personal and professional lives. For Jones and Goddard, in particular, these questions provoked long responses about the difficulties in learning about and responding to reforms.

Other Data Sources

Other data sources also became important as I constructed the cases. These sources included interviews with principals, district administrators, and state officials; and documents collected from the classroom, school, district, and state and from the national reform efforts. They helped me to develop new perspectives on the data I collected through the teacher observations and interviews.

Interviews. A part of my EPPS work included interviewing school, district, and state-level actors. State-level interviews were semistructured and focused on a particular topic (e.g., the state reading policy, the MEAP mathematics test). The interviews ranged from 30 to 90 minutes and were audiotaped and transcribed.

Nancy Jennings, an EPPS colleague, and I interviewed school and district administrators in Derry. We interviewed the Donnelly-King principal, Michael Adams, and his replacement, Tim Kite (in 1992), once each. We interviewed the district reading coordinator, Teresa Jensen, on two occasions. Finally, we interviewed the Derry superintendent, Richard Dole, once. In Hamilton, I did only one interview. Along with David Cohen, an EPPS project director, I interviewed two members of the district research and evaluation unit. These administrators were responsible for the district monitoring and assessment systems. In cases in which I did not do interviews (e.g., with the Sanford Heights principal), I used transcripts provided by other EPPS researchers.

I also interviewed several state-level actors. Either by myself or with David Cohen, Nancy Jennings, and James Spillane, I interviewed several individuals responsible for the state reading and mathematics policies and for revisions in the state MEAP test. We conducted these interviews between 1989 and 1992. These interviews, like those at the school and district levels, proved helpful as I constructed a nested context in which the four teachers worked.

Documents. I collected and reviewed a variety of documents. At the classroom level, I gathered textbooks, homework, in-class assignments, unit tests, and chapter tests. Teachers also gave me copies of materials they gathered at inservices and workshops. The teacher-made materials provided examples of instructional representations. The professional development materials provided a context to talk about what the teacher learned or valued.

At the school and district levels, I collected relevant curriculum documents and copies of standardized test scores. At the state level, my colleagues and I collected a mass of documents related to old and new state curriculum policies and to old and new versions of the MEAP. A close reading of these documents provided additional perspectives on teachers' interpretations of reforms.

DATA ANALYSIS

Data collection and analysis activities interacted throughout this study. I spent considerable time poring over interview transcripts and observation notes after the data were collected, but the analysis of the data really began during the collection phase. Pushing myself to think about conjectures and themes while still gathering data helped me form and reform interview questions and observation points, test emerging ideas, and consider alternative perspectives.

I used several approaches in analyzing the data. One was coding and chunking the data into preliminary categories. Another was drafting analytic memos as a means of exploring developing ideas and themes. A third approach was peer review of analytic memos and case drafts. Finally, I kept a reflective journal for the last 2 years I worked on this study. These diverse approaches helped me to analyze and reanalyze the data as I teased out themes, insights, and illustrative points.

I began my analysis by reading through and hand coding each teacher's interview and observation data. These codes helped me to construct a preliminary set of analytic categories. Some of those categories were views of subject matters, instructional practices, use of textbooks, influence of tests, student groupings, regularities, relationships, ways of managing reforms, and personal background. I then created four documents (one for each teacher), and entered these draft categories. I cut and pasted the relevant data from the interviews, observations (which were in word-processing files), and various documents into the appropriate categories. This rough cut reconstituted the data into manageable chunks. It also helped me evaluate the quality of the data; I could easily see, for example, where my data on a particular reform were thin. I could then seek additional data during the next interview or observation. Chunking the data also helped me begin to build themes and to see similarities and differences across the teachers' contexts, opportunities to learn, classroom practices, and responses to reforms.

At this point, my advisor, David Cohen, suggested I "spend time with the ideas." As a result, I wrote a series of six analytic memos in which I explored nascent themes such as autonomy and uncertainty, and organizational and personal resources. I also explored categories of reform responses such as selective attention, coexistence, proceduralizing, blurring distinctions, and adding on. In each instance, I inserted relevant examples or illustrations from my data. Working with the ideas in this fashion proved invaluable because I was able to write my way into the data in an exploratory fashion and play with ideas, evidence, and arguments in manageable ways.

After writing about what would become the major constructs of the study, I began initial drafts of the teacher cases. To do so, I went back to the chunked versions of the data. Before writing any text, however, I combed through my categories and illustrative data. I eliminated some categories, combined others, and created some new categories. I then constructed draft cases.

Writing and analytic thinking are clearly connected. In fact, Hays, Roth, Ramsey, and Foulke (1983) argue that "*written* language makes logical and analytic thought possible" (p. x). Constructing conceptual categories and chunking the data, writing analytic memos, and drafting cases were important means of analyzing the data. Another useful approach involved sharing my writing with others. I shared the analytic memos with members of my committee and a few graduate student peers. As part of our regular meetings, I shared case drafts with my EPPS colleagues. The ethic of sharing one's writing with colleagues is a vital dimension of the EPPS project. The thoughtful responses helped me consider alternative perspectives and see which ideas needed further development and illustration.

One last approach to data analysis was to keep a personal journal. In the fall of 1992, I began maintaining a daily log as a way to get myself into the day's writing.[2] This journal served several purposes because I found it a convenient place in which to note nascent ideas, to outline developing ideas, and to think across the cases.

WRITING CASE STUDIES

As Buchmann (1994) observed, data alone tell no story. Instead, data allow the telling of many stories and they do not judge how those stories might be told. An important dimension of one's methodology is the rhetorical form chosen.

As I considered ways to tell the stories of these teachers' responses to reforms, I explored two options. The one I rejected took a thematic approach. I would have identified and described key themes in teachers' responses to reforms, such as the need to respond to multiple reforms;

the interaction of policy, organizational, and individual resources; and the management of reforms in the context of practice. Illustrations of each theme would be drawn from across the teacher cases.

I rejected this approach for two reasons. First, I wanted the themes to develop from the teachers' stories rather than to seem imposed on them. More importantly, however, I wanted to emphasize the richness and complexity of these teachers' stories. A thematic approach would not have accommodated this need.

The approach I settled on might be described as a modified comparative case study. Four teacher cases form the core of the study. Those cases focus on each teacher's response to a range of reforms—reading, writing, and mathematics, and I examine:

1. how teachers learn about and make sense of the reforms in light of their past practice;
2. changes in teachers' instructional practices; and
3. changes in teachers' assumptions about teaching and learning.

Two things about this approach differ from conventional case studies. First, rather than construct a separate chapter comparing teachers' responses across the cases, I decided to use epilogues at the end of each set of cases. These epilogues were opportunities to both summarize the cases and to illustrate the cross-teacher and cross-reform variation in teachers' responses. The second difference can be seen in chapter 7. In early drafts, I attempted to address the question of why teachers respond as they do within the cases. The result suffered two problems. One was bulk. Exploring responses to multiple reforms created very thick cases. Adding yet another big section explaining those responses made the cases unwieldy. The other problem was conceptual. Because I wanted to develop the constructs of policy, organizational, and personal influences as explanatory factors, I concluded that the most sensible approach was to pull these ideas from the cases and to write a separate chapter. There, I could explicate the constructs, demonstrate their interaction, and provide illustrations from across the cases.

REFRAMING TO EXPLORE THE PROSPECTS
FOR SYSTEMIC REFORM

The core of this book comes from my dissertation study of the cross-teacher and cross-reform variation in teachers' responses to reading, writing, and mathematics reforms. The principal revision for this book was to reframe that study to consider prospects for the movement toward systemic reform.

One part of that effort meant reading and reflecting on the large systemic change literature, particularly for the assumptions inherent in that theory. Another part involved reviewing the state-level data my EPPS colleagues and I collected to tease out how the Michigan policymakers' efforts compared with the systemic vision. Finally, I reexamined the teacher cases and the explanations for their responses to expand and illustrate my analysis of the systemic argument

NOTES

1. I tried to tape record classroom lessons on a couple of occasions, but found the results disappointing (e.g., difficulty hearing students' voices) and so abandoned the practice.
2. The idea of using a journal entry as a means of starting one's daily work comes from Steinbeck's (1969) *Journal of a Novel.* I highly recommend reading this text. Realizing that even writers as prolific as John Steinbeck can have bad days proved salutary on more than one occasion.

References

Adams, M. (1989). *Phonics and beginning reading instruction.* Champaign, IL: Reading Research and Education Center.

Adams, M. (1990). *Beginning to read: Thinking and learning about print.* Cambridge, MA: MIT Press.

Allington, R. (1980). Teacher interruption behaviors during primary-grade oral reading. *Journal of Educational Psychology, 72,* 371–377.

Altwerger, B., Edelsky, C., & Flores, B. (1987). Whole language: What's new? *Reading Teacher, 41,* 144–154.

Anderson, R., Hiebert, E., Scott, J., & Wilkenson, I. (1985). *Becoming a nation of readers.* Urbana: University of Illinois Center for the Study of Reading.

Applebee, A., Langer, J., & Mullis, I. (1987). *Learning to be literate in America: Reading, writing, and reasoning.* Princeton, NJ: Educational Testing Service.

Applebee, A., Lehr, F., & Auten, A. (1981). Learning to write in the secondary school: How and where. *English Journal, 70,* 78–82.

Atwell, N. (1987). *In the middle.* Upper Montclair, NJ: Boynton Cook.

Baker, L., & Brown, A. (1984). Metacognitive skills and reading. In P. D. Pearson (Ed.), *Handbook of reading research.* New York: Longman.

Ball, D. (1988). Unlearning to teach mathematics. *For the Learning of Mathematics, 8*(1), 40–48.

Ball, D. (1990a). *Halves, pieces, and twoths: Constructing representational contexts in teaching fractions.* East Lansing, MI: National Center for Research on Teacher Education.

Ball, D. (1990b). Reflections and deflections of policy: The case of Carol Turner. *Educational Evaluation and Policy Analysis, 12*(3), 263–275.

Ball, D. L., & Cohen, D. K. (1995, April). *What does the educational system bring to learning a new pedagogy of reading and mathematics?* Paper presented at the meeting of the American Educational Research Association, San Francisco, CA.

Ball, D. L., & McDiarmid, G. W. (1990a). *A study package for examining and tracking changes in teachers' knowledge* (Technical Series 89-1). East Lansing: National Center for Research on Teacher Education, Michigan State University.

Ball, D. L., & McDiarmid, G. W. (1990b). The subject matter preparation of teachers. In W. R. Houston (Ed.), *Handbook of research on teacher education* (pp. 437–449). New York: Macmillan.

Baratta-Lorton, M. (1976). *Mathematics their way.* Reading, MA: Addison-Wesley.

Barr, R., & Dreeben, R. (1983). *How schools work.* Chicago: University of Chicago Press.

Berman, P., & McLaughlin, M. (1977). *Federal programs supporting educational change, Vol VIII: Implementing and sustaining innovations.* Santa Monica, CA: Rand Corporation.

Boulton-Lewis, G., & Halford, G. (1992). The processing loads of young children's and teachers' representation of place value and implications for teaching. *Mathematics Education Research Journal, 4*(1), 1–23.

Brenna, B. (1995). The metacognitive reading strategies of five early readers. *Journal of Research in Reading, 18*(1), 52–62.

Brouillette, L. (1996). *A geology of school reform: The successive restructurings of a school district.* Albany: State University of New York Press.

Brown, J., Collins, A., & Duguid, P. (1989). Situated cognition and the culture of learning. *Educational Researcher, 18*(1), 32–42.

Buchmann, M. (1984). The priority of knowledge and understanding in teaching. In L. Katz & J. Raths (Eds.), *Advances in teacher education, Vol. 1* (pp. 29–50). Norwood, NJ: Ablex.

Buchmann, M. (1986). Role over person: Morality and authenticity in teaching. *Teachers College Press, 87*(4), 527–543.

Byars, B. (1968). *The midnight fox.* New York: Puffin Books.

California Board of Education. (1987). *English-language arts framework for California public schools.* Sacramento: California State Department of Education.

California Board of Education. (1992). *Mathematics framework for the California public schools.* Sacramento: California State Department of Education.

Calkins, L. (1986). *The art of teaching writing.* Portsmouth, NH: Heinemann.

Campbell, P., & Bamberger, H. (1990). Implementing the standards: The vision of problem solving in the standards. *Arithmetic Teacher, 37*(9), 14–17.

Carter, K. (1993). The place of story in the study of teaching and teacher education. *Educational Researcher, 22*(1), 5–12.

Carver, R. (1992). Effect of prediction activities, prior knowledge, and text type upon amount comprehended: Using rauding theory to critique schema theory research. *Reading Research Quarterly, 27*(2), 164–174.

Cazden, C. (1992). *Whole language plus: Essays on literacy in the United States and New Zealand.* New York: Teachers College Press.

Chall, J. (1983). *Stages of reading development.* New York: McGraw-Hill.

Chubb, J., & Moe, T. (1990). *Politics, markets, and America's schools.* Washington, DC: Brookings Institute.

Clune, W. (1993). The best path to systemic and educational policy: Standard/centralized or differentiated/decentralized? *Educational Evaluation and Policy Analysis, 15*(3), 233–254.

Cohen, D. (1995). What is the system in systemic reform? *Educational Researcher, 24*(9), 11–17, 31.

Cohen, D., & Ball, D. (1990). Relations between policy and practice: A commentary. *Educational Evaluation and Policy Analysis, 12*(3), 249–256.

Cohen, D., & Barnes, C. (1993a). Conclusion: A new pedagogy for policy? In D. Cohen, M. McLaughlin, & J. Talbert (Eds.), *Teaching for understanding: Challenges for policy and practice* (pp. 240–275). San Francisco: Jossey-Bass.

Cohen, D., & Barnes, C. (1993b). Pedagogy and policy. In D. Cohen, M. McLaughlin, & J. Talbert (Eds.), *Teaching for understanding: Challenges for policy and practice* (pp. 207–239). San Francisco: Jossey-Bass.

Cohen, D., & Spillane, J. (1992). Policy and practice: The relations between governance and instruction. In G. Grant (Ed.), *Review of research in education* (Vol. 18, pp. 3–49). Washington, DC: American Educational Research Association.

Cohen, D., Spillane, J., Jennings, N., & Grant, S. G. (in press). *Reading policy: The Michigan reading policy.* New York: Teachers College Press.

Connelly, F. M., & Clandinin, D. J. (1990). Stories of experience and narrative inquiry. *Educational Researcher, 19*(4), 2–14.

Corbett, H., & Wilson, B. (1990). *Testing, reform, and rebellion.* Norwood, NJ: Ablex.

Courtland, M. C., & Welsh, R. (1990). A case study of a teacher's changing perceptions of the writing process: The second and third years. *English Quarterly, 23*(1–2), 62–79.

Cuban, L. (1984). *How teachers taught: Constancy and change in American classrooms, 1890–1980.* New York: Longman.

Cuban, L. (1990). Reforming again, again, and again. *Educational Researcher, 19*(1), 3–13.

Cusick, P. (1983). *The egalitarian ideal and the American high school.* New York: Longman.

Darling-Hammond, L. (1990). Instructional policy into practice: The power of the bottom over the top. *Educational Evaluation and Policy Analysis, 12*(3), 339–347.

Darling-Hammond, L., & McLaughlin, M. (1996). Policies that support professional development in an era of reform. In M. McLauglin & I. Oberman (Eds.), *Teacher learning: New policies, new practices* (pp. 202–219). New York: Teachers College Press.

Donmoyer, R. (1995). The rhetoric and reality of systemic reform: A critique of the proposed national science standards. *Theory Into Practice, 34*(1), 30–34.

Duncan, E., Quast, W., Haubner, M., & Cole, W. (1985). *Houghton Mifflin mathematics.* Boston: Houghton Mifflin.

Eicholz, R., & Young, S. (1991). *Addison-Wesley mathematics.* Reading, MA: Addison-Wesley.

Eisenhart, M., Shrum, J., Harding, J., & Cuthbert, A. (1988). Teacher beliefs: Definitions, findings, and directions. *Educational Policy, 2,* 51–70.

Elbaz, F. (1983). *Teacher thinking: A study of practical knowledge.* New York: Nichols Publishing.

Elmore, R., & McLaughlin, M. (1988). *Steady work: Policy, practice, and the reform of American education.* Santa Monica, CA: Rand.

Fenstermacher, G. (1979). A philosophical consideration of recent research on teacher effectiveness. In L. Shulman (Ed.), *Review of research in education 6* (pp. 157–185). Itaska, IL: F. E. Peacock Publishers.

Fenstermacher, G. (1986). A philosophy of research on teaching: Three aspects. In M. C. Whitrock (Ed.), *Handbook of research on teaching.* New York: Macmillan.

Fine, M. (1991). *Framing dropouts: Notes on the politics of an urban public high school.* Albany: State University of New York Press.

Firestone, W. (1989). Educational policy as an ecology of games. *Educational Researcher, 18*(7), 18–24.

Firestone, W., Fuhrman, S., & Kirst, M. (1989). *The progress of reform: An appraisal of state education initiatives.* New Brunswick, NJ: Center for Policy Research in Education.

Fiske, S., & Taylor, S. (1984). *Social cognition.* Reading, MA: Addison-Wesley.

Fuhrman, S. (1993a). The politics of coherence. In S. Fuhrman (Ed.), *Designing coherent education policy: Improving the system* (pp. 1–34). San Francisco: Jossey-Bass.

Fuhrman, S. (1993b). Preface. In S. Fuhrman (Ed.), *Designing coherent education policy: Improving the system* (pp. xi–xiii). San Francisco: Jossey-Bass.

Fullan, M. (1993). *Change forces.* New York: Falmer.

Fullan, M. (1996). Turning systemic thinking on its head. *Phi Delta Kappan, 77,* 420–423.

Glaser, R. (1984). Education and thinking: The role of knowledge. *American Psychologist, 39,* 93–104.

Goodman, K. (1986). *What's whole in whole language?* Portsmouth, NH: Heinemann.

Goodman, K., Shannon, P., Freeman, Y., & Murphy, S. (1988). *Report card on basal readers.* Katonah, NY: Richard C. Owen.

Goodson, I. (1992). *Studying teachers' lives.* New York: Teachers College Press.

Grant, S. G. (1991). The California History/Social Science Framework: A study in the de-professionalization of teachers. *Journal of Curriculum and Supervision, 6*(3), 213–221.

Grant, S. G. (1994). *The variation in teachers' responses to reading, writing, and mathematics reforms.* Unpublished doctoral dissertation, Michigan State University, East Lansing.

Grant, S. G. (1996). Locating authority over content and pedagogy: Cross-current influences on teachers' thinking and practice. *Theory and Research in Social Education, 24*(3), 237–272.

Grant, S. G. (1997a). Opportunities lost: Teachers learning about the New York State social studies framework. *Theory and Research in Social Education, 25*(3), 259–287.

Grant, S. G. (1997b). A policy at odds with itself: The tension between constructivist and traditional views in the New York State social studies framework. *Journal of Curriculum and Supervision, 13*(1), 92–113.

Grant, S. G., Peterson, P. L., & Shojgreen-Downer, A. (1996). Learning to teach mathematics in the context of systemic reform. *American Educational Research Journal, 33*(2), 509–541.

Graves, D. (1983). *Writing: Teachers and children at work.* Portsmouth, NH: Heinemann.

Gray, B., & Davies-Toth, M. (1990). *World of language.* Morristown, NJ: Silver Burdett & Ginn.

Greeno, J. (1991). Number sense as situated knowing in a conceptual domain. *Journal for Research in Mathematics Education, 22*(3), 170–218.

Guskey, T. (1996). Professional development in education: In search of the optimal mix. In T. Guskey & M. Huberman (Eds.), *Professional development in education: New paradigms and practices* (pp. 114–131). New York: Teachers College Press.

Hancock, M. (1993). Exploring the meaning-making process through the content of literature response journals: A case study investigation. *Research in the Teaching of English, 27*(4), 335–368.

Hargreaves, A. (1994). *Changing teachers, changing times: Teachers' work and culture in the postmodern age.* New York: Teachers College Press.

Harris, V. (1993). Literature-based approaches to reading instruction. In L. Darling-Hammond (Ed.), *Review of research in education* (Vol. 19, pp. 269–297). Washington, DC: American Educational Research Association.

Harste, J., & Burke, C. (1977). A new hypothesis for reading teacher research: Both teaching and learning of reading are theoretically based. In P. D. Pearson (Ed.), *Reading: Theory, research, and practice: Twenty-sixth yearbook of the National Reading Conference* (pp. 32–40). Clemson, SC: National Reading Conference.

Hawley, W., Rosenholtz, S., Goodstein, H., & Hasselbring, T. (1984). The need for a systematic approach to school reform. *Peabody Journal of Education, 4*, 1–14.

Hays, J., Roth, P., Ramsey, J., & Foulke, R. (Eds.). (1983). *The writer's mind: Writing as a mode of thinking.* Urbana, IL: National Council of Teachers of English.

Heaton, R. (1994). *Creating and studying a practice of teaching elementary mathematics for understanding.* Unpublished doctoral dissertation, Michigan State University, East Lansing.

Hertert, L. (1996). Systemic school reform in the 1990's: A local perspective. *Educational Policy, 10*(3), 379–398.

Hiebert, E., & Colt, J. (1989). Patterns of literature-based reading instruction. *The Reading Teacher, 43*, 14–20.

Holmes Group. (1986). *Tomorrow's teachers.* East Lansing, MI: Author.

Holzman, M. (1993). What is systemic change? *Educational Leadership, 51*(1), 18.

Hunter, M. (1983). *Mastery teaching.* El Segundo, CA: TIP.

Jennings, N. (1996). *Teachers learning from policy: Cases of the Michigan reading reform.* New York: Teachers College Press.

Kamii, C. (1993). Primary arithmetic: Children inventing their own procedures. *Arithmetic Teacher, 41*(4), 200–203.

Kingdon, J. (1984). *Agendas, alternatives, and public policies.* Boston: Little, Brown.

Kirp, D. L., & Driver, C. E. (1995). The aspirations of systemic reform meet the realities of localism. *Educational Administration Quarterly, 31*(4), 589–612.

Kirst, M., & Walker, D. (1971). An analysis of curriculum policy-making. *Review of Educational Research, 41*, 479–509.

Kozol, J. (1991). *Savage inequalities.* New York: Crown.

Kroll, L. (1990, April). *Making meaning in writing: A longitudinal study of young children's writing development.* Paper presented at the meeting of the American Educational Research Association, Boston, MA.

Kulleseid, E., & Strickland, D. (1989). *Literature, literacy, and learning.* Chicago: American Library Association.

Lampert, M. (1990). When the problem is not the question and the solution is not the answer. *American Educational Research Journal, 27*(1), 29–63.

Langer, J. (1984). Examining background knowledge and text comprehension. *Reading Research Quarterly, 19,* 468–481.

Lanier, J., & Little, J. (1986). Research on teacher education. In M. C. Whitrock (Ed.), *Handbook of research on teaching* (3rd ed., pp. 527–569). New York: Macmillan.

Lieberman, A. (1995a). Practices that support teacher development: Transforming conceptions of professional learning. *Phi Delta Kappan, 76*(8), 591–596.

Lieberman, A. (Ed.). (1995b). *The work of restructuring schools: Building from the ground up.* New York: Teachers College Press.

Lightfoot, S. (1983). *The good high school.* New York: Basic Books.

Lipsky, M. (1980). *Street level bureaucracy: Dilemmas of the individual in public services.* New York: Russell Sage Foundation.

Little, J. W. (1982). Norms of collegiality and experimentation: Workplace conditions of school success. *American Educational Research Journal, 19*(3), 325–340.

Little, J. W. (1989). District policy choices and teachers' professional development. *Educational Evaluation and Policy Analysis, 11*(2), 165–179.

Little, J. W., & McLaughlin, M. (1993). *Teachers' work: Individuals, colleagues, and contexts.* New York: Teachers College Press.

Lortie, D. (1975). *Schoolteacher: A sociological study.* Chicago: University of Chicago Press.

Lusi, S. F. (1997). *The role of state departments of education in complex school reform.* New York: Teachers College Press.

Mathematical Sciences Educational Board. (1989). *Everybody counts: A report to the nation on the future of mathematics education.* Washington, DC: National Academy Press.

McCandless-Simmons, S. (1990). *Discoveries in reading.* Crawfordsville, IN: Harcourt, Brace, & Jovanovich.

McDiarmid, W., Ball, D., & Anderson, C. (1989). Why staying one chapter ahead doesn't really work: Subject-specific pedagogy. In M. C. Reynolds (Ed.), *Knowledge base for the beginning teacher* (pp. 193–205). Oxford, UK: Pergamon Press.

McDonnell, L., & Elmore, R. (1987). Getting the job done: Alternative policy instruments. *Educational Evaluation and Policy Analysis, 9*(2), 133–152.

McGee, L. (1992). Focus on research: Exploring the literature-based reading revolution. *Language Arts, 69,* 529–537.

McKeachie, W. (Ed.). (1980). *New directions for teaching and learning.* San Francisco: Jossey-Bass.

McLaughlin, M. (1987). Learning from experience: Lessons from policy implementation. *Educational Evaluation and Policy Analysis, 9*(2), 171–178.

McLaughlin, M. (1990). The Rand Change Agent Study revisited: Macro perspectives and micro realities. *Educational Researcher, 19*(9), 11–16.

McNeil, L. (1988). *Contradictions of control.* New York: Routledge.

Meadows, B. (1990). The rewards and risks of shared leadership. *Phi Delta Kappan, 71*(7), 545–548.

Meier, D. (1995). *The power of their ideas: Lessons for America from a small school in Harlem.* Boston: Beacon.

Meyer, J., & Rowan, B. (1978). The structure of educational organizations. In M. Meyer (Ed.), *Environments and organizations.* San Francisco: Jossey-Bass.

Michigan State Board of Education. (1985). *Essential goals and objectives for writing.* Lansing: Michigan Department of Education.

Michigan State Board of Education. (1986). *Essential goals and objectives for reading education.* Lansing: Michigan Department of Education.

Michigan State Board of Education. (1990). *Essential goals and objectives for mathematics education.* Lansing: Michigan Department of Education.

Murname, R., & Levy, F. (1996). Teaching to new standards. In S. Fuhrman & J. O'Day (Eds.), *Rewards and reform: Creating educational incentives that work* (pp. 257–293). San Francisco: Jossey-Bass.

National Commission on Excellence in Education. (1983). *A nation at risk.* Washington, DC: U. S. Government Printing Office.

National Council of Teachers of Mathematics. (1989). *Curriculum and evaluation standards for school mathematics.* Reston, VA: Author.

National Council of Teachers of Mathematics. (1991). *Professional standards for school mathematics.* Reston, VA: Author.

Nisbett, R., & Ross, L. (1980). *Human inference: Strategies and shortcomings of social judgment.* Englewood Cliffs, NJ: Prentice-Hall.

O'Day, J., & Smith, M. (1993). Systemic reform and educational opportunity. In S. Fuhrman (Ed.), *Designing coherent education policy: Improving the system* (pp. 250–312). San Francisco: Jossey-Bass.

O'Dell, S. (1967). *The black pearl.* Prince Frederick, MD: Recorded Books.

Ogle, D. (1986). K-W-L: A teaching model that develops active reading of expository text. *Reading Teacher, 39,* 564–570.

O'Neil, J. (1993). Turning the system on its head. *Educational Leadership, 51*(1), 8–13.

Orfan, L., & Vogeli, B. (1988). *Silver Burdett mathematics.* Morristown, NJ: Silver Burdett & Ginn.

Paris, S., Cross, D., & Lipson, M. (1984). Informed strategies for learning: A program to improve children's reading awareness and comprehension. *Journal of Educational Psychology, 76,* 1239–1252.

Paris, S., Wasik, B., & Turner, J. (1991). The development of strategic readers. In R. Barr, M. Kamil, P. Mosenthal, & P. D. Pearson (Eds.), *Handbook of reading research, Volume II* (pp. 609–640). New York: Longman.

Pearson, P. D. (1989). Reading the whole language movement. *The Elementary School Journal, 90*(2), 231–241.

Pearson, P. D., & Johnson, D. (1991). *World of reading.* Morristown, NJ: Silver Burdett & Ginn.

Perkins, D., & Salomon, G. (1989). Are cognitive skills context-bound? *Educational Researcher, 18,* 16–25.

Peterson, P. (1990). Doing more in the same amount of time: Cathy Swift. *Educational Evaluation and Policy Analysis, 12*(3), 277–296.

Pikulski, J., & Cooper, J. (1991). *Houghton-Mifflin: The literature experience.* Boston: Houghton Mifflin.

Porter, A., Floden, R., Freeman, D., Schmidt, W., & Schwille, J. (1988). Content determinants in elementary school mathematics. In D. Grouws, T. Cooney, & D. Jones (Eds.), *Effective mathematics teaching.* Reston, VA: National Council of Teachers of Mathematics.

Pressman, J., & Wildavsky, A. (1974). *Implementation: How great expectations in Washington are dashed in Oakland.* Berkeley: University of California Press.

Putnam, R. (1992). Teaching the "hows" of mathematics for everyday life: A case study of a fifth-grade teacher. *Elementary School Journal, 93*(2), 163–177.

Rabinowitz, M., & Woolley, K. (1995). Much ado about nothing: The relation among computational skill, arithmetic word problem comprehension, and limited attentional resources. *Cognition and Instruction, 13*(1), 51–71.

Remillard, J. (1991). *Is there an alternative? An analysis of commonly used and distinctive elementary mathematics curricula.* (Elementary Subjects Center Series no. 91). East Lansing: Center for the Learning and Teaching of Elementary Subjects, Michigan State University.

Resnick, L. (1987). *Education and learning to think.* Washington, DC: National Academy Press.

Richardson, V. (1990). Significant and worthwhile change in teaching practice. *Educational Researcher, 19*(7), 10–18.

Richardson, V., Anders, P., Tidwell, D., & Lloyd, C. (1991). The relationship between teachers' beliefs and practices in reading comprehension instruction. *American Educational Research Journal, 28*(3), 559–586.

Rosenholtz, S. (1991). *Teacher's workplace: The social organization of schools.* New York: Teachers College Press.

Rowan, B. (1990). Applying conceptions of teaching to organizational reform. In R. Elmore (Ed.), *Restructuring schools.* San Francisco: Jossey-Bass.

Sarason, S. (1982). *The culture of school and the problem of change* (2nd ed.). Boston: Allyn & Bacon.

Sawyer, W. (1987). Literature and literacy: A review of research. *Language Arts, 64,* 33–39.

Scheurich, J., & Fuller, E. (1995). Is systemic reform the answer for schools and science education? Cautions from the field. *Theory Into Practice, 34*(1), 12–20.

Schwille, J., Porter, A., Belli, G., Floden, R., Freeman, D., Knappen, L., Kuhs, T., & Schmidt, W. (1983). Teachers as policy brokers in the content of elementary school mathematics. In L. Shulman & G. Sykes (Eds.), *Handbook of teaching and policy* (pp. 370–391). New York: Longman.

Shulman, L. (1983). Autonomy and obligation: The remote control of teaching. In L. Shulman & G. Sykes (Eds.), *Handbook of teaching and policy* (pp. 484–504). New York: Longman.

Sizer, T. (1996). *Horace's hope: What works for the American high school.* Boston: Houghton Mifflin.

Smith, F. (1979). *Reading without nonsense.* New York: Teachers College Press.

Smith, J. (1995). Competent reasoning with rational numbers. *Cognition and Instruction, 13*(1), 3–50.

Smith, M., & O'Day, J. (1991). Systemic school reform. In S. Fuhrman & B. Malen (Eds.), *The politics of curriculum and testing* (pp. 233–267). New York: Falmer.

Smith, M., O'Day, J., & Cohen, D. (1990). National curriculum, American style: Can it be done? What might it look like? *American Educator, 14*(4), 10–17; 40–47.

Sowder, J., & Schappelle, B. (1994). Research into practice: Number sense-making. *Arithmetic Teacher, 41*(6), 342–345.

Spillane, J. (1993). *Interactive policy-making: State instructional policy and the role of the school district.* Unpublished doctoral dissertation, Michigan State University, East Lansing.

Spillane, J. (1996). Districts matter: Local educational authorities and state instructional policy. *Educational Policy, 10*(1), 63–87.

Spillane, J. (1998). State policy and the non-monolithic nature of the local school district: Organizational and professional concerns. *American Educational Research Journal, 35*(1), 33–63.

Spillane, J., Peterson, P., Prawat, R., Jennings, N., & Borman, J. (1996). Exploring policy and practice relations: A teaching and learning perspective. *Journal of Education Policy, 11*(4), 431–440.

Stake, R., & Easley, J. (1978). *Case studies in science education.* Urbana: University of Illinois Center for Instructional Research and Curriculum Evaluation.

Steinbeck, J. (1969). *Journal of a novel.* New York: Viking.

Stewig, J., & Haley-Janes, S. (1990). *Houghton-Mifflin English.* Boston: Houghton Mifflin.

Thompson, C., Spillane, J., & Cohen, D. (1994). *The state policy system affecting science and mathematics education in Michigan.* East Lansing: Michigan Statewide Systemic Initiative, Michigan Partnership for New Education.

Tyack, D., & Cuban, L. (1995). *Tinkering toward utopia: A century of public school reform.* Cambridge, MA: Harvard University Press.

Walley, C. W. (1991). Diaries, logs, and journals in the elementary classroom. *Childhood Education, 67*(3), 149–154.

Warren, D. (1989). Teachers, reformers, and historians. In D. Warren (Ed.), *American teachers: Histories of a profession at work.* New York: Macmillan.

Weatherly, R., & Lipsky, M. (1977). Street-level bureaucrats and institutional innovation: Implementing special education reform. *Harvard Educational Review, 47,* 171–197.

Weiss, J. (1990). Ideas and inducements in mental health policy. *Journal of Policy Analysis and Management, 9*(2), 178–200.

Wise, A. (1988). The two conflicting trends in school reform: Legislative learning revisited. *Phi Delta Kappan, 69*(5), 328–333.

Wood, G. H. (1992). *Schools that work.* New York: Dutton.

Wright, B. (1994). Mathematics in the lower primary years: A research-based perspective on curricula and teaching practice. *Mathematics Education Research Journal, 6*(1), 23–36.

Yochum, N. (1991). Children's learning from informational text: The relationship between prior knowledge and text structure. *Journal of Reading Behavior, 23,* 87–108.

Zeichner, K. (1986). Content and contexts: Neglected elements in studies of student teaching as an occasion for learning to teach. *Journal of Education for Teaching, 12,* 5–24.

Zullie, M. (1988). *Fractions with pattern blocks.* Palo Alto, CA: Creative Publications.

Author Index

230

Subject Index